NURSING
THROUGH
THE YEARS

In association with The Royal London Hospital League of Nurses

To all the nurses of The Royal London Hospital: past, present and future
and for Barbara Thompson, without whom this book would not have been possible.

NURSING
THROUGH
THE YEARS
CARE AND COMPASSION AT THE
ROYAL LONDON HOSPITAL

LORETTA BELLMAN, SUE BOASE,
SARAH ROGERS AND
BARBARA STUCHFIELD

PEN & SWORD
HISTORY

AN IMPRINT OF PEN & SWORD BOOKS LTD.
YORKSHIRE - PHILADELPHIA

First published in Great Britain in 2018 by
PEN & SWORD HISTORY
an imprint of
Pen & Sword Books Ltd
Yorkshire - Philadelphia

ISBN   HB: 978 1 52670 874 8
PB: 978 1 52674 846 1

The right of Loretta Bellman, Sue Boase, Sarah Rogers, Barbara Stuchfield, to be identified as Authors of this work has been asserted by them in accordance with the Copyright, Designs and Patents Act 1988.

A CIP catalogue record for this book is available from the British Library.

Typeset in Times New Roman 10/12 by
Aura Technology and Software Services,
Printed in Europe through Printworks Global LTD.

Pen & Sword Books Ltd incorporates the Imprints of Pen & Sword Books Archaeology, Atlas, Aviation, Battleground, Discovery, Family History, History, Maritime, Military, Naval, Politics, Railways, Select, Transport, True Crime, Fiction, Frontline Books, Leo Cooper, Praetorian Press, Seaforth Publishing, Wharncliffe and White Owl.

For a complete list of Pen & Sword titles please contact

PEN & SWORD BOOKS LIMITED
47 Church Street, Barnsley, South Yorkshire, S70 2AS, England
E-mail: enquiries@pen-and-sword.co.uk
Website: www.pen-and-sword.co.uk

or

PEN AND SWORD BOOKS
1950 Lawrence Rd, Havertown, PA 19083, USA
E-mail: Uspen-and-sword@casematepublishers.com
Website: www.penandswordbooks.com

Contents

List of Illustrations

1. 2015: New league badge, designed in 2015 for all members of the League of Nurses.
2. A view of the front of The London Hospital and Whitechapel High Street, c 1930s.
3. 1940s: Student Nurses in pre-war style unmodified uniform at Hylands House, Chelmsford. (Image appears by courtesy of Daphne Elliot)
4. 1940s: Wartime Whitechapel High Street, with bomb shelter sign and taped shop windows. (Image appears by courtesy of Tower Hamlets Local History Library and Archives)
5. Location of bombs that landed on or in the vicinity of The London Hospital during the Second World War.
6. 1940s: A wartime ward at Brentwood Annexe with blackout blinds and heating stoves in the centre.
7. 1940s: Student nurses relaxing in Trueloves sitting room. The uniforms have smaller sleeves and no apron straps because of rationing.
8. 1940s: Student nurses eating lunch with aprons on in Trueloves dining room. A Sister tutor is observing them in the background.
9. 1940s: Practical teaching; learning how to change a patient's draw sheet. (Image appears by courtesy of The Royal London Hospital Archives and Museum)
10. 1942: Norman Hartnell's Student Nurse Uniform sketch.
11. 1940s: Practical teaching; washing a patient in a frame. (Image appears by courtesy of The Royal London Hospital Archives and Museum)
12. 1940s: A nurse's bedroom in the Edith Cavell Home; this layout remained unchanged until the 1980s.
13. 1940s: A General Nursing Council Exam paper dated 1949. (Image appears by courtesy of Jean McCrae's daughter)
14. Prize giving and badge presentation in the Medical College Library, 1949. Nurses who had already left the hospital returned in mufti to receive their hospital badge and certificate.
15. 1940s: Rear view of The London Hospital showing patients on the balconies and the covered walkway.
16. 1940s: The London Hospital badge.
17. The London Hospital swimming pool, this was used until the 1980s.
18. A student nurse nearing the end of her three year training wearing a silver 'S'. This badge denotes that she is undertaking staff nurse duties before qualifying. (Image appears by courtesy of Shirley Waterman)
19. 1960s: A sister tutor teaching student nurses in the new library.

Cover photos:

Acknowledgements

This project would not have been possible without the advice, support and wisdom of Barbara Thompson, former President of The Royal London Hospital League of Nurses.

The Royal London Hospital League of Nurses Oral History Project Team would also like to express their sincere thanks for the financial support from The Royal London Hospital League of Nurses, again, without which this book would not have been possible.

The co-authors would also like to express their gratitude to their family and friends, whose support has been invaluable.

The Oral History Project Team would like to express their gratitude and thanks to the following volunteers who generously gave up their time to interview and be interviewed:

Interviewers:

Loretta Bellman, Sue Boase, Juliet Crum, Valerie Dixon, Sarah Rogers, Jane Stokes and Barbara Stuchfield.

Interviewees:

The following generously volunteered to share their experiences of training and working at 'The London' and local district. Without them the project would not have been possible. Their memories have been very moving and a privilege to hear:

Madge Barkaway, Ruth Anne Barkaway, Colonel David C. Bates ARRC QHN QARANC, Rosemary Bayford, Dame Christine Beasley FQNI FRCN, Dr Loretta Bellman, Sheila Billins, Sue Boase, John and Lynne Brown, Patricia Burton, Ann Buxton, Gary Caughey, Dr Claire Chatterton, Susannah Clark, Janet Clements, Cath Comley, Sarah Cooper-Jones, Sue Cowburn, The Baroness Caroline Cox of Queensbury FRCN, Juliet Crum, Margaret D'Anger, Paula Day, Sylvia Denton CBE FRCN, Nina Dickins, Valerie Dixon, Jill Dolman, Adam-Robert Downham, Joy Dunicliff, Rev. Canon Clare Edwards, Eleanor Ella, Daphne Elliott MBE, Margaret Erdman, Patricia Ferguson, Fiona Ford, Doreen Fox, Lilian Fox, Bridget Gibbs, Rev. John Glasspool, Heather Gramkow, Lorraine Gray, Hilary Griffin, Joy Hall, Christabel Holton, Pat Houchin, Jacqueline Houghton, Lucy Howarth, Mary Ingwerson, Yvonne Jacobs, Barbara Jarvis, Mark Jones, Hannana Khatun, Cate Kinsella, Gianna Lee, Joyce Lelliot, Jan Lewis, Catherine Lock, Doris Lomas, Laurence Mary 'Nichola' Lovett, Anna Lynch, Adrienne Mabbott, Stella Mayers, Valerie Moore, Jean Murray, Anita Norden, Bernadette O'Shea, Samantha Parsfield, Hilary Pask, Deva Payaniandy, Amanda Payne, Ruth Perryman, Jules Plumb, Judith Podger, Maureen Pollex, Kelly Read, Adrian Reyes-Hughes, Neil Robertson, Jean Robinson, Sarah Rogers, Professor Jane Salvage FQNI FRCN, Ann Sayers, Maureen Scholes, Rosie Sharpley MBE, Margaret Simpson, Patricia Stevens, Barbara Stuchfield, Barbara Thompson, Marilyn Thompson, Amanda Thorn, Tracy Upton, Linda Wallis, Rev. Canon Dr Frances Ward, Shirley Waterman and Trudy Wood.

Grateful thanks are also extended to:

Jonathan Evans, formerly of The Royal London Hospital Archives and Kate Jarman and Richard Meunier, The Royal London Hospital Archives, Barts Health NHS Trust, for their time and support to the project.

Teresa Doherty, Royal College of Nursing Joint Archives and Information Services Manager.

Fiona Bourne, Royal College of Nursing Archives Operational Manager.

Adele Herson and team at The Typing Works for transcribing all the interviews.

Bernell Bussue, Cassandra Henry and Alice Baille-Lane, who generously arranged meeting space for the Oral History Project Team meetings at the Royal College of Nursing.

David Street and colleagues in the Development & Alumni Relations department, City, University of London and Joanna Peggie, Internal Communications and Engagement, Barts Health NHS Trust, for their help in accessing project participants who trained in the 1990s and beyond the millennium.

Special thanks are extended to Claire Hopkins, Pen & Sword Editor, for her ongoing enthusiasm and support for the book.

Original art work:

Paula Day for her amazing artwork which has captured the essence of each decade so well.

Photographic reproduction:

Many thanks to the following people who have supplied original photographs for the book:

Lesley Berris, Sue Boase, Liz Day, Paula Day, Daphne Elliot, Karen Harris, Jules Plumb, Sarah Rogers, Trish Stevens, Jane Stokes, Barbara Stuchfield, Barbara Thompson, Marilyn Thompson, Shirley Waterman and Trudy Wood.

Thanks to The Royal London Hospital Archives and Museum and Tower Hamlets Local History Library and Archives who have both granted permission for the use of photographs within the book.

Please note that all reasonable attempts have been made to establish who owns copyright and obtain copyright permission for the use of these photographs.

We would also like to acknowledge the influence of Dame Phyllis Friend FRCN, 1922–2013. She trained at The London Hospital between 1940–43. Dame Phyllis worked in a wide range of roles at The London as a sister, sister tutor, matron and Chief Nursing Officer from 1969–71. She was a member of the General Nursing Council, including vice-chairman. She worked in many high-level posts, both nationally as Chief Nursing Officer at the Department of Health and Social Security, and internationally as UK representative to the World Health Organisation, World Health Assembly and European Regional Committees. She was a truly inspirational nursing leader.

Foreword

This book tells us what life and work was like in the words of nurses who trained and worked at a large hospital, serving an impoverished population in East London. The hospital, first called The London Hospital, later The Royal London Hospital, was founded in 1740, moving to its present site in Whitechapel in 1757. Until the establishment of the National Health Service in 1948 it was a voluntary hospital, funded entirely by charitable donations.

In view of the enormous changes that have taken place during the last eighty years in the composition of the population, in social conditions in general, and in the practice of medicine and nursing, it is a matter of great interest to record the experiences of nurses who trained and worked there in former times, while it is still possible to do so. Those who trained during the impoverished 1930s and 1940s are now few, but their stories are all the more interesting for the light they shed on changes in the practice of nursing and medicine.

The war years, 1939–45, provide a rich yield of stories—falling bombs on parts of the hospital, food rationing and the introduction of penicillin. Three years after the war had ended came the introduction of a universal health service supported by taxation. There are those who witnessed great changes brought about by the introduction of the National Health Service. No longer did a nurse have to stand by the door with a begging bowl at the end of visiting time, to collect money for the taxi fare of a patient who needed transport to get home.

The East End of London had long been a place where immigrants settled, in part due to the proximity of the docks. There was a sizeable Chinese community in Limehouse, and, from the 1880s onwards, pogroms in Russia caused a massive influx and settlement of Jews in Spitalfields and Whitechapel. Churches founded by an earlier wave of Huguenot immigrants were converted to synagogues – many have subsequently been converted to mosques by later immigrants from Bangladesh. The Jewish community was notable for its generosity in support of the hospital, and there was even a kosher kitchen. In the 1960s there were still many shops in Whitechapel where only Yiddish was spoken.

In 1942, Norman Hartnell, who designed clothes for the royal family, was asked to re-design uniforms for The London Hospital nurses. This was a time of clothes rationing during the war. His designs, with their distinctive puff sleeves, were individually tailored for every nurse. They turned out to be attractive, practical and comfortable, but were phased out in the last decade of the twentieth century.

A major break with the past occurred when it became increasingly evident that the main hospital building was no longer able to provide the facilities for twenty-first-century healthcare. After many delays, the well-loved eighteenth-century grade two-listed building was replaced by a new, 675-bed, multi-storey, modern hospital, which opened in February 2012. The old building has been bought by Tower Hamlets Council and will remain in use after refurbishment.

Having trained and spent my working life at The Royal London Hospital, including the period of its merger with St Bartholomew's, I have been greatly touched by the stories of my predecessors, colleagues and successors. Over eighty nurses were interviewed for this book whose ages ranged from 24 to 96. I commend this book as a good read for the remarkable glimpses it provides into the rich experiences of nurses, across the years, in service for the welfare of others.

Barbara Thompson
President of the Royal London Hospital League of Nurses (2010–17)

Presidents of The Royal London Hospital League of Nurses

Clare Alexander, Lady Mann.	1941–1961
Dame Phyllis Friend.	1962–1972
Dr Sheila Collins.	1972–1984
Maureen Scholes.	1984–1991
Trudy Wood.	1991–2010
Barbara Thompson.	2010–2017
Cath Comley.	2017-

New league badge, designed in 2015 for all members of the League of Nurses.

Timeline

1943 State Enrolled Nurses with two year training enacted in 1943, General Nursing Council recorded qualification from 1947.

1948 National Health Service introduced. 'Free health care for all'.

1952 Preliminary Training School returns to Tredegar House from Trueloves, Ingatestone, Essex.

1962 Hospital Plan: Separation of the NHS into three parts, hospital, local health authorities and general practice.

1962 Introduction of the 'block system' where work and student nurse education was reorganised in a structured format.

1967 The Salmon Report: Recommended a new senior nursing staff structure. Matron's title was to be abolished.

1967 Princess Alexandra School of Nursing formally opened at Whitechapel.

1968 State Enrolled Nurse training commenced at The London Hospital.

1969 Male student nurses accepted for training at The London Hospital.

1969 Combined degree and nurse registration commenced with two London colleges, Queen Mary College and Goldsmiths' College.

1970 Integrated State Registered Nurse/Registered Mental Nurse training introduced.

1971 Hanbury dialysis day centre, purpose built dialysis unit at the London.

1972 The Briggs Report: Introduced one national body for nurses, responsible for setting standards, education and training, including a move to degree entry and research based practice.

1974 First graduate State Registered Nurse training course for nurses who already had a degree began at The London Hospital.

1983 The Griffiths Report: Established general management of the NHS.

1987 Back to Nursing courses, introduced at The London Hospital.

1988 Shortened course introduced for State Enrolled Nurses to become State Registered Nurses.

1989 First helicopter service at The London, later to become HEMS (Helicopter Emergency Medical Services). Express Newspapers helped start the initiative/charity.

1990s Traditional London Hospital uniform phased out.

1991 The Royal London became a NHS Trust hospital.

1992 Project 2000: Move to degree level education.

1992 UKCC Scope of Professional Practice. Developed guidelines which provided a competency framework for nurses in specialist roles.

1995 College of Nursing moved to City University.

2004 Agenda for change: New grading system for most NHS staff.

2012 Phase 1 of the new Royal London Hospital build completed, costing £650 million.

2012 The Royal London Hospital and St. Bartholomew's Hospital, and their respective schools of nursing, merged.

Introduction

if you don't understand history you don't understand the present. *Louise*

The Royal London Hospital League of Nurses commenced an oral history project in 2013. The impetus for this project was the desire of the League of Nurses Executive to retain the memories of members of the League while it was still possible. Memories of nursing life, training and working in the area had been rekindled by Worth's (2002) highly acclaimed memoirs of life as a midwife in Poplar. The project extended its aim to capture the memories of nurses who trained or worked extensively at The London Hospital from the 1940s to the present day. The hospital was granted royal status in 1990. Many nurses still refer affectionately to the hospital as 'The London'.

The recollections of all these nurses is informative, inspiring, and also controversial, often challenging the myths and misconceptions that continue to surround nursing. While this study was undertaken for The Royal London Hospital, much of the content will no doubt resonate with other nursing colleagues and also be of interest to the public at large. It is hoped that the book will also provide different generations of nurses with an understanding and appreciation of a part of their history.

What is oral history?

Oral History is the 'Recording of people's memories, experiences and opinions' and gives the opportunity for ordinary people's stories to be recorded, which might not be otherwise heard (www.ohs.org.uk, 2014). Although oral history is a recently coined term, 'oral history is as old as history itself' and is a rapidly growing historical research methodology (Thompson, 1978). It is used as a method of recording the histories of ordinary people, including women who might have been previously 'hidden from history' (Rowbotham, 1973).

Oral History is increasingly employed in research into nursing, to uncover memories which may be neglected in more formal accounts of the profession. The memories can provide '[a] source of new insights and perspectives that may challenge our view of the past' (www.ohs.org.uk, 2014). Participants' memories of past experiences can be studied in order to comprehend change across time, and educate the profession about nursing in the past, and steer the profession's future decision-making (Miller-Rosser et al 2009). Although the oral history voice may be immediate, persuasive, and compelling, 'memories must be subjected to the same observant historical analysis as any other primary source' (Boschma et al in Lewenson and Hermann, 2008:85). However, Thompson agreed with Jordanova that within healthcare, oral history could be used 'as a key catalyst in reshaping future practice and policy' (Thompson in Bornat et al, 2000). According to Borsay (2009:18), 'There are occasions when historical data and methods are of direct relevance to nursing practice … as important is the indirect way in which history facilitates critical reflection'.

Exploring Modern Nursing History

At one time, nursing was mainly conducted by nuns, monks and the military. The roots of modern nursing began in the nineteenth century. During this era, Elizabeth Fry, a Quaker and a renowned prison reformer, was also concerned about the quality and standard of nursing. In 1840 she started a training school for nurses at Guy's Hospital. Florence Nightingale was born into a rich, well-connected family. She was greatly influenced by Fry, a distant relative. Nurses trained by Fry's school accompanied Nightingale to the Crimean war (1853–56). Eva Luckes, matron of The London Hospital from 1880–1919, and friend and confidante of Florence Nightingale, was one of a group of influential nineteenth-century matrons. Luckes was noted for her introduction of the Preliminary Training School at The London in 1895, the first in England.

Women have been largely ignored in history. This also mirrors the history of nursing, which, until recently, only focused on the 'great and the good', particularly leaders such as Florence Nightingale. Seminal works of the history of the profession have included Abel-Smith (1960) who examined the development of the profession since 1800, and Baly (1973) who focused on nursing and social change. Subsequently, Maggs (1983) examined the 'nurses below' who were mainly excluded in nineteenth- and early twentieth-century studies of the profession. The importance of examining the views of all nurses is now clearly recognised:

> Where it is appropriate to herald the accomplishments of nursing leaders, a balanced portrait of nursing history should also include their disappointments and failures, as well as the experiences of 'ordinary' nurses. *(Lewenson and Hermann 2008:65)*

To undertake this project the co-authors recognised that, 'Nursing history must seek the voices of nurses and nursing in the past' (Hallett, 1997/98). The oral history project, which spans the 1940s to the present day, provides a wealth of information from 'ordinary' nurses as well as high 'achievers'. It is hoped that it will also provide a significant and worthwhile contribution to the history of modern nursing.

A view of the front of The London Hospital and Whitechapel High Street, c 1930s.

Methodology

The project started with three interviewers, but as the project grew more were recruited. Some of the researchers attended the Oral History Society's one-day training, held at the British Library, others had previous experience of qualitative research, or undertook specific Oral History post-graduate education while working on the project. All the interviewers trained and worked, for varying lengths of time at 'The London', and in the community nearby. They all worked as nurses in various nursing specialties. Participants were recruited via: word of mouth; '*The Review*', the league's annual magazine; City, University of London Alumni; newsletters for Barts Health NHS Trust and social media.

Initially it was intended to interview approximately ten participants per decade, however, it was harder to find volunteers who trained between 2000–14. 1938 was the earliest year in which a participant trained. There were significantly more retired nurses who volunteered to be interviewed. While all interviews are confidential, it may be that some nurses currently working within the profession did not want to highlight some concerns and 'go on record', unlike retired nurses who 'can explore their experiences without placing themselves under undue pressure or facing questions as to the current failings of the system' (Brooks, 2009).

The nurses in this book, although from different generations, have much in common. They have participated in approximately one hour-long interview for an oral history research project and shared their memories of becoming and being a nurse, while working in the East End of London. We have been fortunate in being able to interview one set of twins, both of whom trained at The London in 1946, and also have more than one example of where many nurses trained at The London within one family. Two participants were unable to meet for an interview but sent written accounts instead. All the participants consented to their quotations appearing in this book. The interviews took place between 2013 and 2016.

Interviewees were sent an introductory letter explaining the project, and proposed areas of discussion. The questions and general topic acted as a 'cueing mechanism…' which led to the volunteers recalling a series of memories (Abrams, 2010:84). The shared bond of training at the same hospital, whatever their particular experiences, helped act as an 'ice-breaker'. Critics of oral history argue that 'memory is unreliable because it deteriorates with old age…' however, others dispute this, saying that long term memory is the last to be affected, and that with age may come a special honesty which may enhance memory when reflecting on life's events (Thompson cited in Ritchie, 2011). Following the interview, the participants chose to receive either a transcript or CD of their interview.

A number of questions also guided the interview. Participants reflected on why they decided to train as a nurse; their choice of hospital or latterly university; their experiences of their training, both good and not so good; patients that they could never forget; their major achievements and challenges, and their legacy for current nursing practice, including how things have changed in nursing since the decade in which they trained. Much of the invisibility of the physical work and emotional labour of nursing is revealed throughout the decades. Chapter 8, 'Moving on', highlights how nurses who trained at The London had a wide variety of different career paths, including, for some, reaching high office in nursing and in government. Many of the participants have remained nursing 'at the patient's bedside', providing the 'essential nursing care' that is the bed-rock of nursing. Chapter 9 presents a selection of reflections on 'How things have changed', from across the decades.

Producing the book

The transcripts were analysed thematically and selected memories incorporated into a chapter per decade. The co-authors have briefly set 'their' decade into the context of the period, including local and national events where appropriate. Each chapter reflects what the participants recalled, and cannot, and does not, include everything that may have happened at The London, and in nursing during that period.

Challenges

One of the biggest challenges for the co-authors has been to provide a rich and authentic description of nursing through the years in the participants' own words. The large sample of participants and the book's word limit has meant that, at times, they have had to select a small sample of the quotations, from the wealth of material across a wide range of themes. If further information is required, the transcripts, together with accompanying digital recording, will be stored in the hospital archive and may be retrieved with permission from: rlharchives@bartshealth.nhs.uk. Copyright is held by The Royal London Hospital League of Nurses.

Maintaining anonymity

Initially interviewees' quotations were to be unidentified, however, it was felt that the reader would be less able to 'hear' the different nurses' voices in the narratives. Pseudonyms were randomly selected to replace each participant's first name, chosen according to those that were popular in the decade in which they were born. The use of pseudonyms will enable the reader, if they wish, to follow the memories of a particular nurse, but maintain participants' anonymity.

Artwork

Overall, the recollections contribute to the history of nursing and the artwork supports the historical context within each decade. The artwork was provided by Paula Day, currently a senior sister at The Royal London Hospital, who is also a graduate of the St Martin's College of Art and Design, London.

The memories captured paint a vivid picture of nurses' lives, training and working in the East End of London, both in a large teaching hospital and the local community. Through these interviews, insights were gained into some of the everyday issues that have previously been neglected by some nursing historians and practitioners. While 'This legacy of nurses' wisdom is, at times, extremely challenging and controversial...' (The Royal London Hospital League of Nurses Oral History Project, 2016), it is hoped that this project will help student and trained nurses and nursing leaders to 'understand the past as a guide to present and future action' (Davies, 1980: 15).

> actually recognising that there's always been flaws and positives in every era of history and I think sometimes some people do look at the past and think it was all great and it wasn't. But I also think they look at the present and think it's all bad and it's not as well ...there's still lots of compassionate nurses out there doing a hard job in difficult circumstances and I think sometimes that gets forgotten .... *Louise*

1940s, Mixed media on canvas, 2017, Paula Day.

Chapter 1

The 1940s – War and Peace

When the war broke out I was in the sixth form at school and all noble-like I said I'd nurse. … I was doing modern languages, nothing like nursing, English, French, German and Spanish … and my aim was to be a secretary to a diplomat and travel. So in the end I ended up, like a lot of people, volunteering to nurse. *Joan*

The whole of this decade was dominated by the Second World War (1939–45), its impact and consequences. Life during the war in the East End of London, the history of the devastation suffered, and the resilience of the population still resonates today, so many years later. This chapter captures a snapshot of life for some nurses, during, and immediately after the war.

It's very strict but the standard is the highest in the world

During the 1940s nursing may have seemed an obvious choice for a young woman as either a temporary or a lifelong career. However, with the majority of men signing up for military service, there were increasing opportunities for women to contribute to the war effort. Women of all ages and marital status now stepped into what had previously been considered 'a man's job'. There were, though, those such as Edna, who from childhood, had always wanted to nurse:

It was a childhood ambition. I did nothing but play nurses with my dollies. I visited my mum … at The London Hospital when I was three, and apparently said I'm going to be a nurse when I'm a lady. Well, I achieved the nurse bit, but never mind about the lady.

Whether it was to fulfill a childhood ambition, contribute to the war effort or for an entirely different reason, what remains puzzling is why, at that time, did young women choose to train as a nurse at The London Hospital? The hospital stands in close proximity to both the Docks and the City of London. These commercial, financial and trade centres of the capital were key enemy targets. It would seem that the reputation of the hospital far outweighed the risks that they faced:

Oh a friend of my father's said, 'There's only one place for a nurse to train really well and that's The London Hospital … you don't hear so much about it and it's very strict but the standard is the highest in the world'. *Joan*

The impact of war

During the Second World War, the hospital played a central role in organising emergency medical services to the north and east of London. It also suffered heavy damage due to enemy action during the Blitz, as Dorothy relates:

1940s: Student Nurses in pre-war style unmodified uniform at Hylands House, Chelmsford.
(Image appears by courtesy of Daphne Elliot)

On the 7th of September, 1940, the major blitz on London started, and continued without a break for fifty-seven days. Hundreds of bombs fell on the East End, particularly around the docks, which were situated a short distance from the hospital. On one occasion, myself and another nurse were instructed to open up a ward that had been closed … a high caseload was expected, as a burning [closed] ward had fallen on seventeen firemen [firewatchers]. Bomb after bomb fell, and many incendiary bombs, on the hospital, which were expertly dealt with by the many trained volunteers. From the hospital window, the sky was aglow with dock fires. The fires caused such a wind that all the large windows cracked, that were fortunately covered with mesh wire. These mesh wires had been put around all the windows. The next day, the King and Queen came and visited the very burnt firemen on the ward, and I was sure that the King and Queen gave comfort to the suffering firemen.

When there was an air raid you stayed on duty, you knew the patients that had got to stay in bed and you knew the patients that you could get up from bed, but you stayed where you were. *Marjorie*

Many staff and patients were evacuated to sector hospitals outside London, but essential services like A&E, midwifery and outpatients remained at Whitechapel. About 200 patients remained at The London with skeleton ward and teaching staff.

> I was returned to The London [from working at Chase Farm Hospital] on July 10th, 1943 … only been back a few days when we had 'that bomb', as we called it. I shot under the bed with several people … and the glass all came under the bed as well but I wasn't hurt really and I remember the next morning, as I was coming from the hospital back to Cavell Nurses' Home, a man was sweeping up the road and there among his rubbish was my needlework basket, so I went and reclaimed it and I had that basket for years afterwards and I used to look at it and say, you went through the bombing … It was the ward that was bombed and it was the blast from that that took the windows out of Cavell Nurses' Home. *Eileen*

> After one of the terrible nights of bombing I went into central London and will never forget St Paul's, it stood majestic, surrounded by such devastation, rubble and dust everywhere. *Dorothy*

The London received injured and sick civilians and military staff, as Marjorie recalls:

> Turner Ward had Dutch sailors, [some] … were very sick indeed and of course none of them knew what had happened to their families at home so they were

1940s: Wartime Whitechapel High Street, with bomb shelter sign and taped shop windows.
(Image appears by courtesy of Tower Hamlets Local History Library and Archives)

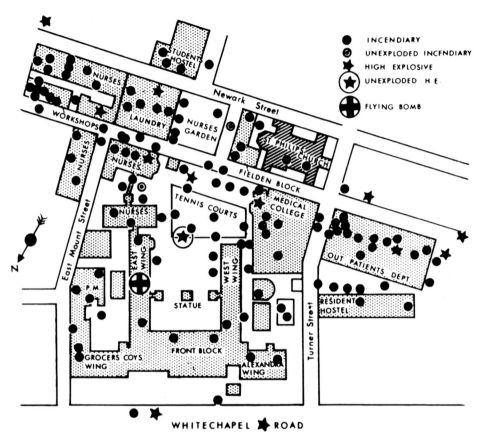

Location of bombs that landed on or in the vicinity of The London Hospital during World War Two

very anxious and apprehensive men.... Now the soldiers and the sailors ... the ones who were basically orthopaedics, were allowed to go out and have a little bit of normality ... they used to go down to Charringtons, the brewery, and the brewery used to give them plenty to drink so we were often coping with drunks. But this particular sailor who had his left arm in plaster and right leg in plaster [also] wanted a pass and Sister [X] ... said, 'No, you were disobedient and you were late coming in last time you had a pass, you're not having a pass'. The ceilings, because of the war, had huge metal poles to keep them up and didn't this young man shin up to the top of the metal pole and he sat there and said, 'Sister, ze pass, Sister, ze pass'. 'No, you're not having a pass, come down at once'. And he sat there until he got his pass because that was the only way he intended to come down. And he had been in the Dutch opera company, he had a lovely, lovely voice. And he very often sang at night, I think just to relieve his miseries. And in the ward on Christmas Eve there was a young sailor ... dying of tuberculosis and he begged him to sing *Ave Maria* ... he sang that *Ave Maria*.... And the lad died ... and I can hear that voice now.

Nurse training continued with the training school now spread between eleven different hospitals encompassing the outlying sector hospitals. Memories of the Doodlebugs, which rained down on the East End towards the end of the war, were very vivid. Marjorie again:

> I started at The London at the end of the war when the doodle-bombs [flying bombs] were still falling…. The east wing of The London had been hit by a bomb and so there was only half of that wing working. The third floors of The London were not in operation and Croft Ward was used entirely for casualties…. One of the first things that I had to do was to fill sixteen stone hot water bottles and put them in those sixteen beds ready for the casualties.
>
> And … the last doodle-bomb happened … it fell behind the … private wards. And I was on night duty so I knew that it had happened, I mean we heard the wretched thing coming and we'd counted to thirty and we were still alive … we went out into the street … to see if we could help and … there was a little …[child] about four who had the most enormous broom that you ever did see and it was sweeping up the glass saying, 'Bloody old Hitler, bloody old Hitler'!

Edna too remembers:

> sheltering babies under their cots in David Hughes … when there was an air raid … Doodlebugs, V1s and V2s. And they were nasty because they were insidious, they were quiet, and we didn't often have an air raid warning because they came out of the blue.

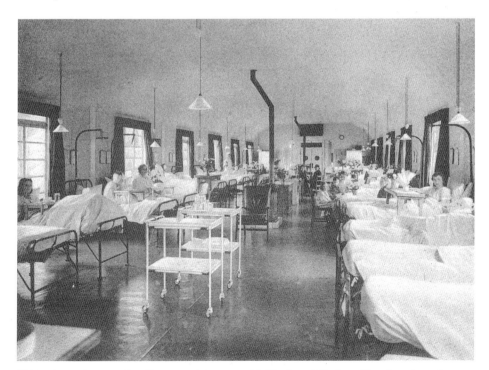

1940s: A wartime ward at Brentwood Annexe with blackout blinds and heating stoves in the centre.

The introduction of penicillin and streptomycin

War accelerated the development of new drugs. The sulphonamide drugs were introduced in the 1930s, augmented by Penicillin in 1943.

> I remember Penicillin being introduced, and we had to gown and glove and mask, because they didn't know what it would do to us. *Edna*

> Penicillin by ... injection which was very painful indeed. .... [O]nly soldiers were allowed to have Penicillin, it was just for the Army. And it was a brown solution...it was grown in the lab and the mould on the top was basically saved and the solution was taken off and put in the vessel to give [to patients]. *Marjorie*

The poor living conditions of the East End community contributed to the spread of tuberculosis. Streptomycin was eventually used to treat this disease. However, for some patients there were significant side effects, as Kathleen recalls:

> I'll never forget ... a young boy ... we did a ward round ... and we came to ... where this young man ... was sitting up in bed, and he smiled at us all, and Dr X said, 'He can't hear us. He's deaf, and that has been caused because we've given him Streptomycin for his ... tubercular meningitis. ... [A]t that time, Streptomycin of course hadn't been refined ... so this fellow, he'd got his brain back, but he was totally deaf.

The war also contributed to the rapid spread of tuberculosis:

> people won't believe this but I actually nursed ... in a ward where there were twenty-five young women under the age of 25 and I happen to know that all those girls were dead within a year.... It was the living conditions. You have to remember that people went down into the Tube [underground station] and slept in the Tube so that it spread. *Marjorie*

Food rationing and why I don't like Marmite

> Well the food was very good. Bacon, we only got one rasher and I used to laugh and say, rather than waste a plate they should have held it on a fork and we just took it ... But what amazed me, we were allowed a bottle of beer! I think it was provided by Mann, Crossman & Paulin, the brewers. That surprised me a lot because I'd never drunk beer and I didn't have it then but yes, there was beer provided. *Eileen*

Marjorie describes the food available for both the nurses and the patients:

> very strict rationing. You know we had our own two ounces of butter, four ounces of sugar and two ounces of tea ... and when you'd eaten it or drunk it, it had gone. We were well fed ... breakfast, we always had a cereal of some description, we always had something hot and we always had toast and marmalade. And we had some very good orange jelly that had been sent from America and we were allowed it because we were under twenty-one ... [and] had to have the extra vitamin C.... At half past nine in the morning we had bread and margarine and Marmite, hence the reason why I really do not like Marmite ... for lunch we had soup, a meat course and a pudding.... At four o'clock we had a sticky bun or we had jam to go with our bread. In the evening

we had soup, a meat course and a pudding … and with the milk … we could get our hot drink in the evening. … [W]e also had the hospital shop where we could buy Horlicks and Ovaltine at cost price … things that were very scarce like salad cream … if you went to the shop and they'd got them then you bought them simply because you had to grab them…

Oh the patients' meals were very good. Despite the rationing, The London insisted that food was part of the treatment … food was all cooked on the premises. The sisters … always served the meals … We had to lay each patient a tray set correctly with knife, fork and spoon and cruet and you took the tray complete to the patient. … [V]ery precise in the amount and how it looked … and if you had a patient who the consultant had said in the ward round, 'Sister, I think we have come to the stage of TLC please', anything that patient fancied they were given and I have been up to the kitchen at midnight and collected a kipper because someone fancied a kipper.

These nurses are to be admired for their courage and resilience and the tough work they had to do often in very dangerous surroundings. The women who trained immediately after the war considered themselves very fortunate. However:

we were always hungry … I always remember, just after the war … being by the docks these men came up and they had all these rotten bananas and … well, they weren't rotten, they'd gone really ripe … because we hadn't seen bananas for years and years … everybody queued up to buy them. They were alright if you ate them straight away. *Irene*

we did have a big hangover from the war. We had to take our ration books, give them in, we also had clothing coupons taken for our uniform. And you know how much we got a month? £4 4*s* 4*d*. In a little brown envelope which was handed to us, I think it was Home Sister that gave it to us, you had to queue up for it. *Vera*

Post-war applicants

Nursing is often referred to as a vocation.

I had a father who would have liked me to work in a bank. That was not at all what I wanted to do, so he made me take a secretarial course once I left school, and I worked for different companies in Liverpool, and when I became eighteen, I pestered him again, and this time he said, 'Alright, if that's really what you want to do', but he didn't help me at all. *Kathleen*

There were also diverse reasons for deciding to train as a nurse.

Probably because my mother had trained and so I knew a bit about it, but I'd had ideas of wanting to do psychiatry, psychology … I needed a degree and we couldn't afford to send me to university, the headmistress had actually asked my parents to visit to see if there was any way we could deal with the funding, but it wasn't possible so it rather took me to either teaching or nursing as suitable careers at that time for women. *Gladys*

I really wanted to be a teacher but I came from a poor home … they couldn't afford to keep me with the fees and things to pay so I gave that idea up, so I finished up being a nurse teacher instead. *Betty*

I left school then, I had no idea what I wanted to do at all and my great friend said, 'Well why don't you join the Bank?' ... so I became a bank clerk, but I was so bored ... there was one girl ... she was going to be a nurse and she was telling me about it and I said, 'oh I think I'll do that' and my friend said, 'You wouldn't like it, you'll see dead people and you'll always be giving bedpans.' *Winifred*

With so much devastation in the East End of London, what made the hospital seem such an attractive option for post-war nurse training?

[Father] said, 'Well I think it would be better to train in London, that's where the best hospitals are' so I started looking at them all, getting the brochures, and I chose The London because it had a swimming pool ... St Thomas's, Bart's ... they didn't talk about swimming pools. They may have had them, but The London made a point. *Kathleen*

this particular girl said, 'Well I'm going to train at The London', I said oh no, I want to train at the best, she said, 'it is the best' ... there was St Thomas's, St Bartholomew's and Guy's Hospital, they were the only ones I knew of as very good, so I applied for an interview with Bart's, and The London ... I went in to see the matron ... and she said ... 'Well why did you want to come to The London Hospital?' and I actually told her, to all my friends' astonishment, I said, 'Well matron, I like them both but the London Hospital's got a swimming pool', so everybody roared with laughter ... 'You didn't say that to the matron?'... I've still got the little booklet, I was seeing the swimming pool and the garden and the tennis courts. *Winifred*

Starting out and fly cake

Prior to the war newly appointed students lived at Tredegar House in Bow. The Preliminary Training School, or PTS as it was known, was also in the same building, as Dorothy recalls:

I arrived with nineteen other soon-to-be nurses, all of whom were very friendly. At Tredegar House, the daily schedule included lectures and practical training and at the end of two months we had an exam, and if you failed this exam, you couldn't go on to train.... The first three months at the hospital was a trial period. They established if you could handle nursing and the hours. There was no pay ... during the three months of work. Our salaries were modest, receiving an annual salary of £25 the first year, £30 the second, and £35 in the third.

Tredegar House was closed during the war. The PTS was transferred firstly to 'Hylands' near Chelmsford, and then new students went to Trueloves House, also in Essex. Even 'straight inners', those nurses who had undertaken some previous training, for example children's or mental health nursing, still went to Trueloves first but for a shorter period of time. Set sizes varied considerably.

We had about forty in our group.... There were one or two who sort of did about three months, decided it wasn't their job and they didn't think they'd ever like it and they left.... But out of about forty of us I think only about three left. *Betty*

1940s: Student nurses relaxing in Trueloves sitting room. The uniforms have smaller sleeves and no apron straps because of rationing.

1940s: Student nurses eating lunch with aprons on in Trueloves dining room. A Sister tutor is observing them in the background.

there were twelve of us in the set from different parts and ... status ... there were some people who ... had ... rather nice backgrounds, posh backgrounds ... and then there were the ordinary people like myself who had nothing, and my parents had said they'd keep me at school 'til I was 18 and then ... I wouldn't get a penny after that, and I didn't, which was hard. *Vera*

The thing that today is a wonderful memory is entering the front door of Trueloves with a huge fireplace and on either side of it huge pots of Michaelmas daisies and on a table in front of the fire there was a lovely spread for tea. *Marjorie*

we all sat round the table and had bread and red jam and fly cake ... we used to call it fly cake 'cos it just had the odd sultana here and there, and mugs of tea ... there were thirty-four in our set. *Winifred*

There were also 'rude awakenings':

We had one weekend off in the middle of our three months PTS when we were allowed to go home. *Marjorie*

it was rationing ... I went to have a bath and filled up the bath, looked down, it was full of flies ... I went and reported the fact and Sister said, 'You'll have to wait 'til it rains'. Well, all the water for that sort of thing came from the sky you see and we were there from January 'til March. *Elsie*

Early learning

You were called at six [am] and you had to present yourself for breakfast at half past six when your name was called from the register and then you started your day. *Marjorie*

Oh we had lessons in ... hygiene, first aid and a few I think on behaviour and courtesy ... I seem to remember about being polite even if people were rude. *Betty*

We spent our days cleaning the house because we were taught to clean, we had proper cookery lectures, we had lectures on bandaging ... we had to make a many-tailed binder ... a splint and generally we were taught bed making, how to blanket bath, and generally how to behave on the wards, that was our task in life. *Marjorie*

[we were] told ... about flower arranging, no, not ever should we have red and white flowers together. *Vera*

We went out on several trips ... [The] London Hospital had its own factory in the East End ... I remember seeing catgut all across the ceilings ... there were no pre-threaded needles ... you thread in theatre but of course they're all different sizes ... And I asked about violins because my sister's a violinist, yes some of the catgut went for that. And we were told how it was soaked and scraped and all the rest of it. They guaranteed it was free of anthrax. Another external visit was to a sewage works ... I can still smell it. Another visit was to a rubbish disposable group and we've been through the war, we'd done a lot of salvaging ... they had a conveyor belt where all the rubbish was tipped out and people picking off the different things and actually salvaging at that time. *Elsie*

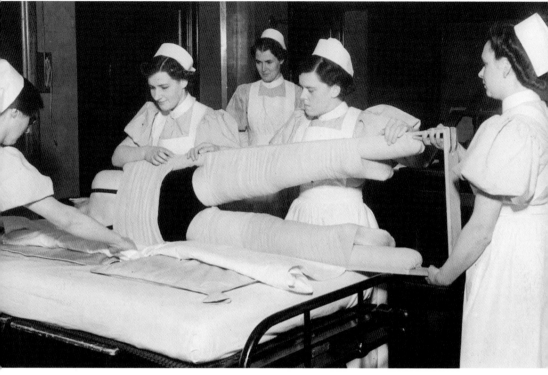

1940s: Practical teaching; learning how to change a patient's draw sheet.
(Image appears by courtesy of The Royal London Hospital Archives and Museum)

An early taste of hospital life could be rather daunting:

> one day a week we went … to have an experience on the wards and I found this
> very interesting, but rather alarming when I seem to be the only person at that
> time on the ward and a patient … called up 'Nurse, nurse', and she looked at me
> and I looked down at her and said … 'I'll go and get you one'… I just felt I …
> wouldn't have known what to have done or anything, and also I was told if you see
> a man … in a white jacket, would you tell the sister or staff nurse there's a doctor
> in the ward … one particular occasion I went straight into the office and said
> there's a doctor in the ward so she [sister] goes out and looks and said, 'Where?'
> and I pointed to this gentleman and she said, 'Nurse, that's the barber'. *Winifred*

> the tutor in charge of us at Trueloves, and she warned us … that we were liabilities
> not assets in the ward, so we'd better mind our Ps and Qs so all we were really
> allowed to do, that I remember, was to clean bedside tables. *Kathleen*

> they were very busy … and the senior nurse said to me, 'Now could you bath
> Mrs X?'and I said, 'Yes of course but I've never bathed [anyone] before', 'Well
> surely you know how to bath someone?' well you'd say yes … [Later on] a
> tutor … [asked] 'Were you shown how to bath Mrs X?' I said, 'No, the nurse said
> surely I knew how to do it' … and she said … 'Would you like your mother to be
> bathed by someone who didn't know how to go about it?' *Winifred*

From 'purple passions' to Norman Hartnell

The uniforms, worn during PTS, were called 'purple passions', and were certainly not in vogue.

> I think they were some purple kind of dress, black stockings, and I can't remember what we wore on our heads … but the greater aim was that we would do well enough so that we could get The London Hospital uniform, with its caps and its puffed sleeves. *Kathleen*

On successful completion of PTS, as Marjorie describes, every nurse was fitted for a bespoke uniform:

> we wore the Norman Hartnell uniform which was the most comfortable uniform that I ever wore. Yes, it had a wonderful front with … four big pearl buttons on … lovely puffed sleeves, but the bust was always adequate and out the back we had an enormous, I mean enormous, pleat so that we could stretch our arms forward in comfort. It had to be twelve inches from the floor. … We had four dresses and we had twelve aprons and you wore the apron that you had worn the evening before in the morning to do what I called the dirty jobs and when you went to coffee, which was half past nine to ten, usually then you changed your apron and came back with a clean [one], but you also had to bring another clean apron with you just in case your apron got spotted with anything like blood or sputum or anything like that, and it was very strict indeed
>
> We were all as nurses disgusted that [at a nearby hospital] nurses went out into the street in their uniforms. Unheard of love. We weren't allowed to go even down as far as the Post Office and by jove if you were caught love you were in trouble, I mean big trouble.

However, wartime rationing of fabric meant that uniforms had straight sleeves not puffs, until royalty intervened.

> Queen Mary, who was our President, …. [c]ame to the hospital and said, 'What are my nurses doing with straight sleeves?' And they said, 'Oh because of the rationing' and she said, 'Right, I shall send Norman Hartnell down to redesign'… we then had much smaller puffs. *Vera*

1942: Norman Hartnell's Student Nurse Uniform sketch.

Early ward experiences and the white book

A white book was given to every student nurse to record their practical experience throughout their training. When sister or staff nurse thought a nurse proficient in a practical task they signed it off in their white book. A student nurse could not complete their training without their white book as evidence of clinical skills. Specific practical skills included for example: simple enema; a starch and opium enema; hypodermic injection; application of antiphlogistine poultice (kaolin poultice); removal of stitches; a test meal before certain X-rays; cleaning and sterilising of catheters; passing a catheter; taking a specimen from a catheter; dressings; colostomy care; lifting a patient; bed making; urine testing with a Bunsen burner and litmus paper; preparation for intravenous infusions (in glass bottles); infant feeding; typhoid fever nursing, etc. Completion of the white book was supervised by Matron's Office. Later in the decade the white book was covered and became a nurse's essential blue book.

What else were these student nurses required to do?

> Oh yes, everything was sparkling clean, damp dusted and … sister would go along like this [with her finger] and she would look under there and round here … I can remember cleaning lavatories and sinks every morning, when you're a junior you have to do that. *Joan*

There was no time to linger as Kathleen explains:

> those wards were 40 beds in size, long like a corridor, and after a little while, I was told by one staff nurse that I really would have to quicken my pace otherwise I would never make it, so I started to become a little quicker. Also, in the refectory, where we ate, and where we were signed in each morning on duty, I was always the last to leave, because I took so long to eat, so I had to learn how to get quicker in all departments.
>
> and my first ward … was a men's medical ward, and I can remember that we had patients with eye difficulties, mostly it was a case of lens extractions, and in those days, they were kept in bed for ten days, they had sandbags each side of their heads, and you had to be very careful not to make an unnecessary noise to make them jump, otherwise … it was thought that the operation would not be successful. That was on one side of the ward, and then I remember on the other … the five skin [dermatology] beds. I felt so sorry for those men … you put them in a cold tar solution in a bath … they didn't improve very much…. Of course this is before the time of antibiotics.

Some encountered their first death very early in their training. Winifred recalls:

> the senior nurses were very good because one of them said to me, 'I'd like you to help me this afternoon, we're going to lay out Mrs X… have you ever seen a dead body before?' and I said, 'No', and she said, 'Well, you remember Mrs X, she was very poorly and she really was in a lot of pain and she always looked so sad, well if you come and look at her now'… and there was this very peaceful lady lying in bed, but I thought from that nurse's point of view what a marvellous thing to do, rather than just take me in and we've got to lay this dead person out you know.

Everything was strictly controlled

Becoming a nurse included learning and obeying the rules and adapting to the hospital routine. Much of the time was spent being respectful to senior staff:

> there were quite a few rules. Some of my set had to leave for unruly hair ... and another one for not wearing suitable night attire. *Eileen*

Irene explains:

> we never knew anybody's Christian name ... you only called people by their surnames ... you trained for three years with someone and you never knew their Christian name.
>
> If you met a sister and you were talking to her, you had to take it [cape] off, whether it was raining or not, until she said, 'Okay, you can put it back on again' [*laughs*]. Ridiculous, isn't it?

Visiting times were strictly controlled:

> The thing that hurt me most ... no parent could see a child awake ... the children had to be asleep at night before the parents could come and visit. There was though one child that we let mother see because he spent most of his life in hospital. *Elsie*

Even the time that medical staff were permitted to access their patients was controlled:

> Most of the doctors ... respected the staff, especially the sister, and they had to abide by the sister. The sister was in charge of her ward and whatever doctor came on, however senior he was, if the sister said no, he had to go by it.... You see, like dinner time, you couldn't have a medical student or a doctor [coming to the ward], however high up he was, because that was the rule. *Irene*

Also, student nurses such as Vera were told to 'keep your distance' and not to get too 'close' to patients:

> it always bothered me this slight remoteness between the patient and the nurse. But that was wrong.

They were taught the price of everything:

> We were not allowed to waste a thing. All our dressings were sterilised on the premises ... so that if we had anything left from a pack that was clean, we hadn't touched, then it had to be reused.... Needles ... scissors, scalpels, everything was re-sharpened.... If as student nurses we broke a thermometer it cost us sixpence. If we broke a large china bowl because everybody washed in a china bowl.... Two and sixpence ... and you earned £2 a month. *Marjorie*

'You're not here to think nurse!'

Sisters are portrayed in many ways.

> We had a sister in charge who had trained at St Mary's Paddington ... she was extremely efficient and able, and if anything was going wrong in any of the nine

theatres, she would appear like magic. She knew about everything. She was amazing. *Kathleen*

a very, very strict sister … I did something wrong one day and … I said, 'I'm sorry Sister, I didn't think.' 'You're not here to think, nurse, you're here to do as you're told'. *Edna*

Sister X, she was very nice, of course she was strict with her little black book, she used to go round … noting everything, if the curtains weren't straight or the screens put straight and the particular bugbear were the wheels … woe betide anybody who … was in charge of a bed and the bed wheels weren't straight. *Edith*

Because of the discipline, many students lived with fear:

And if I'm honest I think I was frightened the whole time, not with the patients, the rapport with patients seemed to be alright, but it's when I saw anyone in authority I just used to shrink. *Vera*

They were very strict you see … we were all afraid of the sisters. *Joan*

For some though this type of discipline was unacceptable.

Years later I was doing district in Ipswich, midwifery, and there was a doctor … and I said, 'Oh, you don't happen to have a sister'. 'Yes' he said, 'She was at The London … she's left …'cos the discipline was too fierce and she didn't like it'. *Vera*

How to survive

Living in [the nurses' home] … thank goodness … and the 'colleagueness', and the friendship. Support from each other was brilliant. *Edna*

Often they were able to benefit from the generosity of others, which included free theatre tickets:

they used to put a notice up on the board in The Luckes [nurses' home] to say there were tickets for … a show. *Vera*

One morning we were all laughing, I don't think the sisters were though … there was … [a bedpan] on top of the Queen [Alexandra] statue … it was medical students. … Never heard how they got treated. *Hilda*

The patients come first

Winfred remembers how the nurses' social lives were also strictly controlled.

one of my school friends, she was getting married and would I go … I hadn't got a day off … a nurse on my ward … said, 'Oh I'll change with you…', so I went down to Matron's Office and I said, 'My great friend was getting married and I … would love to go and I have got someone to change [with]', but then … I don't know who she was, said to me, 'Nurse, I want to ask you a question, which comes first, the patient or you?', and I said, 'The patient' so she said, 'Well there you

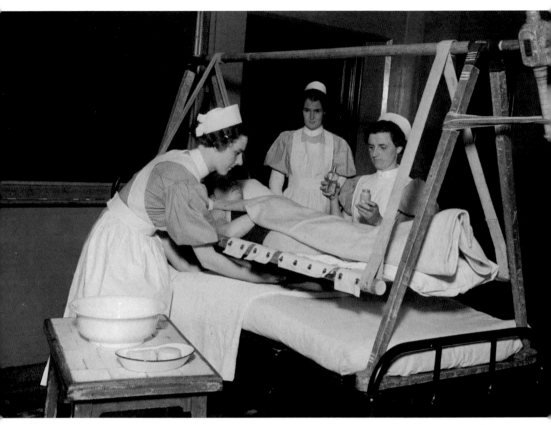

1940s: Practical teaching; washing a patient in a frame.
(Image appears by courtesy of The Royal London Hospital Archives and Museum)

have your answer, you can't change'.... Again, it was very much, 'that is the rule and you can't change it' ... so I never went to her wedding.

To request a specific day off Vera remembers:

Oh you had a piece of paper, you had to cut off the corners ... and then you put your name on and said, 'May I have such and such a day off' and it always had to end with 'Please Sister'.
  The one day that you were promised you could always have off duty was your 21st birthday, and of course matron was *in loco parentis* because you didn't come of age 'til you were 21, so she had to sign a consent for operation and things ... I mean for really, it's going back to the dark ages.

Clandestine lives and no mingling with the medical staff

'Living in' was also strictly controlled.

Of course, everybody lived in a nurses' home, everybody ... had to be in by ten pm every night. You could have late passes ... but one of the night sisters stood at the nurses' home and ticked your name off as you came in. *Irene* the rules were rather strict … I mean my father when he brought something, I think he brought a radio up for me from Yorkshire, was not allowed to come into my room in the nurses home 'cos he was a man, so I mean that … was quite extraordinary. *Gladys*

There were clandestine meetings with men. If you wished to marry you had to leave as Marjorie recalls:

One girl of my set was in love, went out, got married, had her wedding ring round her neck for the rest of the time and … we kept our fingers crossed that she didn't get pregnant. Or found out…

There was no mingling with the medical staff. No, no, no, no mingling with the medical students, that really was beyond the pale.

I do remember … a girl in the same year, she'd been up to no good and she was told to get out of the hospital by nine o'clock the next morning … I think she'd been to the Medical School or something like that … it was fierce. *Vera*

However, there seemed little time for romance as they were so tired after work:

by the time you've recovered from the day's chores you didn't want to go out anyway. *Edith*

no, no, no, not at all.… One day off a week and you'd have split duties … if we were off in the afternoon, would go to sleep 'cos we were so tired. *Vera*

when I got home … this aunt who brought us up, apparently I went to bed and I slept for nine hours, and she brought me a cup of tea the next morning, and I drank the tea and went to sleep for another nine hours. *Kathleen*

Someone said, 'Why didn't you get married?'…'Well two things, first of all there weren't … that many men … [a]nd you couldn't go out and socialise because I mean all we had was a day off … spent a night and a day at home and came back … that was it. *Betty*

Their lives revolved around hospital life:

one didn't see news or anything, you didn't have a newspaper … I don't recall that we knew much that was going on outside, that was our little world. *Pamela*

Religion, rituals, and routine practice

Religion played an important part in the hospital. At eight am, the ward sister would kneel on a hassock in the middle of the ward and say the prayers, and every two weeks, a vicar, known as Holy Joe, held a service in the ward.… There were two orthodox Jewish wards … [o]ne was for men, and one other was ladies. The wards were called Rothschild and Helene Raphael … they had their own kosher kitchen. There was strict Jewish religion on the wards. Candles were lit on Friday evenings, and Saturday was their holy day. *Dorothy*

Patient care rituals included:

all new patients had to have their hair combed for nits. And the patients didn't like it, especially if they'd just had their hair done.… The other peculiarity I remember was the patients were allowed to have an egg for their breakfast if their visitors brought them one and we had to collect up these, write their name on them and whether they wanted soft or hard and then we had to cook them before we left ... in the morning [after night duty] and I never got mine right! *Eileen*

Mealtimes were quite a ritual where a trolley was brought onto the ward and the sister would stand up and then you stood down in rotation ... patients who needed to be fed were served first, and allocated a nurse, and they stayed with them to either feed them or to see that they really fed properly. *Irene*

Routine work included:

the strict scrubbing of hands before everything and between everything, scrubbing of bed mats and cleaning casters. Bed table cleansing ... [r]egular bedpan rounds, not when required, but you were on a bedpan now whether you wanted [it] or not. Daily bed baths ... and talking, getting to know them [your patients] and getting to know their families, as well, greeting them and making them welcome. *Edna*

If a patient developed a pressure sore it was considered poor nursing care.

I only ever saw one pressure sore and that was a lady ... who'd come from another hospital. *Vera*

Laying up trolleys and carrying trays was always insisted upon and had to be done correctly.

On Friday nights we always laid up a trolley for removal of fish bone, well people ate fish on Fridays. *Vera*

Sunday [in theatres] was cleaning out the theatre, trolleys upside-down, clean out the wheels, count all the things that we had to count. *Elsie*

Finding X-rays were also part of routine work:

I can always remember X-rays being missing ... you can't find them and you spent ... the night before a clinic ... it was one of your duties to get everything, all the paperwork, all ready, and the wretched X-rays were never with it. So the next day, you're chasing the X-ray people up, you know, the same old story. *Irene*

Medical staff - wise, fractious and famished.

it was such a ritual when the consultant was coming round ... everybody had to ... sit up in bed, and the bedclothes had to be as though you were in the Army... very often these consultants ... were of course surrounded with medical students, but sister was there too.... I've heard consultants doing this more than once, telling their medical students that if they are wise, they would consult sister, she has years of experience. *Kathleen*

I did my theatres [experience] ... [the] neurosurgeon, threw his tools all over things ... you had to grab them up and sterilise them again. *Elsie*

Student nurses not only cared for the patients:

> Well Blockbusters were a milk drink made with Horlicks and Ovaltine and mixed together and we used to make them … for the medical students … we weren't allowed to eat or drink on the ward. *Winifred*

At the Annexes

The annexes, to which some of the students were sent during their training, included Banstead in Surrey and Brentwood in Essex. They were considered a welcome break although they did have their down sides.

> it was very pleasant, Banstead, because it was in the country more or less, and I used to love to watch the squirrels rushing up and down the big trees. *Kathleen*

> it was a bit dreary…. It was a long walk from the station … we always walked, I mean there weren't any buses or anything in those days…. And we didn't like the mice when they came in, it was summer and it was very hot … [s]o they opened the doors which was fair enough, 'til the mice came in, I wasn't keen on [that]. *Betty*

Brentwood was a much bigger annexe providing 345 beds. The beds were inside huts that included seventy for patients with tuberculosis.

> I went to Brentwood … I liked being in the country, it was medical and surgical, tuberculosis and neuro surgical wards. *Pamela*

> One of the jobs was trying to fill up those horrible stoves, coke stoves … that was the only heat … they were just sort of left over from the war, it was extraordinary. *Vera*

There were compensations as Gladys recalls:

> There were still a lot of soldiers from … the camp at Brentwood … and they were fit and healthy young men … they were on complete bed rest and it was an absolute nonsense, they probably just had an appendix out or something, fortnight before … the moment the day sister had gone they got out of bed to go and say hello to their buddies and it wasn't easy to … keep them under any kind of control, we were too young…. It was quite a lot of fun.

Night duty – stress, smoking and sister's visits

Being on night duty, for three months at a time, from 8.30 p.m. to 8.00 a.m., whether at The London or at the annexes, was an entirely different experience.

> there were still stoves then in those days. In the middle of the ward on the internal wall, one each side. Two stoves, one for each half of the ward. … I did nights on Turner and we used to sit round the fires at night and we'd pack the drums with gamgee swabs and other dressings. It was quite nice and restful because someone would sit at the desk, or that's where a staff nurse … would sit, but we'd sit by the fire and pack these in and it was quiet. We always had a cloth that we put round the lamps so the lamp only shone on the bed, wasn't the whole ward. And you could hear what was happening. You recognised people's breathing. *Elsie*

1940s: A nurse's bedroom in the Edith Cavell Home; this layout remained unchanged until the 1980s.

I didn't mind night duty at all because it didn't contain all the hustle and bustle of the daytime. *Edith*

I remember working twenty-four nights … in a row. I nearly died when I saw this … it only happened to me once … you did what you were told. *Vera*

There were always challenges:

Used to hate it when the [night] sister came on, you'd only been on, perhaps, the first time on that ward, and you had to know the name, the age and what the patient was suffering from, and what treatment they'd had that day … [r]idiculous, wasn't it? *Irene*

the staff nurse … was so dreadful to me … I mean she was disgraceful, I don't think I ever could have gone and worked with her again. *Vera*

There were routine jobs at night, as Edith recalls:

I remember filling tins with dressings … swabs and cotton wool balls, which we used to make, and we used to have to order dressings if we were … getting on the low side … which was quite enjoyable really … and checking drips and making sure patients weren't in pain, and if they were we'd call night sister and of course the dreaded sister's visits, I think she used to come round twice.

I had to count the teaspoons every night and if there was one missing you stayed there 'til you found it…. Well you always did find it, 'cos otherwise we'd still be there!

An ever present feature were cockroaches:

there was a big kitchen … and you could make your cup of coffee [for a patient] … by the streetlight, you didn't have to put the light on, so you opened a very big cupboard … [c]ockroaches rained down on you. … We always had problems with cockroaches … where we had the hot plates … and every week they were … trying … but they never managed to get rid of them. *Elsie*

I was never told what my routine jobs were … like making incontinent pads … I knew about cleaning … polishing the inkwells and that sort of thing … I cleaned the hotplate down with all these cockroaches running around! *Vera*

Apart from these routine jobs, there was recognition of the burden of responsibility that young nurses also carried at night. Kathleen recalls:

I think it was an acute medical [ward], because there were things like patients suddenly having fits and things like that, and the night sister came round and she said, 'How old are you, nurse?' I said, '19.' She said, 'This is an awful lot of responsibility we're giving you for this ward' … she realised what a challenge this ward was … and we were on night duty for three months at a time … so anyway, we got through it somehow … because we could phone for the night sister … we had to learn what we could cope with ourselves and what we needed help with.

In this decade smoking for women was increasing and becoming fashionable. It also helped to relieve stress:

And there was a night nurses' sitting room … somewhere in the basement, which was solid with smoke, because we were all at the cigarettes by then. *Edna*

Never to be forgotten experiences

My second night duty … was in a women's surgical ward, and I remember that one of the patients … said, 'Nurse, get me some newspapers', so I thought 'I wonder what she wants these [for]'… she said, 'Now spread them over the bottom of the bed.' I did this. I didn't know, I thought she must be a little bit, you know…. When the night sister came round, she said, 'Nurse, what are these newspapers doing on this bed?'… I said, 'The patient asked for them,' and she took my hand … she was very nice about it. She said, 'Nurse, these people are poor. They come from the East End of London, and they use newspapers for blankets. Please go to the cupboard and get her a blanket'… [s]o that was another lesson learnt. *Kathleen*

it was on a woman's medical ward and an elderly lady had come in that day … for investigation, she spoke beautifully and she was very aristocratic and people said … 'We keep taking her out to the toilets, she doesn't seem to want to go, so would you make sure she goes … before she goes to sleep?' So I said … 'Would you like to go to the toilet?' 'No', so when she went out to wash … I said, 'The toilets are next door, would you like to go?' 'No', so I said, 'Well would you like me to bring you a commode?' and she didn't know what I meant so I showed her, 'Take that thing away', she said, so I thought 'Well what can I do?' … the ward was dark and I sat down to write something down on the chart … and I could hear a sort of tinkly noise and I turned round to find the elderly lady sitting on top of her slippers spending a penny, but she turned to me in a very beautiful voice and said, 'the sanitary arrangements in this place are disgusting'. So of course I had to help her get back into bed, change her nightie and … mop the floor up … the next day she'd been admitted to a psychiatric hospital so obviously she wasn't very well. *Winifred*

In order to get through the work before the day staff arrived:

I know we used to wake them [patients] up far too early, at a ridiculous hour, and of course very ill patients who needed complete care … maybe they didn't know much about it … they used to have a blanket bath … and made the bed of course … if any catheter … needed emptying, and make sure that everything was working as it should be. *Edith*

At the end of night duty no one wanted to receive a poor ward report, as Marjorie recalls:

I had the worst [ward] report I ever had … we had reports that we had to sign in the presence of the sister who'd written it … [s]he'd taken no consideration of the fact that I officially was in charge of the children's ward on night duty and every time there was a theatre case I had to go and do theatres … so I duly went down to see her [matron] and I said, 'well if that's the sort of nurse I am at the end of … basically nearly three years … I'd better go now'. And she said, 'Now nurse … [j]ust listen to me for a moment. There are, I would think, nearly a hundred doctors at The London and if all of those wrote a report about me one of them would have written a report like that.' She said, 'I'm very sorry but you're completely incompatible'…. I said … 'The thing that hurt me most was that she hadn't the courage to give the report to me so I could sign it face-to-face'. …And she said, 'I do understand and I will see sister X … and you are to go to the ward and see her and she will apologise to you', and she did. But I mean that was how easy it was for us to talk to our matron. *Marjorie*

East End folk, you could walk anywhere

Although The London received patients from all over the country and beyond for specialist treatment, most of the patients were the local community who lived and worked in the poorest part of London, the East End. Many were first and second generation of immigrants, Jewish people originally from eastern Europe and Russia.

Parts of the East End were considered to be 'rough' areas but:

any London Hospital nurse could walk round any back street in the … area, and no one would ever touch them or abuse them. They were so well respected. *Irene*

Nurses learned much about the local culture:

> I was brought up in a little village in Essex and you didn't meet anybody different … but meeting East Enders … of course, that was fascinating … I went to a Jewish youth club with an ex-patient, there was a young girl who was about sixteen, and when she was discharged she said, 'Well, come to my youth club', I said, 'Yes, lovely.' It was great. *Edna*

> the patients that stood out … it was the way they spoke to each other, 'are you there Dolly?' … 'Well don't forget we're going home soon.' 'Well I can't go home, I haven't got a hat.' 'Well we'll have to buy you a hat' … I've never forgotten. *Winifred*

Vera remembers the patients in Fielden House, the private wards. They included:

> people who'd made money out of the War, they weren't very nice to us. Whereas … what I call the … aristocracy, they were always lovely to us … another person I looked after … was the organist at Sandringham and [he] very kindly said, 'you must come and see me', what he hadn't realised [was] I couldn't afford the fare, that was a sadness. … I don't think people realised how hard up we were, and did you know we weren't allowed to … accept any gifts? Well I remember there was a lady there who had an account at Harrods and she'd got nylon stockings for us all … and we'd never had anything like that, they lasted me for years. *Vera*

Patients made an impression on them in different ways:

> I … remember a young lass … on a medical ward and she was diabetic and she said to me, 'I know I'm going blind so I'm learning Braille…', I was just absolutely full of admiration for [her]. *Vera*

> I nearly became a Communist … one of the patients couldn't sleep and he was the head of the Communist Party in London and he spoke so glowingly about the dreams and desires for people, for poor people to have a chance for … good education and he made communism really sound an ideal sort of lifestyle … I was very impressed by him. *Gladys*

> I nearly got killed [in Casualty] … this poor chap who was obviously 'doolally' and I think he thought I was a Japanese … he'd been in the war and he'd been torpedoed and he was trying to strangle me. *Vera*

> I can remember a little girl who was obviously going to die, who had … kidney failure … and there was very little she could eat, but she could eat … an apple. And I can remember … making a big effort to peel this apple for her, and doing it so that it stayed in a whole, the peel. Just in order to make her smile, and I managed to do that … the poor soul, she was really sick. … The London at that time was a research place for kidney disease … [n]ever heard about dialysis in those days. So there was very little on offer for such patients. *Kathleen*

> I can remember … a chap who'd got an aneurysm and at the bottom of the bed was a bucket of sand. So if the aneurysm burst and there was all this blood we had to throw this…. Horrible. *Vera*

There were some diversions:

> I was in the TB ward … it was a very hot summer, we had all the windows open, the patients … were very mischievous because they wanted to know what our Christian names were so they'd grab us and pull us across the bed to try and find our label on the back of our aprons. *Elsie*

A special tea and the tradition of Christmas at The London

Among these vivid memories of patients were also the very special occasions, in particular the royal visits and the Christmas experience. Before a royal visit:

> everyone was excited, a special tea for us … we looked out of the windows and … we saw these people going … upstairs so they could look down on Queen Mary. And Queen Mary didn't go in the front door, she went round the side, she was greeted with a whole lot of bottoms! *Elsie*

Everyone worked at Christmas. Wards were decorated and presents were found for all the patients.

> We actually were asked where we'd like to go [for Christmas Day] and naturally I said the children's ward, not really appreciating how sick the children would be.
> none of the nurses were allowed Christmas Day off, which was fair enough. *Irene*

> we took in patients … they were the sort of down and out types … [a]nd they … loved it but that they wanted to smoke … or drink more, so they were ready to go home again, but they enjoyed coming in for Christmas, so in fact Christmases were quite fun really. *Gladys*

Patients still had to be cared for as Marjorie relates:

> the nursing staff sang carols and started over in the Block, they walked across the garden singing … they went right to the top of the building [hospital] and came down in a zigzag all the way and ended up at midnight … in the front hall … so you would hear these lovely carols all coming through the hospital. If you were on the wards then you were there watching to see the reactions of the patients so you could go and comfort them if necessary.
> On Christmas Eve we had Christmas tea … in the medical college. How they did it I do not know, but we had meringues, we had choux buns, we had Christmas cake and when you think that it was all on ration, to this day I don't know. But you have to remember we were still voluntary and there were lots of people who were wealthy who sent gifts to The London which included the gift of violets from somebody down in Devon, the sisters always wore a little … posy of violets … and they always wore their 'tails' for Christmas Day.

On Christmas Day:

> Father Christmas came, he was brought in on a stretcher with the fairies around him who distributed more gifts to the patients. *Elsie*

instead of us being sent to coffee … on Christmas Day we went and had sherry with sister. Well us green as grass like [*laughter*] were spliced with this … I can't say that we were overcome but we were quite relaxed, let me put it like that! … It's the only time we ever let our hair down…. And on Christmas night the nursing staff went over to matron's party, which was held in the medical college and the sisters did charades … which was great fun and matron was always there, we had a very nice time. *Marjorie*

Intelligence of the brain and heart

The students received regular classroom teaching sessions:

We had consultant lectures … if we were on night duty we had to stay up and still go to those lectures…. But in my second year all the student nurses were called together … matron told us that we were going to change from our present way of receiving our lectures to having a study day … we were going to have a block of three months with study days and it meant that you had your study day, you were then free at five o'clock and you had your day off the following day which caused quite a lot of havoc with nursing staff on the wards … matron informed us very firmly that as we were the first set … [to do this,] if we didn't get our state registration it would doom the whole of study days. So with fear and trembling we began this new system! *Marjorie*

The Dean of the Medical School … [used] a wonderful phrase, '… because you're sitting here, you must have "intelligence of the brain" … but you also need to have "intelligence of the heart"' … [it's] something I carried [with me]. *Vera*

she'd [matron] done a tour in America … and she gave us a lecture of what she had found … she was appalled at the way the Americans treated their patients in hospital. The bed table was at the bottom of the bed with a dinner on it and no one helped them, or they got an arm in plaster and they couldn't get to it, if they didn't eat it, it got taken away and they had these orderlies who didn't know anything about patients, [she said] 'I hope it never comes here.' *Elsie*

When matron gave us one of our lectures and she was trying to emphasise that we must treat everybody the same, and apparently one day a gentleman came in … [dressed in] a shabby raincoat, arrived at the Porter's Lodge, and said he wanted to see matron … he … said, 'I want to build your nurses a swimming pool'. And he did … I think … he was a sort of millionaire … that was why she told us the story, you never know! *Vera*

I can remember [my tutor] … she looked like a great-grandmother to me … she gave us our practical nursing experience and there was a doll in the bed and … [she] said to me would I give this patient the medication and she said, 'it is written on the blue board'. I picked the blue board up … but there were some other things I didn't know … so I immediately asked her what the other things were, and she said to me … 'You're the first person that's asked me … and that's very important' … people [should] not just do as they're told. *Winifred*

THE GENERAL NURSING COUNCIL FOR ENGLAND AND WALES.

The Board of Examiners by whom this paper was set is constituted as follows :—

Miss M. M. C. Louden, m.b., b.s., f.r.c.s.   Miss F. Taylor, s.r.n.

W. G. Sears, Esq., m.d., m.r.c.p.   Miss A. E. A. Squibbs, s.r.n.

FINAL STATE EXAMINATION FOR THE GENERAL PART OF THE REGISTER.

Wednesday, 9th February, 1949.

MORNING.

MEDICINE and MEDICAL NURSING TREATMENT.

(First Paper.)

Time allowed 1½ hours.

IMPORTANT.—*Read the questions carefully, and answer only what is asked, as no marks will be given for irrelevant matter.*

Credit will be given for legible handwriting.

NOTE.—You must answer THREE questions and not more than three.

1. Describe an attack of bronchial asthma. State what you know about the causes and treatment of this condition.

2. Give an account of the symptoms and complications of diabetes mellitus. State how a case of diabetic coma would be treated.

3. What symptoms may be present in a case of early pulmonary tuberculosis ? Discuss the treatment which may be employed in a patient who has one lung affected by the disease.

4. Describe the symptoms, complications and treatment of scarlet fever.

5. What conditions may cause the appearance of blood in the urine ? How may this be recognised and what investigations might be carried out to ascertain the cause of the bleeding ?

6. State briefly what you know about :—
    (a) venesection ;
    (b) quinsy ;
    (c) infective hepatitis (catarrhal jaundice) ;
    (d) paraldehyde ;
    (e) thiouracil.

A General Nursing Council Exam paper dated 1949. (Image appears by courtesy of Jean McCrae's daughter)

Marjorie remembers the work of the pharmacist:

> the head pharmacist, he was a little tiny man … he picked all the [herbal] plants that he had grown in the hospital garden and brought them to us … they were all in nice little pots … and then we were shown the pills that he made … and they [also] made up all the things like intravenous injections at that time. And he really was incredible, I was very fond of him. … I was on a medical ward and we had a patient with tuberculosis and the drugs were just beginning to come in … [such as] Isoniazid [antibiotic for TB] … and he used to come up to the ward and discuss the flavours that he was putting in the medicine [with patients] and they would discuss it like discussing cocktails!

Role models

Strong leadership was demonstrated:

> Matron … was absolutely brilliant. Wonderful woman, full of dignity, compassion, and we practically had to flatten ourselves against the wall if she did a round, we just stood to attention. *Edna*

Qualified nurses and senior students saw training the next generation as part of their role.

> Everything you were taught … always they'll ask, 'Have you done this before or seen it done before?' So we never did anything on any patient that we'd never seen and sometimes a senior [student] nurse, say third year, would teach us. *Betty*

> someone taught me about taking out stitches … it was fantastic … she said, 'What you do is, you have your scissors and you cut the stitch, you do not just pull it out, you take your scissors, lay it by the side of the wound and then pull the stitch out', oh I blessed that staff nurse for years afterwards because it worked, it stopped that tension. *Vera*

> if you were taught how to do anything a 'London' sister would show you how it was to be done. She would then instruct you to do it … while she observed you … she never ever found fault with you at the patient's bedside, you would be taken aside and it would be explained to you why certain things should have been done better. You were given a pro [probationary] staff post [as a third year student] which taught you the ropes for the beginning of the administration of a ward. *Marjorie*

Good learning from 'outsiders' too:

> Sister X… said to me, 'You're making beds with me tonight', now if you said that to most people they'd think 'Well, so what', it wasn't like that at all, by the time she'd finished with each patient she knew how they were, whether they were in pain, how their family were … the last thing, I can still see her doing this … was to put the bedside locker within reach and the bedside table…. I remember standing at the end of this man's bed and looking at this patient and I thought 'You look so comfortable, I know how to look after a patient now' … basic things without all the technical stuff … I've never forgotten Sister X… not 'London' trained … and I think she was the only one at that stage. *Vera*

The impact of the NHS

The hospital became part of the National Health Service (NHS) in 1948 when the voluntary hospital system came to an end and the state took control of health care. The London, like other teaching hospitals, relinquished its independence to government control.

> And the change from being voluntary hospitals to NHS … didn't really concern us, we just went on nursing … but … for the hierarchy it must have been very difficult. *Edna*

> You have to remember that 'the men' at The London were very, very anti [the NHS], even though we were down at our heel, I mean we were completely dependent on free monies. I mean the patients had to pay … if they could, we had

an Almoner [precursor to social worker]. … No one was turned away. And most importantly … the Samaritans Society, you see, was where the free monies went directly to patients. There was a whole lot of money because there were wealthy Jewish people in Whitechapel … [b]ut you see The London knew it [the NHS] was coming, so there were lots of things that we needed, so money was spent in that year because the amount of money you were granted by the government depended on what you had spent in that last year. *Marjorie*

Changing roles and paying for the privilege

Once you had qualified there appeared to be no support for role transition:

when you did your Finals you had to go to the office [Matron's Office] and ask, which was a bit horrendous, and I remember going into the office … very formally, and they said, 'Yes you've passed', so I was obviously pleased, sort of dancing up the stairs … by the time I got to the [ward] of course it was back to the formal thing…. I said, 'Sister, I have passed my exam', and she said, 'Right, go and check that naso-oesophageal tube' … you weren't allowed to do that … [as a student]. *Vera*

when I left, I hadn't completed this whole four years [training] because I had my appendix out … was sent home for a month and I had to make up that sick leave before they would give me this certificate of training … I didn't make it up, my husband paid for me. He always says he bought me! But we were only earning about £5 a month. *Eileen*

Friends for life

Strong bonds formed between students which, for many, have lasted a lifetime:

[we] were friends until she died … the same set, we started together … I mean I didn't know she was going to be matron [here] then, neither did she, but she was always cut out for that sort of work, she was always very proper…. Yes, I could see the power in her … she was very nice. *Joan*

I'm still in touch with one girl who's in Australia … you could go to Australia, I think it was £10, and she, of course, got a job as a nurse straightaway. She then married a sheep farmer and was out in the country, and her nearest neighbour was about five miles away … but I've since met her daughter. *Irene*

Beyond Training

On qualifying:

they tried to encourage everybody to stay on for a staff year, they said it was worth it, it was most valuable, you learnt such a lot … they went on about it … well we hadn't made up our minds for anything else so we thought we'd stay. *Betty*

all my colleagues either wanted to be air hostesses or go to Australia on that £10 journey, or look after men and I decided no, I'm going to look after women, that's what I'm going to do. So, I did the staff year … big mistake. Sister did not like me! *Vera*

Prize giving and badge presentation in the Medical College Library, 1949. Nurses who had already left the hospital returned in mufti to receive their hospital badge and certificate.

> I did my staff year in medical outpatients, I really wanted to have some evenings free. *Eileen*

For Marjorie this led on to promotion:

> on this particular morning as a staff nurse … [sister] said, 'Nurse I wish you to go to Matron's Office …', so I scratched my brains and thought 'Oh lord, what have I done now?' So off I trotted to Matron's Office … 'Nurse you are to go down to the linen room and be measured for a blue dress'. That's the first I knew. … I said, 'But Miss X, I do not wish to have a blue dress.' 'Oh, what do you mean nurse? …In that case you'll have to see matron' … I saw matron and she said, 'I understand nurse that you do not wish to be measured for a sister's uniform … Well I would like to know the reason why', so I said, 'Well I'm going to do my midwifery in three months' time, there is no point in my … going into blue. And so she said, 'I understand' and I said, 'also,'… 'I wouldn't consider it either, because I do think that in order to have authority you need to go away for two years and then come back when there is no one that remembers you as a student nurse.' 'Oh …in that case I understand, but nurse I'm afraid I do need you to go

onto night duty tonight and you will wear 'gates', which was a little notice to say sister's duties … And the other thing she said to me was, 'If ever you would like a blue dress you have only to let me know', and I felt very honoured.

From general training to midwifery

I finished in '45 and then I did midwifery in Edinburgh because I wanted to get as far away from London and the bombs as possible and the war. *Joan*

I left after training, because … I had an elderly father and this aunt who had … a fractured hip, and … I felt I ought to be … nearer home. I was the only girl. And so I did my midwifery training [in Liverpool]. *Kathleen*

From one extreme to the other:

I [became] a midwife … [a]nd one thing I can remember distinctly was … looking after a lady who'd lost her baby some time, like in the eighth month … we knew the baby would be born stillborn and it was Christmas Day and I was in the theatre, delivered the baby, and the mother … well she knew it was going to be stillborn, but the whole thing was so sad … we did everything and made the mother comfortable and I opened the door to go out and suddenly one of the other girls saw me and said, 'Oh come on, we're all following Father Christmas, we're all doing the hokey-cokey'… and it seemed … I'd come from one world into another world. *Winifred*

1940s: Rear view of The London Hospital showing patients on the balconies and the covered walkway.

Edna describes the time when her midwifery skills were called upon, despite not having completed the specific training:

> I went to do midder [midwifery] … I didn't like midder … so I didn't finish it, and my friend who I was with … she failed her midder [exams]. And carrying on from that … before the NHS came in, The London private staff used to do private nursing, obviously, in the community, rich and famous and royalty. They also did voluntary work, part of which was nursing the hop pickers in Kent, because they came from the East End, mostly. … [An] assistant matron, sent for us … and we wondered what we'd done, and she offered us this post in hop picking … very minimally paid … [s]o we went to the hop fields … and we were housed in a hut. And the first morning, we were just having a scratch breakfast in our hut, and a knock came at the door, a lovely lady, 'Quick, nurse, can you come, can you come? My friend's having a baby.' Me not finishing midder, [my friend] having failed it, and we have seen in our hut a great big box signed 'midwifery outfit,' and I thought 'No way' … but … [we] ran across to the hut … and it was her seventh child, so she knew a darn sight more about it than we did, and we delivered a little girl, easily, who was called [after us]. I wonder where she is now.

Towards the end of the decade Britain celebrated the marriage of Princess Elizabeth to Prince Philip, and London hosted the Olympic Games. India and the Republic of Ireland gained independence from Britain. In the same year that the National Health Service was established, 1948, the Empire Windrush brought excited and hopeful young people from the West Indies to London. Technology advancements during wartime included the jet engine, nuclear fusion, radar, and rocket technology which later became the starting points for space exploration and improved air travel. Medical innovation at this time included the mass production of penicillin, plastic surgery development for burns, and the safe storage and transportation of blood.

Learning to nurse in this decade, during and just after the war years, was a unique experience.

> It was hard but we used to think well 'Well we're here to train so get on with it' … that was the attitude. *Betty*

> I just think we all felt we were…very lucky being trained at The London because you do not forget the basics that you were taught and the respect [you had] for your seniors. *Pamela*

Despite the strict discipline and social control there was a deep appreciation:

> when I left The London I always hoped I would be able to maintain London standards wherever I went because I always felt that I had been taught by … very wonderful people to a wonderful standard and tradition of which I'm very proud now. *Marjorie*

The London Hospital badge

1950s, Mixed media on canvas, 2017, Paula Day.

Chapter 2

The 1950s – 'Getting over the war'

don't forget, the war, we were all suffering, we were all beginning to recover from the war, they were building everywhere. *Mavis*

By the beginning of the 1950s there had been five years of peace. However, the effects of the war were still being felt. Rationing was to continue for another six years, and the damage caused by bombing was very evident throughout London. Some of the damage to the hospital was yet to be repaired. Many of those who were interviewed felt that this was very much a period of 'getting over the war'.

Life was tough and austere, with little money to spend. At the beginning of the decade very few people had a washing machine or fridge, and only ten per cent of the population had a phone, though the Coronation of Queen Elizabeth II in 1953 prompted a boost in the sale of TVs.

The 1950s was a challenging time for healthcare. Although 1948 marked the birth of the NHS, conditions at that time caused many of the maladies that befell those who lived in the East End, who in turn were nursed by those who trained during this decade. This included respiratory diseases that were a result of the pollution and smogs that characterised cities such as London at the time, until the Clean Air Act of 1956. Large scale vaccination programmes for children only began towards the end of this decade.

Women had worked in many responsible roles during the war, but now the men had returned job options were more limited. Many were not expected to have a proper career and gave up work when they married. The choice appeared to be working in a clerical role, a shop, or training to be a nurse or teacher. However, there is evidence in the interviews that reasons for deciding to train as a nurse were varied, and some of them chose this route instead of pursuing a more purely academic role:

> I had a headmistress who very much wanted me to go in for teaching and go to university … and I was interested and would have liked to have done history or literature … those were my two favourite things … but the other half of me very much wanted to do nursing. *Marina*

> I shocked the school, I was head of the school, you were meant to go on to Oxford and Cambridge and so on and I said, 'No, I'm doing nursing,' and they were horrified. 'You're doing nursing? What on earth are you doing nursing for? *Norma*

Some had a very clear desire to become a nurse dating back to childhood, influenced by family experiences:

> I always wanted to be a nurse from the age of three … my father was a medical orderly, stretcher bearer in the Royal Army Medical Corps at Ypres and Passchendaele in the First World War and he spoke so enthusiastically about the nurses he worked with, especially Edith Cavell…. He knew of her in Brussels, in Belgium, they all knew of her. *Elizabeth*

Others had already tried some other form of employment, and their decision to train as a nurse was influenced by those they subsequently met. One individual travelled to Yugoslavia with students who belonged to the National Union of Students, where she became convinced that nursing would provide her with a professional qualification that she desired:

> I went off to Yugo[slavia] … I gave up my job just like that, went off with a whole group of students, I was the youngest in the group … and we had a wonderful time and I met various trained nurses and doctors and they thoroughly brainwashed me … [by saying] if I didn't have much education that I was the type to go nursing … there was no idea of nursing the sick – I just somehow had to get a bit of education … I needed a professional qualification. *Iris*

Choosing to train at The London Hospital was for some due to being in a medical family, who for generations had trained and worked there:

> I chose The London … very much for family reasons because my father, he trained there and he worked there and so it was a hospital I knew and respected and … had a very good tradition … of charitable work and compassionate work for the poor and the needy, in a very poor part of London and, of course, they had a lot of very famous mission families such as Barnardo's. *Norma*

For others, such as Elizabeth, it was the experiences of their family who lived in the East End:

> My mother's family came from Spitalfields, her dad had had half his tongue removed with a cancer from a clay pipe, and they turned it around, they took half one side, turned it around and sewed it together, and then taught him how to speak again and that was in the '20s … [s]o they were very impressed with The London.

Pre-training experience

Although it was not possible to start training as a nurse at The London before the age of 18, there was opportunity to work in some pre-training capacity as a nursing cadet. The placements were often in convalescent homes linked to The London Hospital, such as the one Marion describes as the 'beautiful old house … right on the seafront' in Felixstowe, bequeathed by Hermann de Stern. She continues:

> We wore purple overalls and dresses, and … we were called nursing cadets, because downstairs … I think it was convalescence for The London … and upstairs were East End kids, who needed some convalescence, and we used to take them for walks along the sea front … controlling these, about half a dozen of these kids along the beach … that was an initiation of fire.

Mavis, working alongside her mother, a matron in a nursing home, gained a great deal of experience prior to undertaking her training:

> I'll tell you something very strange. New Year's Eve when I was nearly 18, my mother had been sitting with a patient all evening and I had gone out to celebrate, and came back and she was still sitting in the same room with this person who was, what we used to call Cheyne Stoking … and I said, 'Look, I'm wide awake, you

go and lie down and get some sleep,' and so I sat with this lady. And after a while I was noticing that I couldn't hear her breathing, so I waited a while … tested to see she wasn't breathing, turned her over to the wall to change the sheets … I don't know if you still lay people out in the same way, but we have to wait a while … [t]urned her to the wall and washed her, sponged her down in tepid water. Then turned her this way. As she turned towards me her arm swung loose and banged my leg. Air came out of her lungs and went, 'Arghh!… I thought, oh gosh, I've washed one half of her and she's still alive. … She wasn't … but it took a while for me to kick in.

'Grand looking women in their blue dresses and frilly hats'

Mothers were requested to accompany their daughters to the interview to gain a place as a student nurse at the hospital:

> I remember sitting in the Matron's Office waiting to be called in, and all these rather grand looking women in their blue dresses and frilly hats. *Beryl*

The process was not as straightforward for some as for others:

> I was really quite concerned because there were several other girls waiting to be interviewed and they came out and each one had been told whether they had been accepted or not but I wasn't told anything and about two weeks later I got a letter – signed by the matron … I'm Jewish and the letter said, providing my religious observances did not interfere with my duties they would be pleased to have me! *Rita*

Preliminary Training School (PTS)

PTS continued to take place at Trueloves in Ingatestone until 1952, when it moved back to Tredegar House.

The memory of arriving at the hospital and being shown the accommodation remains strong for Brenda:

> I started on 31 December, 1957, I remember going to Tredegar and we got there about five o'clock, my parents took me, and we walked into this room where there was an iron bedstead and chair, one table, and chest of drawers … I think my parents were a bit horrified at first. Anyway, I was on the top floor and of course at midnight what happened on the Thames, all the boats sounded their sirens and I heard this and it made me feel very homesick because I'd never been away from home before.

And for June:

> my first day at Tredegar, we all sat in a circle, 36 of us, and … had to introduce themselves. Now, I'd come from quite a humble background, and when it started off, 'Daddy was a doctor, daddy was a bank manager'… I'd had this before when I was a scholarship girl. … They'd all been paying and I was in there … and I'd already had to fight my way through that lot and I thought, I'm not having this again … so when it got to my turn I said, 'Right, I come from a row of 150 houses.

We're as poor as church mice and happy as pigs in muck,' and there was silence, and then [three of the student nurses] came over to me and said, 'Thank God somebody's normal,' and we stayed friendly for the rest of our training.

Marina, who began her training in 1951, reflects on her experience:

I do think the Preliminary Training School was a very, very important part of the introduction ... not just to nursing but to the whole attitude and the respect of the patients and the dignity of the patients, it was so drummed into us ... they emphasised the creation of a healthy and healing environment, and the importance of fresh air, and the cleanliness was absolutely everything, around the bed as well as the bed itself, and the nutrition and the invalid cooking, and ... absolutely everything was always taken on a tray, even if it was one tablet on a teaspoon and the glass of water, very important. And we practiced feeding patients in bed when we were lying flat, because you don't realise how difficult that is ... we often did bandaging practice out in the gardens. ...With great hysteria going on because, you can imagine, all the complications ... we got into. *Marina*

Audrey describes not only the cleaning, but also some slightly more unusual activities:

We had to start off by doing housework ... dusting ... clean the toilets and clean the silver.

we had to do foot exercises and pick up a pencil with our toes ... we were told we were going to be on our feet all day long, so to strengthen our feet ... and I think we had to tie knots ... with a piece of string with our feet.

Many were filled with trepidation and embarrassment:

And we used to have to go up to The London, by coach, on a Saturday morning, which we all absolutely dreaded ... it was just the last few weeks, and we were terrified because we'd never actually been in a ward. *Marina*

while we waited for our Norman Hartnell uniforms to be made, we were dressed in a sort of [purple] overall ... [s]ome were too long, some were too short, some were too wide and some were too narrow, but we all shared the embarrassment. *Elizabeth*

Audrey recalls:

I remember being very self-conscious walking up the wards and thinking everyone was looking at me, and one of the patients called me over and said, 'You think we're all looking at you don't you?' I said, 'Well yes, I do,' she said, 'Don't worry, we're not, we're just getting on with our own lives'.

I came straight from school, so into nursing was such a contrast. Immediately you were called nurse, you know, right from the doorstep, it was nurse this and nurse that, and that I found a bit difficult.

Moving up

Once the preliminary training had been completed and the examination had been passed, the student nurses moved up into the Luckes Nurses' Home next to the hospital in Whitechapel:

and then went up to the Luckes Home where we had to share rooms in the basement for the first three months … until we got a room of our own … I slept on a camp bed I seem to remember. *Pauline*

The plumbing and washing facilities appear to have been very memorable:

Another thing that I remember about our room there, it had a wash basin in it … there wasn't a proper plug as we know it, it was a sort of cylindrical thing that … stood in the plughole so that when the water got a bit too high it would float. *Rita*

it was interesting being in the Luckes, because these ginormous baths with brass taps, and overflows that went straight out into the outside … and three washbasins in marble. *Marion*

Close bond

Many of the interviewees referred to the close bond they had with other members of their set, often with friendships lasting a lifetime. The nurses looked to each other for support, sharing their thoughts and experiences:

a lot of us [in our set] would crowd into a bedroom and drink coffee and chat away. *Iris*

The nurses also referred to feeling supported by those who were in charge, and acknowledged the existence of good leadership:

It felt safe … because … there was somebody in charge, and people who knew what they were doing … [a]nd the staff … the ward sisters on … most of the wards I worked on, they knew all their patients. *Marion*

'Still on rationing'

During the 1950s the nurses ate in the main hospital, with the cost of their food taken out of their salary:

there were separate dining rooms for the sisters and the doctors … and they took board and lodging at source so there was a never a question of, oh we can't afford to have lunch or whatever because it was already deducted. That was one good thing but … we lived on biscuits and things because the food was not that brilliant. *Pauline*

Up until July 1954, some rationing was still in place, as June recalls:

Don't forget we were still on rationing…. We were on rationing of things like butter, jam.

I mean on the amount we earned, I remember buying a coat, a beautiful red coat with brass buttons, but I couldn't afford the shoes and the handbag for weeks and months afterwards … I mean you really didn't have many clothes, and we were used to that because the war was not that far [away].

And of course everybody smoked, so you would rush through the food and then rush outside … to have a cigarette.

Marion also remembers:

> I think our first pay cheque was about £9 for the month.

The first ward

Life in the 1950s was disciplined and regimented, with student nurses expected to fall in line with behaviour and rules that had to be obeyed:

> you went into breakfast, and some of the mornings were freezing cold because it was winter, and you weren't allowed to wear cardigans, you'd got your capes, and the night sister signed you in for breakfast ... I mean, we were well conditioned ... unconsciously, perhaps, but it was certainly conditioning, and I suppose a level of institutionalisation. *Marion*

On their first ward, the junior nurses were given the more menial tasks:

> The sister in those days gave their orders via the staff nurse ... [a]nd as a junior probationer you spent most of your time in the sluice room... *Marina*

> setting up trolleys, which seemed to occupy most of my day, and scrubbing macs, and cleaning bedpans and putting them in the machine and stuff. They had a smell about them, the rubber. *Mavis*

> the work was absolutely regimented. *June*

> there was a Kardex, and there was a workbook ... [s]o it was very ordered, and you knew what you had to do, and you did it ... and there was a process. *Marion*

> In the morning when we went on, dirty work was done, the senior nurse did the dusting, 'cos it was considered very important ... keeping everywhere clean, so you prepared ... instruments that were boiled, dressings that had to be got ready, we made up our own packs, they didn't come ready made. *Elizabeth*

Various work patterns existed, but mainly the nurses worked split shifts, with a few hours off in the afternoon, returning for the busy late afternoon and evening time:

> mostly sleep ... we perhaps went to the sitting room and read or perhaps went over to the market in Whitechapel ... that was the worst bit about split shifts, really there was no time in between. *Pauline*

There was apprehension for tasks that would eventually become part of everyday life:

> I think answering the phone ... if the phone went and you had to answer it, whoever was nearer ... it took me a long time to get used to that. I had ... to answer the phone and this chap said he was at Grocer's, I'd never heard of Grocer's [ward] ... and I thought he said he was at the grocer's. *Audrey*

It became clear some things were not as straightforward as they seemed:

> I remember on my first day there was an old lady who badly wanted a bed pan and the staff nurse asked me what I was doing and I said, 'I'm off to get a bed pan for [the lady]', and I got a right ripping off because I hadn't been observant and she'd

got a catheter and she'd got a Dix bottle under the bed and how was she going to manage a bed pan to pass water, which is what she wanted to do! *Rita*

Some preferred nursing those patients who were on total bedrest:

My first ward was Turner which then was a male medical ward – [I] preferred total nursing care … I mean heart attack patients … that were on complete bed rest for goodness knows how long … I felt that was proper nursing. *Pauline*

'This is real nursing'

Sometimes first warders found themselves witnessing conditions they were not prepared for, nor had anyone given them any warning. These experiences forged strong, lasting memories for student nurses such as Mavis:

and then the sister came to do the dressing, and she said, 'You can come and stand in and observe at the end of the bed.' And I thought, this is it, this is real nursing … and the chap had bandages over most of his head and face, and she just looked at me to see that I was watching, and she started to take off the dressing, and then the last piece was a half piece and she just lifted it away, and half of his face came with it, and that shocked me. Because I hadn't seen any surgical stuff before … he had cancer, but that's all I was told. And when I saw the dressing come away with half of his face with it, it really shocked me…. I think she could have warned me. But then maybe she was testing me, I don't know.

Nothing was said afterwards, the nurse was just left to clear up the trolley.

The curse of counting

As in the previous decade, one recurrent theme throughout the interviews of those who trained in the 1950s was the daily task of counting cutlery, each piece being engraved with the name of the ward. This burden lay heavily on the junior student nurses who, as in Pauline's case, found themselves disciplined if the full quota had not been identified:

Throughout my whole three years and subsequent eighteen months as a staff nurse, there was only one time when I really thought I would have to give up … I was the one counting the cutlery this particular night and … there was a small knife missing. Well … you'd think that was the crime of the century and I said to sister … the counting is correct except for one small knife. So she told [me] I would have to find it before I could go off duty…. We used to have to go and look in the pig bins and things, I mean it was quite humiliating … after a while I said, I don't [know] where it is and she said, 'Have you looked in the patients' lockers.' So I said, 'Well I haven't looked in their lockers but I have asked the patients'. So she said, 'Well I suggest you look in the lockers nurse.' So by this time my supper time had gone, I knew I wouldn't get any, I was very tired, very tearful, I went round and one of the patients said, 'Oh yes, I've got a small knife in my locker, I'd forgotten.' So I said, 'Oh well at least it's found.' So she said to me, 'Please don't tell sister because I got told off yesterday, the same thing happened.' So when I went back to tell this particular sister that I had now found the knife, she said where was it. I said it was in a patient's locker. 'Whose locker,' she said. So I said, 'Well the patient has asked me not to say' and she absolutely came down on me like a ton of bricks, she said, 'When I ask you a straightforward question nurse, I expect a straightforward answer.' Well of course by this time I was all crying, tears and … I said, 'I can't … the patient has specifically asked me not to say and I'm in a difficult position.' And she took me to Matron's Office for insubordination … [I saw an assistant matron] and she asked sister to leave me there and she was most understanding and sympathetic and she said, 'I expect you've missed your supper.' And I said, 'Yes'… and obviously she couldn't be disloyal to the sister but … she was very reassuring and yes, she was very nice. I thought … being taken to Matron's Office, I thought I'd be dismissed.

So on my next day off when I went home, I said I wasn't going back. So my father promptly put me in the car and took me straight back, which was perhaps the best thing he could have done.

School of Nursing

Teaching continued once the nurses had started working on the wards, with lectures from the sister tutors, and consultant doctors and surgeons, which took place on the top floor of the Luckes Nurses' Home. Sister tutors were often described as formidable and austere, but there were many references as to how good they were at teaching, alongside some amusing recollections:

> I always remember [the nurse tutor] standing up in front of us giving a lecture of some sort on gynaecology and she took off … her detachable middle sleeve [of her uniform], and she held it up in front of her, she said, 'Imagine,' she said, 'This is the vagina!' *Rita*

> the sister tutor I remember most was Scottish … but she used to say, she used to long to talk about 'pathogenic microorganisms,' and we'd do anything to make her say it. *Mavis*

Volunteers were sought from the local area to help with some of the practical sessions:

> what I did like, we had very big practical [sessions], and they would get people from the East End to come in, and I remember having to apply an eye bandage to a person, and they'd obviously done it many times, and they whispered, 'Don't forget the bit that goes underneath.' *June*

'East Enders, tremendous guts, tremendous courage and I loved them'

There was a strong affection and respect for the local people:

> Well, certainly on the wards they were the local people and I loved them, both the women and the men had the typical Cockney resilience and humour … East Enders, tremendous guts, tremendous courage and I loved them. *Norma*

As throughout history, the East End was a vibrant mix of different races and cultures, reflecting the movement of races as a result of war and political changes:

> East London was very different in the late fifties … I mean, it was very, very Jewish, and delightful, lots of eastern European Jews, refugees. *Marion*

Beryl remembers the special diets required:

> People who were particularly Orthodox … you ordered kosher meals for them …
> [a]nd I suppose it was this time of year the rabbi would come in and blow a ram's
> horn … Yom Kippur … their New Year.

And the prayers said to everyone:

> and what I find interesting is that we used to have prayers in the ward every
> morning and I don't remember any [non-Christian] patients objecting.

There were also the characters seen both in and out of the hospital:

> Mrs X… was an old lady and she lived locally and … was a patient of the skin
> department, she was a very bedraggled old lady and fairly foreign in her ways,
> quite grubby, she had leg ulcers and she would come up to the skin department for
> dressings a couple of times a week … and while your back was turned, she would
> nick things off the treatment trolley and she could later be found, with a very old
> pram, peddling them in the Whitechapel Road. Any old bottles that were empty or
> nearly empty, she would take those and certainly bandages, I think she was found …
> [selling the bandages] … and she was not only well known in the skin department but
> I think she was also well known in Whitechapel. And she always told us that she had
> a sick daughter with heart problems at home, we never quite knew if this was so. *Rita*

'there was always something for the patients'

Nutrition seemed to be central in the nursing of the sick:

> the good thing was that before the patients had their meals, you offered them a
> bedpan and you sat them all up in bed and you put their bed tables straight so that
> they could reach their food and you went round with the sister and you served the
> food and they got a choice, if there was nothing there they liked then you used
> to go and make them scrambled egg … so there was always something for the
> patients and you went round and made sure that they had eaten something. *Brenda*

> I even spent some time in the diet kitchen, preparing the liquids for tube feeding
> and all the special diets that we had, salt free, diabetic, slimming, childrens'
> wards, but it was mostly the tube feeding, knowing what nourishment to give
> somebody that was having to be fed by tube. *Elizabeth*

> And the wards were closed from half past 12 'til 2 for the patients to have a rest
> and the consultants didn't come in, nobody came in and that was it. *Brenda*

'You could barely see the other end of the ward'

The condition of many of the patients reflected the condition of London in the 1950s, as
Marion remembers:

> you got the [ward with] two fourteen beds on each side, and the gaps, and
> the gas fires on each side, and because [many patients had] bronchitis … and
> bronchiectasis, spit pots … and of course, those were the days in the late fifties,
> early sixties, of smog, and sometimes you were on a ward and you could barely
> see the other end.

But on a more positive note she recalls:

> Sunday afternoons were lovely, and Saturday afternoons, because you did the
> flowers … they used to buy the flowers from … the market stalls across the
> road … that smell of mimosa … that takes me right back.
>
> because Charrington[s] was just up the road, and the smell of the brewery used
> to come in in the summer through the windows.

Empathy and unpredictability

It was felt that the whole ethos of compassion and listening to people was integral to the
way in which patients were treated, as Elizabeth describes:

> [we] learnt to care for the whole patient, medical, physical, emotional, spiritual,
> everything we did had to be well done, we had to be observant, knowing the
> patients and what they'd received as treatment.
>
> I think the empathy came from we knew our patients very well. We spent time
> with them and we were aware of their fears and their discomforts … sheets were
> smoothed, pressure areas were treated, tongues were cleaned if they were dry.

Iris remembered how different sometimes the patients were, and how unpredictable the
likelihood of recovery could be:

> a man died … he was young, having an appendicectomy, had a lovely young
> wife and a very young baby, 6-month-old baby and he started to deteriorate and
> deteriorate … and it was almost as though … this is what he'd decided … I mean
> I go cold now when I think about it … it was devastating for all of us.

In contrast, she cared for another patient who recovered despite his prognosis, and the
expectation of the houseman:

> the houseman said, 'You're wasting your time, that man's going to die anyway,'
> you see, in fact that old man walked out on a stick … a real chirpy old cockney,
> who'd made up his mind that he wasn't going to die, and I was so impressed by
> the [difference between] the young man and the old man.

'You really gave your life'

At times during their training, nurses, such as June, would be sent to different wards with
no warning:

> you would go down to breakfast one morning at half past seven, and sister would
> be sitting there, first of all to see that you had got no make-up on, 'Wipe that
> lipstick off, nurse,' and then she'd say, 'Oh, nurse, you're going to … X Ward'….
> No preparation at all … or, 'You're going to Brentwood [Annexe], so get your
> stuff packed' … you couldn't make plans.

There were few days off. Although it was possible to request time off for a special family
event, many of the nurses gave the impression they rarely bothered as it was so difficult
to gain permission:

> and I'd been to the office and asked to have the night off and they said, 'can't
> you ask your cousin to change … the date of her wedding? '… yes, I was her

bridesmaid at that wedding. I had to go on night duty afterwards at midnight, after being up all day. *Audrey*

No, you couldn't really plan anything particularly 'cos you could get it taken away, if you bought theatre tickets, we used to rush around trying to swap them with each other, 'Can you go to the theatre, I can't,' … you really gave your life. *Elizabeth*

The ward sisters were often scary and difficult to work with, but also often seen as role models. Nurses spoke of the fear that they had of doing something wrong and how this was heightened by the closeness of working with the sick:

Oh, terrified, terrified most of the time. Absolutely terrified … it's a sensitive business touching people, sensitive business looking after people when they're ill and [you are] terrified of doing something wrong. *Norma*

if you broke a thermometer you had to pay for it. Everything was your fault in those days. *Elizabeth*

Dealing with death and trauma

For many their first experience of death came as a shock, the memory never leaving them:

the mortuary wagon came and all the curtains were pulled and all this sort of thing and we all stood while it … went out [of the ward]. *Beryl*

Marina recalls:

I remember one patient coming in … she must have been in her late twenties, but she had two children and … was on her third pregnancy, and … had been advised to have the pregnancy terminated, … she was absolutely terrified because she was Roman Catholic, … I remember reporting this to sister … I seemed to be the only one that was really worried about this…. I took her up to the theatres, and very, very sadly, she actually did die on the table. … And that was my first [death] but if you can imagine [me] a second ward nurse … it really was terrifying, and the person who was sent to help me, I can remember her giving me the shroud and saying, 'Just carry on with this and I'll be back in a moment or two'… and … I think it made such an impression on me that, by the time I became a tutor, I always made quite a thing about the importance of doing the … last … rites and then last offices, and how one should do it with the greatest dignity possible, thinking it could be somebody very dear to yourself.

and of course the other thing was when a Jewish patient died you tried to get the body out of the ward before the ritual or the professional mourners came in and … they had a separate part of the mortuary. *Beryl*

Sometimes, especially at night, black humour became a way of coping with what otherwise could be overwhelming:

We were laying out a patient, we'd had four deaths that night, and the last one, I was so exhausted and I'd forgotten the [name] tag, you know? So we'd laid him out and I said to the nurse, 'Just put the shroud on, I'll go and get the tag.' When I got back, pulled the curtains back, 'Ah!' She'd put the shroud on herself! … Woke up the whole ward! … It was about four o' clock [in the morning]. *June*

This narrative, also from June, provides an example of the traumatic experiences some nurses had, and how this quite often impacted on their choice of specialty once they qualified. It also exemplifies the empathy of the other staff in the hospital:

> the second ward I had was … the Children's Ward … I was on night duty and there was only a Staff Nurse and myself. She went for supper, and the phone rang … they said, 'We're rushing a child up who's got severe head injuries,' … he was a little one of about 18 months … he had to go to theatre immediately … [I was told] to shave his head, and he had a little mass of curls. And luckily … a medical student came up, and he did it, because I really didn't want to do it … because I'd got a sister of that age, it really, really upset me.
>
> … on top of everything they said to me … 'You go with the child and take it to theatre,' and I had to go into theatre, it was one of the top neurosurgeons … he was very tensed up because this was dramatic … I can remember him kicking something across the room because he wanted everyone to hurry, and the child died on the table … it was the most traumatic thing for me. … I came downstairs in the lift, and they'd given me the little boy's coat, I don't quite know why … I had to go and see the parents and get them into a car. He'd fallen out of a car … this was my baptism of fire … part of it stayed with me because I always wanted to do neurosurgery afterwards, that's why I did it for my staff [nurse] year … because I can remember coming down in the lift when that little boy died … and crying, and the porter was in the lift and he offered me a sweet, a boiled sweet … he didn't know what else to do with me.

Progress and variety

Pioneering work was being done in medicine during this time, with the early approaches to dialysis treatment and the first heart valve replacement operations. Some of the wards began to focus on medical research:

> the kosher kitchens had gone, and … Helen Raphael and Rothschild were kosher wards … originally, but not when we were there … they were medical research wards, one male, one female. *Marion*

But at that time even routine surgery meant a long hospital stay for patients:

> these ladies were flat on their backs having their cataracts, double padded for two weeks, and we would … get very fine scissors and put Vaseline on the scissors to cut their eyelashes … we had steady hands. *Marion*

For other surgical procedures it was necessary to make sure that the patients rested and convalesced, despite it not being that popular with their husbands:

> And also of course, if anybody came in, say for a hysterectomy, first of all they had to sign to say they'd go to a convalescent home for two weeks … and they needed rest, and they all got it … I think we had to get them to sign because the men didn't want it you see … [a]nd so we used to say, 'No, this is part of the operation, they've got to go,' and oh, they loved it. *June*

Some conditions that were still being treated in the 1950s were thankfully on the decline:

When I went to the skin department as a student nurse, we still had a Lupus Vulgaris [tuberculosis luposa] clinic, which continued all my times that I … worked in the skin department and in 1968 when I left it had diminished to about half a dozen patients …. I think it was reduced to a monthly clinic so hopefully there were no new cases, these were all old cases and they had the most dreadful disfigurement sometimes, their noses and their ears eaten away and prosthesis and stuff on their faces … quite sad. *Rita*

Nurses remember the earlier antibiotics:

Streptomycin [was] thick and gloopy … the insulin syringes and needles, we had a little steriliser in the lobby … [a]nd you checked to see the [needles] weren't barbed, and I remember my first Streptomycin [injection] and the man was so thin. *Marion*

And the unknown danger of air entering the veins when using the opaque intra-venous 'giving sets' as Beryl remembers:

Well to give a blood transfusion or any infusion we had these red rubber giving sets and if it stopped you had to massage it. When I think about it … however many emboli have I caused! I don't remember anybody dying but we used to do all these sorts of things to get the tube, get the infusion going … it was quite a performance.

The lack of hermetically sealed and sterilised bags for intravenous fluids led to the occasional spill:

I got covered in a pint of blood 'cos it was a rubber cork in a glass bottle and it came out, and the sister said, 'Oh go and get changed,' but to go and get changed was in the nursing home, and I had to walk … it look[ed] as if I'd had an axe in my head, it had covered down my face, down my uniform, you can imagine a pint of blood. She made me walk through the hospital. *Elizabeth*

Nurses were also required to work in the private wing during their training, although not everyone enjoyed this:

I mean the nurses weren't terribly happy looking after the private patients but … that was part of the training in those days. *Brenda*

'Bringing the parrot into the ambulance'

Occasionally nurses were required to accompany patients when they were being transferred from the hospital to another locality. This gave them a welcome break from the routine of the wards:

But I had one or two occasions where I was asked to accompany a patient in an ambulance to another hospital … I used to like that because that got you away from the hospital … [one patient on], the neurosurgical ward at The London, he'd been smashed in the back of the neck with a rifle during the war, and he was left paralysed … but they didn't quite know what to do with him because he was a total quadriplegic, and they'd had him at The London to try and do something for him, and they decided there wasn't anything more they could do... he had to be taken back to the coast where he lived, so I had to accompany him, and there was another man also, he'd had an operation, he was being dropped off en-route, and we had ... hospitals that were in touch, that if he stopped breathing or anything like that, we could dive in there.... [O]n the way home, I took him to see my mother in Belvedere, and we'd come through Blackwall Tunnel, and I said, 'Oh, if we divert to my mum's we can have a cup of tea, and I remember her bringing the parrot in to the ambulance to show him ... it was lovely, it was all very informal then. *June*

'You do not talk over the patient'

A great deal of teaching came from working alongside the more senior nurses, seen by some as an apprenticeship style of learning.

One of the things we were taught ... two nurses working with a patient, you do not talk over that patient ... you talk to them, and that's stuck ... and if you say you're going to do something for a patient, you jolly well do it. If you're busy ... you say, 'I'll be back as soon as I 'can' ... I suppose they're not rocket science ... but it's those little things that mean a lot to a patient. *Marion*

Well it was mostly you had people with you to show you procedures ... as you were going along, that sort of teaching, not formal sitting down teaching. *Pauline*

It was clear that the sister of the ward was very actively involved in the day-to-day running of the ward:

Sister had an office but she was rarely in it because she was busy. *June*

She also supplemented the lectures nurses received with on-ward teaching:

Sister, on Sunday afternoons, would sit down with you in the ward and do a teaching [session], and that was wonderful. ... Because you were looking at Mr so-and-so with chronic nephritis or whatever ... because you could associate the patient with the complaint. *June*

Challenging bad practice

Some, like Mavis, experienced situations that taught them how to stand up for the values that had been drummed into them:

there was a chief, a surgeon, [who] was coming to demonstrate a procedure. I don't even remember what the procedure was, but the staff nurse had laid out a trolley and I had to observe her laying out a trolley, and everything was absolutely perfect, and the sister had come by and said, 'That's ok.' And then as the staff nurse turned around, her apron caught on to one of the receivers, [which] clattered ... to the floor, and she looked round quickly and she picked up and put it back on the trolley.... Now for me that was a mortal sin, and I couldn't believe that she was just going to leave it there, but when the consultant came she didn't say anything, and he started doing his stuff, and I spoke. I realised that maybe I shouldn't have afterwards, but then part of me still thinks, well I should have.

And I said, 'But you can't use this trolley because the receiver dropped on the floor and it's [tainted]' ... [s]o she says, 'You don't know what you're talking about, nurse, take no notice,' and shut me up in other words. ... Well I thought it was such a betrayal of everything that we'd been taught.... But what's the point of learning the aseptic technique ... I was outraged.

Night duty

The nurses would have mostly remained on the same ward for their first three month block of night duty. The night sister would do her rounds and expect any nurse she picked on to take her round the ward, and provide her with the names, diagnoses and other details of all the patients:

> on one night sister round I used the name and diagnosis twice, and there were thirty-six people in the double ward, when we'd finished she said, 'You repeated one name, when I come back you will know all your patients.' *Elizabeth*

> Oh we had a terrible night sister, everyone was scared of her ... she'd always find something wrong. If she couldn't find anything, she would say, 'what's the temperature of the ward, nurse?'... it was jolly cold sitting there and it was draughty ... and so I had my cape on and she came in and said to me, 'Are you cold, nurse', and I said, 'Yes', I was. She said, 'Well if your brain was more active ... you wouldn't be so cold'. *Audrey*

There was little time off and some worked long stretches of nights without a break:

> on night duty, when you got the three months, twenty-one days without a day off. ... I've got a photo of me somewhere ... and I look about 40 because I was grey. *June*

Sometimes it was extremely busy, and it was tempting to try and start the early morning work early, even though it was forbidden as Elizabeth recalls:

> Nobody was allowed to get up before six, nobody was allowed to be washed and we were so busy one night, so dreadfully busy, rushing around, hardly time for meals, and one chap who was not quite conscious, we thought we could get him washed earlier, he wouldn't know and he'd be comfortable. We made the bed, changed his pyjamas, washed him, combed his hair, laid him back and he died, so we had to take all the clean sheets off, all the clean pyjamas off, put his old dirty pyjamas back and dirty sheets and then call sister. Who then said, by now it's half past six, I mean you know, we spent ages doing this and she came up and said, 'Yes he was dead and would we make the bed and put [on] the clean pyjamas,' I mean just to not admit that we'd got him up before six, we made so much work for ourselves. *Elizabeth*

'Overload of responsibility'

The second round of night duty created a great deal of uncertainty and responsibility at times for the nurses. Norma remembers:

> second night duty was a nightmare, I do remember that because you had to fill in and therefore there would typically be the junior nurse, the second year and then the

staff nurse and depending where the gap was, you had to be their replacement. So one night you might be junior nurse, that was OK, and then you had to take on staff nurse responsibilities, that was very, very nerve-racking. I remember, it was [an] open chest surgery [ward] and I remember in the middle of the night and I had staff nurse's responsibility, and this guy came down from theatres, a porter, and desperately wanted a replacement chest drain … and was going to take one from a patient and I didn't really have the knowledge or the authority but I said, 'I'm sorry, you cannot take that because … this patient needs it'. … In the morning when we had handover … the sister just said, 'No, it's a good thing you did so, nurse, otherwise the patient would be dead.' But terrifying responsibilities and because you tended to rotate from ward to ward, you never really got to know the patients and so you'd be taking big responsibilities … if I had a criticism, I'd say that was an overload of responsibility on young students. We didn't have the training to give them the authority to take that responsibility. It didn't happen too much but I think it was a fault in the system that … that patient might have been dead and then of course you hardly sleep the next subsequent nights, you never know what responsibility you're going to have. I used to have huge worries too about letting things like drips run through and that kind of thing. So I did find second [year] night duty very stressful. *Norma*

Working alone at night on a smaller ward such as Uppers was also nerve-racking:

I was alone at night in Upper wards. At the top of the hospital where treatments were given.. I was given a tray … I was told, 'Here's a tray, if they can't breathe you'll have to do a tracheotomy.' … On my own in the night, and I said, 'I won't be able to do it,' and [the doctor] said, 'If they're dying in front of you you will.' It was a lot of responsibility for a student up there. *Elizabeth*

'The benevolent Elephant Man' and others

Myths and tales of ghosts abounded for those working on night duty:

one night I kept hearing footsteps on the stairs and I opened the door to welcome night sister, no one there, about a quarter of an hour later this happened again, still no one there, the third time it happened I was a bit shaken but sister was there, when I told her that I was feeling a bit nervous she replied, 'I expect it was the Elephant Man, he was in these rooms.'… On upper wards. And she said, 'Don't be afraid, he's quite benevolent'. *Elizabeth*

But other people used to say… that the taps came on at the sinks because there were sinks strategically placed down the ward, and that lights would come on, things like that. These were ghosts of people who'd thrown themselves down lift shafts and things … all these stories used to abound. *Pauline*

The need for mutual respect

There was a strong element of hierarchy between the different professions and roles. On the one hand nurses were not encouraged to mix with orderlies and domestic staff but:

Yes. I found … I got on better with the older orderlies … the kitchen staff … the older staff nurses, I got on better with them … they wanted to keep the groups separate so that the nurses and the doctors weren't encouraged to speak to the domestic staff. … and I was much looked down upon because my ward orderly … invited me to her wedding anniversary party. And I thought that was great … and she didn't live far away, and I went to her house, but when I came back the next day and spoke about it, it was very 'infra dig', 'We don't do that, we don't…'. *Mavis*

In fact going to this anniversary party became a significant event:

I fell in love with a man who was at the anniversary party that I went to with my ward orderly. *Mavis*

On the other hand, nurses could be poorly treated by the doctors with whom they worked, and there was a strong unstated requirement for the senior nurses to be able to 'control' those who had a tendency for tantrums and rudeness, especially in the operating theatre:

I had to count the swabs, you know … [for] these massive thoracoplasties and I was stuck on the [counting] stand, and I'm counting these six swabs … and at the end I said to him, 'There's one missing.' 'Nonsense, count them again', so I counted them again; 'There's one missing.' Well, he was furious, you know, that his operation was being held up, and I was petrified, but he rummaged around inside the chest, pulled out this great big swab and threw it at my face. *June*

Ward rounds were a performance:

all the notes and X-rays had to be out, if they weren't there you had to find them … and there was deathly hush when the consultants walked in … and you always had to help the housemen find the X-rays … if they couldn't, especially when they were new. *Brenda*

Key to the role of the sister was dealing with the consultants, some of whom were notorious with their short tempers and inflated egos.

you had to control him, you didn't let him control you and I know what he expected … he expected [us] to stand with him when he was teaching the students all the time and I decided he didn't need me standing there, so I thought I'm going to go on as I want to go on with him, and so I said to him, 'When you're ready sir, I will come and chaperone'… and he never did it to me again. *Brenda*

It was also clear that the ward sisters went a long way towards training the young doctors, a fact which occasionally was acknowledged by the senior medical staff:

[he] was known to be a bit hot tempered, he was okay and I got on very well with him and he said to one of his housemen one day, 'If you listen to the ward sisters you'll learn a tremendous amount young man', which was true. *Brenda*

Annexes – fear, flood and fun

Most student nurses also spent some of their days working in one of the annexes. Brentwood was the largest of these, where several areas of nursing were experienced, such as caring for those with tuberculosis, and patients who had pioneering surgery, particularly neurosurgery, as Marion recalls:

> the only thing I remember about night duty down at Brentwood was being put on the kids' ward, and … the neurosurgeon … he would tackle stuff that nobody else would tackle … and loads of children on this ward with hydrocephalus … I suppose Brentwood was my second year, so I was beginning to … know a little bit, but I have never felt so scared in all my life … my memory of it is that I was left in charge for some time on that ward, and it scared the living daylights out of me…. Because I'd never worked with kids before, they were ill, ill, ill children…. But I think it was just not knowing enough. I think that was the issue … and I mean, that was the only time I didn't feel safe … it was really scary.

There were also memories of the flood that occurred one day:

> I remember there was an enormous storm and … that passageway down the middle of … The Hard … was flooded, I mean it was like a waterfall and the water seeped into all the wards and I remember being ankle deep in Alexandra Ward … and sweeping out through the French windows, sweeping out the water, that was quite an event for the annexe. *Rita*

Practical jokes and bending the rules appeared to abound in the annexes, where perhaps life was slightly more relaxed. Norma remembers:

> Again, I'm afraid it's my dreadful propensity for practical jokes. I was sent down to Brentwood and was on first night duty…. And then I cannot think why I ever did these ridiculous things but … I knew that [the House Officer] was going to come to visit me after night sister's ward round and I just got a large bladder syringe and filled it with cold water and they had this kind of opaque glass on ward sister's office and I could see this figure coming round and I thought, 'This is [he].' So I hid behind the door with this huge bladder syringe and as he came in, directed it into his ear. Unfortunately it wasn't him, it was night sister. It was a lace cap and all the lace tail, it just … sort of crumpled in the water … I didn't stay, I rushed into the ward and I gave some poor unfortunate lady the most unwanted bed pan she ever had in her life.

June recalls managing those patients who were not necessarily on bed-rest:

> down at Brentwood, on the TB Ward when I was on nights, they were young men … most of them, and they wanted to go to the pub over the way. So I would say, 'Look, you can go over to the pub but you've got to be back by ten because sister does her round', and they had French doors going out because they had lots and lots of fresh air, so they'd put their clothes on, go out, because they were quite mobile. Whether they were supposed to go and have beers in a pub, I don't know, but I let them go, and then I'd be sweating because it would get to five to ten, they weren't back, I would think, oh please, God. I'd pull the curtains round so that it looked as though they were busy … and they'd all sneak in, get in bed with their clothes [on].

And Elizabeth remembers the needs of one particular patient:

> one [patient] I can remember very clearly [at Woodford Annexe], he was a poor Cockney lad who had TB but he was slowly dying, we weren't getting anywhere

with him, every day for tea we offered bread and jam or cake for three o'clock tea 'cos he needed feeding up … and when I got to him he'd say, 'Can I have a salmon sandwich?' and because there was only bread and jam and cake he didn't eat anything … we couldn't tempt him. One weekend at home I told my mum and she said, 'I'll make him a salmon sandwich', so off I went that night ready for the Monday and when it got to tea, he said, 'Salmon sandwich please?' and I said, 'There you are', and he ate the lot. He grinned from ear to ear.

In my third year I was sent to Banstead [Annexe].… It was a lovely place, countryside, and I was there in the winter and another girl and I went into the kitchen one day, there was loads of snow and we pinched the big silver trays and we went … tobogganing. We got into trouble for that. *Pauline*

Tuberculosis

Tuberculosis was still common in the 1950s, with many people being treated and convalescing in the annexes, most notably at Brentwood:

Yes, I went to Brentwood early on and oh my god I hated it there, I mean I'm born and bred Londoner and what would I be doing in Brentwood … it had its ups and downs, because it was the thoracic ward, and of course they hadn't controlled tuberculosis then and they were doing thoracoplasty with these poor people with the tubes coming out and sitting bolt upright and every which way. *Iris*

The following description gives the idea of some of the treatment and the social context of the disease at the time:

the surgical ward was doing operations, they were removing ribs to collapse lungs and they were doing air treatment to collapse lungs, and PAS, antibiotic … was coming in … don't forget [in] the fifties we had the smogs and people coughed a lot, coughed and spat, there were signs in the buses, do not spit … £50 [fine].… People coughed and spat a lot with all the pollutants, so if you had TB it wasn't always picked up … and there was also a big stigma about it. It was thought that it came from dirt and that you had a dirty home … you weren't looked after or you were poor or you didn't eat properly … so to actually be diagnosed wasn't easy anyway. But some of the surgical treatments were a bit rough and ready. *Elizabeth*

'Unauthorised entrances'

Back at the Whitechapel site, the 'Garden of Eden' was an area given to the nurses to use in their off-duty time, together with the swimming pool built alongside.

For social life beyond the walls of the hospital, much of the focus was on circumnavigating the rules and regulations:

There was a very strict curfew time for returning by, I think it was ten o'clock … and of course we got to know the unauthorised entrances … there was one via the electricians' department in the Alexander home and there were others through various windows … but they were quite high windows, round the nurse's homes, so they weren't the easiest, you had to be hoisted up into them. *Marina*

The London Hospital swimming pool, this was used until the 1980s.

you had to be in by [a certain time] … you couldn't bring a man past a certain doorway. And we had a wall we used to climb to get in. *Mavis*

Discipline was strong both within the wards and off duty:

one of the girls in my set, she was seen coming back, she wasn't actually in the [medical] students' hostel, but she was walking back from there, and she was hauled up over the coals and she was asked if she'd been there and she said yes, she had, and so she was confined to her room for three days while they decided what they were going to do with her. *Audrey*

my best friend had a Lambretta, and we'd been out on this Lambretta … we were in our third year then and we got back to The London and it was after time so she said, oh I'll leave the scooter in the front of … the hospital … and either side of the main entrance were consultants' car spaces … well we hadn't realised that [it] was all alarmed and we put the scooter in there and all these alarms went off and porters were running out to see … so we just joined in the sort of, ooh, what's happening…. So we got away with that. *Pauline*

What was acceptable

There were formal events during the year:

> we always looked forward to the Christmas balls, and we had one in Grosvenor House, and we had one in the Royal Festival Hall.... And another one at the Hilton, and we used to have excursions afterwards, and it was usually parties of us, and I remember in those days when Heathrow was very much just an ordinary airport, it hadn't grown ... but you could actually go out there and [after a ball] get breakfast early in the morning. *Marina*

The Christmas show provided a time for the nurses to mix with the doctors and medical students as Iris recalls:

> I was in the Christmas shows, you know, as a pair of legs in the chorus.
> ... wonderful parties we used to have, and of course we weren't supposed to go into the medical students' hostel but we were in the Christmas show and I'm afraid we used to.

Christmas on the wards was a memorable time especially with the long tradition of each nurse on duty being given a bunch of violets:

> it was quite fun at Christmas decorating the wards and the carol singers coming round and that was lovely, and a lot of the patients loved that. And Father Christmas came with the fairies and you got your bunch of violets. *Brenda*

> I remember, on night duty we used to have deliveries of violets, which were delivered and had to be placed in the mortuary so that they kept alive ... and they were distributed on Christmas morning ... and then in the springtime we used to get huge deliveries of daffodils from Sandringham because of the Queen, of course, being patron to The London, and ... that was wonderful. *Marina*

There was mention of the Coronation of Queen Elizabeth in 1953, when inevitably some were not able to join in the celebrations:

> Well I recall that I was on night duty and I was fed up and all my friends were going ... to line the streets and to sleep there [for the Coronation]. *Audrey*

Marriage and challenging the status quo

On completion of their training many nurses remained at The London in order to gain further experience. It was usual to stay for at least a year as a staff nurse. Midwifery was also seen as essential further training, the nurses often moving to other hospitals to complete this.

For others, the limits on their life outside their nursing role had been lifted, much to their relief:

> I married within thirty-six hours of finishing my training because I'd been engaged from my first [year].... In those days ... you didn't marry while you were a student nurse. *Norma*

Now they had completed their training there was a clear indication that some of the traditional ways of doing things were being challenged, such as the counting of cutlery and the saying of prayers. Iris recalls:

> I mean it was just ridiculous … but as a student nurse … you had to just put up with the situation, that's what they wanted, that's what you had to do. However, when I got to be a staff nurse it was something else, because I could take the responsibility and I did sister's duties once for [sister] when she was away … I was in … a very busy surgical ward … I used to say to them, 'Forget those teaspoons, if we're short I'll go out and buy them some,' … I mean ridiculous … my twenty-eight men were more important than a teaspoon.
>
> [the sister] went off on her holiday, I took sister's duties, and the first thing I decided was, right, I haven't time to get down on my knees and do all this praying … and when [sister] came back and you know, the ward went back into absolute routine again … she said to me, 'You never once did the prayers did you?'

For one new staff nurse waiting for a post in a ward at Whitechapel, working elsewhere gave her the opportunity to respond in her way to the needs of her patients:

> so I had to go to Woodford [Annexe] … it was three big old beautiful Victorian houses joined together, and it was men one end and woman the other, and I got the men's end, and I quickly could see that this wasn't like a ward. These are people who've got brain tumours or MS … and their quality … and time of life is not going to be long. So I quickly set about disrupting the whole of the system and taking them out to Woodford Green, to the coffee shops in chairs … I always remember [one man], he had no legs, and he wanted to watch a football match so we took him to see a football match. *June*

Working in blue and beyond The London

Many of those nurses who were interviewed and trained in the 1950s continued in the profession, reaching high levels of seniority and responsibility. Moving to the next step, into 'blue', often came within the same decade, with some interesting insights into life as a sister in those days, as described by Brenda:

I was written to by the [matron] who asked me … if I would come back in blue … I think I was one of the youngest ward sisters so I did come back and I was a relief sister …

A student nurse nearing the end of her three year training wearing a silver 'S'. This badge denotes that she is undertaking staff nurse duties before qualifying.
(Image appears by courtesy of Shirley Waterman)

you would go to somebody's ward and you would be expected to run that while they were on holiday and you were very junior … you did it and you got on with it but it was quite frightening at first. … The good thing about it was they had wonderful food in the Sisters' Dining Room, but you had to be very careful where you sat because they'd all got their allocated tables … and one or two people took me under their wing and that was fine … silver service and salmon on Sunday, and sometimes … duck on a Saturday, it was wonderful.

I was in one of the bigger rooms, sisters' rooms in Cavell Nurses' Home, and if you were going on at eleven o'clock, the maid always brought you breakfast in bed.

Fashion of the times managed to unknowingly penetrate the formal uniform:

when we were night sisters wigs came in … if you couldn't get to the hairdresser you put on a wig. *Beryl*

When a vacancy for a sister's post became available, it was not a matter of applying for an advertised post, you had to wait to be asked. In fact it was frowned upon if you did express your interest even if you had already worked as a sister elsewhere, as Audrey discovered:

they told me off really for asking for something so presumptuous as to ask to be a sister.

Some of the nurses took time out over the course of the next few years, and it was not unusual for them to team up with other nurses:

Oh I did the full year [staffing] … and I went away … we all hitchhiked in those days so we hitchhiked around Italy for a couple of months … a girl that I trained with and myself. *Iris*

Others went to work abroad in Canada or to the US, such as Beryl, who went for a year with a friend to a hospital in New York:

[It] was quite a change. Because things were still pretty austere here…. Rationing had finished but there wasn't much money about and there certainly wasn't much in the way of choice. We got to America and we were earning more money and there was just choice everywhere, and people ate out all the time, whereas here … let's say it was still … it was a big thing to go out to dinner and things like that…. But we felt that we raised the tone of nursing there.

Life as a nurse in the 1950s was strict and regimented with long hours and little pay. It reflects a time when for everyone, just after the war, life was hard. References to the cleaning and the counting of cutlery illustrate the extent of work required on the wards, alongside the caring of those who were sick. Hierarchy was strong, both within the nursing profession and in relation to the medical profession. Living conditions followed the same strict codes. However, within the narratives there is a strong sense of identity, pride and strength that came from such a training, along with a confidence in the ability to cope with all aspects of nursing the sick, as well as an obvious sense of fun.

1960s, Mixed media on canvas, 2017, Paula Day.

Chapter 3

The 1960s – 'The Times They Are a-Changin'' (Bob Dylan 1964)

> By the time I'd reached the sixth form I'd decided I wanted to do nursing and my mother couldn't understand why it had to be London because we lived in Devon and she said, 'We've got a perfectly good hospital here', but it was the sixties and I had to be in London … I had no idea of any of the London hospitals but one of the girls in my class … applied to The London and that's how I heard of it. *Carol*

The 1960s was a great turning point in history. 'You've never had it so good before and you'll never have it so good again'; the words, in 1960, of the UK's then Prime Minister, Harold MacMillan. By the end of the 1950s, war-ravaged Europe was completing reconstruction and there began a tremendous economic boom. The Second World War had brought about a huge leveling of social classes and, by the 1960s, almost any working-class person in Western Europe could afford a radio, television, refrigerator, and motor vehicle. Motorways were being built and new universities were opening. UK rock music, with groups such as the Beatles and Rolling Stones, had a global impact and London became the fashion capital of the world. The sixties were also dominated by the Vietnam War, Civil Rights Protests, the Cuban Missile Crisis, and the assassinations of John F. Kennedy and Martin Luther King, as well as the end of the race to land a person on the moon.

The post-war baby boom produced a generation that seemed to challenge everything that had gone before. Politicians, parents, grandparents, the media poured scorn on their rock music, their miniskirts and their hairstyles. Peace, love, and often drugs, was the hippie mantra. The momentum of the civil rights and women's liberation movements and the emergence of the contraceptive pill reflected the dawning of a new era. Yet, messages of equality of opportunity had yet to impact on everyday life. A career for a young woman was still perceived as less important compared to the expectations for a young man. In general it was still assumed that most women would marry, become a housewife and mother. Combining family life with a career was not to be encouraged. Traditional attitudes and values prevailed.

Career choice from limited options

> having just done A-levels in zoology and botany … I suppose the decision to be a nurse was made about two years previously when, at school, we were encouraged to decide what we were going to be and it was either … a nurse or a teacher … only very few people were invited to apply for university. *Diane*

Family members and teachers had an impact on career choice:

> Well, my mother was a nurse, and I'd said all the way through my childhood I wanted to be a nurse, but I'm very unlike my mother, she would say … 'You're not suitable', which made me want to do it more and more. *Angela*

> I worked in the Foreign Service for six years doing typewriting and secretarial. I went abroad to Laos and my father died, I came home. Then I went to work at a school for the headmaster…. By the time I reached over 40 I thought, blow me, I don't wish to spend the rest of my life behind a typewriter … my mother had been head of the Red Cross … I thought I'd better follow my mother and train as a nurse. *Sandra*

> I got my inspiration from a Sunday school teacher… who had been a fever nurse and had worked abroad in Africa, and I was absolutely mesmerised by her stories of nursing. *Wendy*

Positive memories of being nursed influenced career choice for Hazel:

> So I started in 1965 … I was working in a bank, and I had a medical condition … my GP … referred me to The London Hospital … I needed surgery … and the operation I had now would be a day case, but I was bed rest for a week, post-operatively, and then another week of mobilisation, and then discharged … on the agreement that I would have a month's convalescence. … I was so fascinated by the nurses…. And the sister … was very pleasant and patient, went round to see the patients at least two or three times a day … the nurses were very efficient, always smiling, and bearing in mind, they were the similar age to me. And we were in the sixties …it's The Beatles and miniskirts … and there's these girls wearing this wonderful uniform that looked so fantastic, and I thought when I got home … 'I think I'm going to write to the hospital and see if I could do my nurse training', and my father's reaction was, 'You'll never do it'. So I had to prove him wrong.

The more focused such as Beverley did work experience:

> at school I did a pre-nursing course at the local hospital … I was interviewed by matron [at The London] and she said at the time that I had enough GCEs and to go off and find a job for a year as I was too young…. So that was very good advice.

Why The London?

> I applied to various London teaching hospitals … got into two, but I chose The London, I loved The London because it served its' population. *Wendy*

> The London Hospital was in a Jewish area and I felt comfortable training there. It was close to my foster parents and also to my mother who was an immigrant living in the area. It is also a famous hospital … and the training and care was excellent. *Florence*

> So I applied to the Westminster [hospital] … [and] I got accepted … I can remember what [matron] said to me at interview … 'I did realise I would be handicapped because I wore glasses because the steam from the steriliser would

1960s: A sister tutor teaching student nurses in the new library.

mean I wouldn't be able to see properly?' … I thought 'I'm not coming here'…
and my mother, who was with me in the interview, in those far off days, was sort
of outraged. *Janice*

Medical connections included:

I was good friends with two other people at school, and neither of them knew
what they wanted to do. They said, 'Well if you're going to be a nurse we'll come
too'. And one of them's brother was a medical student at The London, so … we
applied to The London. *Helen*

[I] thought it will have to be a London teaching hospital. It will have to be
somewhere like St Thomas's. … My GP … said, 'Absolute rubbish, you've
got to go to The London…. That's the best hospital in the world'. He trained
at The London. … He got onto the phone there and then, 'I'm going to ring
[matron] … I've got a most marvellous young lady here, I would highly
recommend that she would be most suitable to be a London Hospital nurse'.
And that was it. *Gillian*

Matron was very insightful and often looked beyond age limit and formal qualifications:

> I applied to two other hospitals in London … they wouldn't touch me [because of my age]. … I … sat with lots of youngsters [at the interview]. I waited a long time, at the end I was the only person left. I thought they'd overlooked me, and the nurse came out [of Matron's Office] and said, 'Oh, I thought you were one of the mothers.' *Sandra*

> So I actually left school at 16 and went to work in the city, typing, but I had a friend who … got a place at The London, and I sent off for an application form, and in those days The London did a brilliant thing. You had to fill out your application form, but you also had to write a … small essay on your life so far, and I presume it was my life so far that got me a place, because I certainly didn't have the qualifications. *Angela*

In 1968 Mile End Hospital, together with St Clement's Hospital, was transferred to the management of the Board of Governors of The London Hospital. Its designation was changed to The London Hospital (Mile End). Mile End's School of Nursing merged with The London Hospital School of Nursing to become the Princess Alexandra School of Nursing and Midwifery. The London also trained nurses from the Mildmay Mission Hospital in nearby Shoreditch.

> In 1968 … I had been accepted to commence my State Registration Nurse training at Mildmay Mission Hospital, Shoreditch, East London, [after] passing the entrance examination. I held no formal qualifications other than RSA [Royal Society of Arts] in Shorthand and Typing. I heard about Mildmay through the church I attended in Northern Ireland. It was exactly as described, small, cosy and full of warmth and care. This was what I longed for after leaving my close-knit, although somewhat troubled, family behind. … Mildmay had no facilities to train their own staff, so students were seconded to The London Hospital for training. *Veronica*

> as a Mildmay [nurse] … [people] were slightly suspicious to start with, which was understandable … I think they realised [then] … I wasn't going to preach at them. *Elaine*

Uniform-diverse opinions

The 'purple passions' of the earlier decades were still worn for the first twelve weeks of training; then, as before, students were measured in the linen room for their 'designer' uniform:

> The seamstresses … were always saying … 'You must consider yourself so lucky, because … you're having a designer label uniform', but in those days … we'd never heard of it … we'd be told, 'Well this is designed by Norman Hartnell …'. And although all your peers were wearing miniskirts and our uniforms then were twelve inches from the ground … I personally just loved it … they were so well made … natural fibres…. And the way the bodice was made, with the inverted pleat at the back, was just wonderful … and particularly working on men's wards, I mean, you never felt that you were putting yourself into a difficult position by bending over. *Hazel*

The Mildmay was the same colour uniform, but …we had straight sleeves…. Caps, lovely caps…. What could you do with those! *Elaine*

The whole uniform was built to last but, at first, wearing it was challenging:

one of the first things that we were asked to do was to report to a specific lesson with a toothbrush and a tooth mug, and we had no idea what this was about, but it was … teaching you how to make your hats, and releasing the starch … for the ribbons to be tied up. *Hazel*

those starched collars were horrible … and the hats were ridiculous. I had very short hair and it would never stay on, trying to make them was a work of art … I used to have to put a little roller in the front of my hair, and … thousands of clips round the side to get it to stay on. *Carol*

Challenging the uniform rules regarding jewellery:

I decided to have my ears pierced. I was told to wear 'sleeper' ear rings for a few weeks until they healed. … I was summoned to Matron's Office who told me they would have to be removed. I refused, saying my ward sister had pierced ears and if she could wear them so could I. I never heard any more about it. *Veronica*

A new way of life

The Preliminary Training School (PTS), of twelve-weeks duration, continued, preparing students for their training by integrating theoretical and clinical knowledge with fundamental nursing skills. This new way of life included, for most, a new way of living:

I grew up in quite a rural area where it was all clean air and marvellousness and … I hit Whitechapel and it was really thick and smoggy … I can remember going home and my mother being completely outraged that all my underwear, which in those days was white … was all grey and she was insistent that I hadn't washed it properly … rather than the fact that the smog had got to it. *Janice*

New students initially lived and learned at Tredegar House in Bow which was both exciting and petrifying.

The first day was … very exciting … my parents took me … we were put in rooms with two of us together … it was done alphabetically. *Janice*

I was petrified, absolutely petrified. And I can remember sitting on that bed in that room with my trunk and thinking, well, this is it…. That afternoon … we all went down and we bonded because we were all together in this situation. *Wendy*

the principal tutor … she was a formidable woman … I remember one of the first days there she asked everybody in the set with a connection to The London, and everybody had either had a mother train there, father train there, aunt, uncle train there and they got to me, my only connection was The London, I'd been born there and I was the only East End girl that they'd really taken at that time … I thought everybody was really quite posh compared to me but I felt I was more mature because I'd been brought up in London. *Jennifer*

I remember the curfews … you weren't allowed to … run bathwater after a certain time, and … lights out at ten o'clock, and they'd come round and check…. [There were] restrictions on when you were allowed out; the closest cinema was in Mile End, which we would walk to, but we could never ever see a complete film show because we couldn't get back in time. *Hazel*

Learning nursing

In 1962 the General Nursing Council syllabus was revised. The study-day system was superseded by a tutorial system in 1963. The London was the first training school in the UK to receive approval to train students according to a new syllabus.

the classrooms were in Tredegar House and we then started to meet patients about the end of the first month … we went up to the wards we had been allotted for an afternoon and then it lengthened. *Wendy*

we'd come back totally exhausted after a half day on the wards, and we'd gather in each other's rooms with our feet up on the bed and some of the least fit with their feet in a bowl of water. *Helen*

Learning to clean included their own residence:

[We were taught] anatomy, physiology, we even had a tour of a sewage farm … how to make a bed, how to put a pillowcase on, with the open end facing away

1960s: A ward sister supervising a student nurse learning to take a patient's blood pressure.

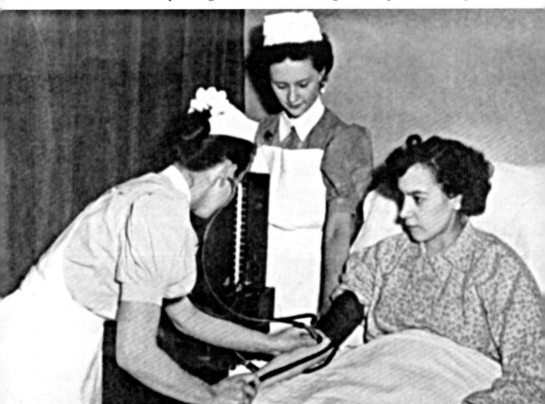

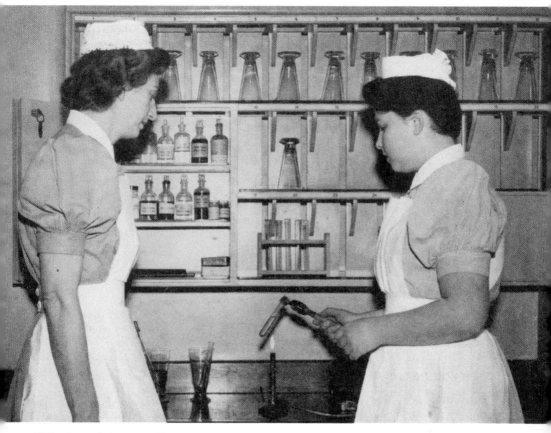

1960s: A ward sister teaching a student nurse how to test urine using a Bunsen burner.

from the door. Damp dusting … how to clean a toilet, we cleaned every morning because we kept Tredegar House clean. *Wendy*

we also did cooking, we made junkets … I never had occasion to ever make a junket when I was a nurse…. The sort of throwback to a slightly different time. *Janice*

Hazel recalls:

[The] head of nurse education … what a daunting lady…. [S]he came to do a last practical test with us before we left to go up to The London, and my story, which gives me nightmares … was to measure out a dose of iron medicine using the old glass measures … and I was so nervous … we'd been taught … once you'd identified your correct bottle and shaken it, take the top off, but the top never was put down … it was held in your opposite hand, in your little finger. Then you poured your mixture out. … I had a little tray, because we [carried] everything to the patient's bedside. … I measured all this out, I was just so nervous, and I put the medicine container with the mixture on the tray ready for the patient, and then I've got to put the top back onto the medicine bottle, and I caught the bottom of the medicine bottle on the container, which tipped over … and ended up a brown river flowing down Miss X's white apron, and my lasting memory is, 'That's it, I won't start my training.'

There was some light relief:

in the practical room … teaching … the Australian lift, and I remember, in my group, the 'guinea pig' who was in bed and having to be lifted, the two girls dropped [her] on the floor. I mean, we all laughed … it taught you a wonderful lesson … you'd never do it to a patient…. [We also learnt] how to wash a patient's hair in bed. *Hazel*

next door to Tredegar House was the training school for the Police, so quite a few of my colleagues ended up with policemen, and…the song *'I Want to be Bobby's Girl'* was in the charts, and that was played frequently in Tredegar House! *Janice*

When Tredegar House closed students then lived at the Luckes Home situated in Whitechapel, immediately behind the hospital.

The Luckes Home – firm, fun and over forty

The Luckes [Home], named after Eva Luckes, a previous matron at the hospital … was a magnificent building with beautiful wood panelling and big brass door knobs. It felt like a palace to me after leaving a two bedroom, modern, prefabricated bungalow (made with asbestos panelling) in which ten of us lived in Northern Ireland. *Veronica*

we all sat down for tea in the Luckes and met up with the other girls, one of whom is still a very good friend…. Some of the girls decided, when we'd settled in, to go to the Prospect of Whitby [pub] and I thought that was very adventurous. *Beverley*

Settling into the Luckes included:

There was a very fearsome lady [warden]… in the Luckes… who used to keep a firm eye on us. *Beverley*

We had our own domestic assistant who dusted and tidied our rooms regularly, often telling us off when it became too messy. A resident receptionist took phone calls and messages for us and pinned them to the notice board for our attention. The event's organiser … cared deeply about the new intakes. She encouraged us to explore our new area…. Often she would provide us with free tickets for theatre, shows, and events such as … Wimbledon. *Veronica*

we had a churn of milk every evening with one of those pail dippers so that we could make a milk drink. *Josephine*

I do remember the white line… in the hall of the Luckes over which visitors could not step. *Diane*

Some took longer to settle:

I was desperately homesick though I loved being away from home … I had to write every week and my mother wrote to me … her letter always included some

1960s: A group of sister tutors outside a nurses home.
(Image appears by courtesy of Karen Harris)

money, not that we really had to pay for anything … the end of my first month's pay … it was something like £16 or £18 … but then all our food was taken out and our accommodation … the best thing was to try and find a boyfriend to … buy you some nice meals. *Carol*

Most students were under 21 but there were also older colleagues.

There was only one girl older than me, she was 34 and we thought she was really old. *Josephine*

[Being 40] well, it made me feel young, I enjoyed the company of the youngsters. Luckily I was advised to carry on with my basement flat … in London … I could escape on days off. *Sandra*

In 1967, just around the corner from the Luckes Home, the new School of Nursing was opened by Princess Alexandra.

I remember the school because it was shiny and new. … And Princess Alexandra coming and … John Harrison House [new nurses' residence], it was all very exciting. *Gillian*

At that time, in 1968, two new developments in nursing were: the introduction of a two-year practical pupil-nurse training to become a State Enrolled Nurse (SEN), and the option of a combined 4½-year degree course in Economics or Social Science and Administration at the University of London with training for State Registration (SRN).

one of the biggest changes that's happened at The London, during my time … State Enrolled Nurses … began to be trained at The London, which was completely new. … [S]omebody who was in our set in PTS … when she didn't pass the end of PTS exam … she was offered to be one of the first enrolled nurses. … [S]he declined. *Angela*

we had the first people who were doing a degree course, and a man! And he was the first man to do [general] nurse training at The London. *Josephine*

A testing time

You learnt the ward routine very, very well and you forgot it at your peril. *Wendy*

[It was] very, very strict … and don't speak … to people unless [they speak to you.] But, really … there was no time to talk to patients … anybody who was nursed in bed had to be turned and the draw sheet pulled through, and that's what we seemed to do all day, and the bed pan round. *Diane*

in the sluice … scrubbing … the rubber draw sheets … IVI [intra-venous infusion] poles, cleaning those, commodes … endless locker rounds. … [I]f they thought that you were OK you got onto temperatures and blood pressures and I felt I'd hit a peak … when I realised that if I put six thermometers in at the same time, they'd all be warm by the time I went to number six instead of one at a time. *Jennifer*

there were several people who dropped out in the first six weeks. *Beverley*

Veronica remembers the value of sound advice:

my heart was not in continuing the training. I was homesick. A tutor [tried] to encourage me to stay. I remained adamant…. [She] advised that if I did not want to stay another 2½ years to complete SRN, then I should join the new Pupil Nurse combined course ending with a State Enrolled and Queens District Nursing Certificate. This in comparison was only a further eighteen months. She said, 'If you leave now you leave with nothing…. If you continue, you have a qualification for the rest of your life'. Her advice proved to be invaluable in setting me up for life. It was on this course that I met my best friends to this day.

'Scary, and you knew your place very, very well'

I was scared to walk on the ward, I learnt that the staff nurses probably were more scary than sister, and I learnt my place in the team, and … to know the sluice very, very well. Because the sluice was my domain. And a refuge without a doubt. And the times I let the catheter steriliser burn dry. *Wendy*

I found [children's ward] very stressful … a very high proportion of the children had had neurosurgery … and I remember being asked to bath these babies, and never having bathed a healthy baby … I was told … to do neurological observations and when I said I'd never done them was told to just use my common sense. *Helen*

I remember we had several cardiac arrests in one day, and … being the most junior nurse, being allocated to cleaning up afterwards, and going to the treatment room, which was just absolutely filled with used trolleys, and looking at it and thinking, 'Where do I start?' and the sister … she was standing behind me, said, 'If you survive this, nurse, you will go on to become a really good nurse'. I've never forgotten that … I remember being quite relieved when I had days off, and going home … seeing so many poorly people, it was really daunting. *Hazel*

I can remember … bringing a patient back from theatres who'd had a bronchoscopy and he collapsed in the lift … it was only within the first few weeks of being on that ward … it turned out this man was having a stridor attack, which was quite scary,…he was okay when we got back to the ward, but that was very much like an episode of *Casualty*. *Hazel*

I found it terribly, terribly stressful … the ward sister, I don't know if she actually gave me eye contact very much at all, probably to tell me to go and do the 'bottle round'… I certainly knew my place. *Carol*

I wasn't used to discipline, and the discipline, in every respect, was pretty strict. The uniform had to be absolutely right, your shoes had to be absolutely right, your hair had to be absolutely right, no make-up, no jewellery, nothing to make you an individual, really … I struggled with the time keeping. *Diane*

Coping – just

we had to do a blanket bath on our first ward, which was observed by our sister tutor, and the patient I was allocated was quite demented. I spent the quarter of an hour before [she] arrived literally chasing him round the ward in his pyjama top and nothing else to try and get him back into bed. I just achieved it … she made strong criticism that I didn't observe his modesty adequately during the blanket bath. *Helen*

one particular patient … a Greek businessman …. they allowed smoking then … and he smoked cigars. And he was a lovely, lovely man … I was the junior nurse … and if I'd done my jobs, I'd sit and talk to him, take him a cup of tea … and got quite attached to this, this elderly man, because he reminded me of my grandad, and his English was pretty good and I remember being absolutely devastated … coming back from … my nights off, to find that that day he died. …I was given the job of … bagging up all his property. And doing it in floods of tears. *Hazel*

I can tell you my most uncomfortable moment … sister said to the staff nurse, 'Oh Mr X has just died, would you take Nurse X … and lay him out?' I'd been there a week! She believed in throwing people in at the deep end. … I'd never seen a dead body before! … I just was numb … my first ward, but the traditions and the way things were done had already begun to be imprinted in your brain and you just went … with the flow, you did what everybody was doing. *Cynthia*

Good experiences

> So my first ward experience was at the Mildmay, but after six months we returned to The London … orthopaedic and neurosurgery. It was the busiest ward I ever worked on. Very interesting, very heavy, fantastic patients, fantastic staff … sister … fantastic lady, full of life. Very, very dedicated to her job, very knowledgeable. *Elaine*

> my first ward…was in the private wing, so that was really quite an easy way in because there were fewer patients and the sister was very nice, and there didn't seem to be too much wrong with those patients either. *Diane*

> [On] my first ward … [t]he sister had a reputation for having a bad temper, very strict and impatient but I later found her to be an excellent teacher. Coming on duty … one day I heard a patient choking, it sounded dreadful. This patient had a tracheostomy and I had never received any tracheostomy training … I thought the patient was dying. Immediately I grabbed the suction machine and catheters and tried to clear the obstruction. Suddenly the ward sister appeared looking fierce, but cool and collected and instructed me in the proper technique. Afterwards she thanked me for using my initiative and gave me a glowing report when I left that ward. *Veronica*

> the support of the senior nursing hierarchy was tremendous. They were strict with us but they gave us wonderful support in everything we did really … they had great expectations of us and I suppose we had great expectations of them, that they wouldn't sort of leave us too much to our own devices. *Cynthia*

…and not such a good experience as Angela recalls:

> Now, I'm going to try and think of something charitable to say about … [sister], and all I can say is most of the nurses who survived working with her or for her, I think, got very good training, but she was very, very hard … some days were unbearable. *Angela*

'I could have given up'

Although personal resilience was often needed, it was the friends you made, often during PTS, who gave you most support throughout the three years and beyond.

> It was during PTS that I met the friends that I have to this day and there were six of us who formed a group … they're my friends for life and that's what I really do value … leaving home and finding them and they were a great support … especially those early years. *Carol*

> I think it was very hard … I could have given up … we all stuck together and talked about our times on the wards and the difficult times, several times I thought I was too young for some of the things I was faced with. I remember being in charge of the ward when someone died and he wasn't very old … thinking, 'I'm not sure I can cope with the relatives and the whole thing about it', and it was very hard sometimes. … I kept going but I think I could have given up quite a few times along the way and several people in our set did. *Beverley*

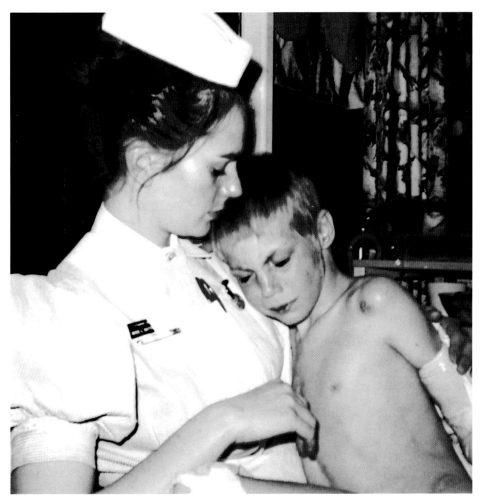

1960s: Care and compassion.
(Image appears by courtesy of Lesley Berris)

Routines and rituals amid change and innovation

In 1964 The London was the first hospital in England to install its own computer. Initially computers were used to store patients' medical records. New ways of working with computers had yet to be introduced for the nursing staff and many of the traditions, as in previous decades, continued:

> We all knelt down…and she [sister] took prayers and we looked like a flock of little doves, it was just beautiful, it must have been very touching to watch. *Josephine*

> if we needed to write a note to the sister on the ward, we had to cut all the corners off. I never knew why that was but much later on I was a matron of a nursing home and I worked with a girl who was six years behind me at The London, so we used to do things that way, if I wrote her a note, I used to cut the corners off. *Beverley*

Ways of working mostly continued in a similar vein:

> You always greeted people.... Nobody crossed the threshold without [being greeted], it was a security measure ... you represented the organisation.... It makes a lot of difference, particularly in a hospital. *Gillian*

> you do everything a certain way ... lay out your dressing trolley, everybody lays it out the same, they all take out the stitches the same ... everybody at that time did everything the same. *Jennifer*

> Twenty-six eggs on a Sunday morning, boiled eggs in the chip pan was a nightmare because you could never get them all right and I hated Sunday mornings. *Josephine*

> the wonderful thing you learn at The London Hospital is that we never are *on* the ward, [we have to say] we are *in* the ward. What a load of rubbish! *Angela*

In fact signs of change were becoming apparent even then:

> We had a male tutor ... and we were shown [in the school] how to do a blanket bath, two of us, you washed the far side first so you don't drip on the clean side ... and we washed the wrong side first and then he arrived [in the ward], and we thought 'Well we'll just do it again and hope the patient doesn't say anything', and it took us an hour between the two of us. We told him this afterwards because he was a nice approachable guy and he said, 'You know I think if we just gave you a flannel and a bowl of water and said, "Wash him" you'd do much better'. *Josephine*

On duty and never late

> We worked in a team of three and we all came on together and we were never, never late. *Josephine*

> Split shifts were unavoidable.... It meant you had the hard work of patient care in the morning and again in the evening while the day staff had reasonably quiet afternoons. *Veronica*

> I didn't mind doing split duties ... we had the afternoon off. ... I put my feet up and read a book. *Sandra*

Split shifts disappeared when a system of internal rotation was adopted.

> No splits, no ... two days off after seven days working ... and you worked with the same people. ... You actually had a good team, and you supported one another. If you didn't get on with them, that was just bad luck. *Elaine*

Doing the rounds

> we did ... all the things that nurses don't do now ... there would be a bedside locker round where you cleaned the lockers, took the flowers out, changed the water, cleaned the bed tables. *Helen*

> Pressure sores were frowned upon ... we used to go round with the oil and spirit and rub, rub people's bottoms. Yes, that was a strange concept. *Beverley*

I learnt how important it is to care for your patient, and I think it was implicit in the amount of contact we had with our patients, because we were going round and pulling the draw sheet through and preventing bed sores, we had a lot of contact. *Diane*

Too much responsibility?

I went on duty, I found that my staff nurse had gone off sick, so I was the senior nurse … this was the time of the Krays, and these two guys … had been in … a gambling den in a basement … somebody threw a homemade petrol bomb down, and both men sustained really nasty burns … and they needed to be nursed on sterilised linen, and we didn't have disposable sheets and pillowcases then … because their wounds were being nursed in an open fashion, as soon as their sheets or pillowcases became wet, we had to change them … it was constant. … And being absolutely terrified, because I was the senior nurse … when sister goes off … you're left, and the man who sustained the worst injury … there was always this possibility, 'Is he going to need an emergency tracheostomy?' and the equipment was left in the room, and we were shown how to do it, should we need to … terrifying. *Hazel*

everybody hated … going to 'special', [a patient] … it was quite scary because you might be sent to neurosurgical … when really you haven't had any experience of neurosurgery at all. So people did feel … very apprehensive about it. *Jennifer*

The first Intensive Care Unit (ICU) at The London opened in 1965 with space for six patients. It was the early days of life support technology and patients were also still nursed in side wards:

in those days we didn't have ICUs, we nursed the patients who'd had cranial surgery or … major thoracic surgery … on the ward and you'd go on trembling at night … [there] were the Beavers [respirators] … and you'd hear that noise, [*makes whooshing noise*] … and of course the patients were 'special[ed]', that was a tremendous responsibility. *Wendy*

a very scary thing on night duty where I was asked to … relieve someone for a meal break and it was … a patient in a side room on a ventilator. So never having seen a ventilator before … I went in and the handover was fleeting and … I sat there absolutely petrified, praying that nothing would happen to this patient for the hour while the staff nurse went off for her … [meal break] and nothing fortunately did happen. *Carol*

Surgical experience

I was very impressed with the surgeons and the standard. I'll never forget the long hours they worked … the nurses there, they had to be strict, of course. It was tough … but inspiring, and the music was played all the time. I enjoyed the music … and counting the swabs. *Sandra*

In the mid-1960s the first open heart surgery was performed at The London:

> it was quite salutary, going to the open-heart surgery [theatre]. *Sandra*

Cynthia recalls the preparation of the patient before and following surgery, and the cleaning of the theatres:

> They [patients] always came on a trolley [to theatres] or in their bed. … The patient was prepared in the ward … the bed was prepared … the sheets and blankets … would be folded back … and then just pulled over the patient [to conserve body heat] when they returned. … You would be assigned a patient on the day and you would prepare them for theatre … you would accompany them … into the anteroom of the theatre…. [After the operation] you would go down to the theatre door and the patient would be wheeled out and it was your responsibility to keep their airway open during the transition from theatres to the ward … so then you made sure that their airway was viable and then you had to take the airway out of their mouth when they started to cough it up.

Theatre responsibilities included:

> Sterilising everything, packing things into the autoclave. …They had some CSSD. … You cleaned the theatre table…. The orthopaedic side of it … the theatre had to be double cleaned. You would clean it all through and then you would start again and you'd double clean it … prevention of cross-infection … bone infection and don't forget, this was 1960, although we'd got antibiotics, hadn't got the range … and … we've got problems with antibiotics now but then we were still giving Penicillin by injection…. You certainly learnt your instruments very quickly … I loved the time [there].

She also remembers many of the operations were performed for cancer although the word was rarely mentioned.

> doctors particularly would talk about metastatic growths, I don't remember the C word being big in the vocabulary, it really was that you've got this condition which we need to do something about … I think most of them guessed.

It appears that some patients were told:

> I remember when I was very junior I was walking past this bed and this young man called me and he said, 'I've just been told that I've got cancer and I might die', bearing in mind this was a long time ago, there wasn't a treatment for it and I just didn't know what to say, nobody had prepared me for that and I thought, here am I, 19 or 20, being given this young man who probably wasn't that much older than me and … not knowing what to say to him. *Jennifer*

Health and Safety?

> we had certain tasks to do on night duty and we were responsible for boiling the bed pans in a big bed pan boiler … and then it was lit underneath by gas and one of my outstanding memories was trying to light this thing, turning the gas on, wouldn't light, turning it on again and the third time I turned it on,

it went boom and blew my eyebrows off. So I had to go the following morning to Matron's Office and explain what had happened and fill in an accident form. *Beverley*

Hazel recalls:

I badly scalded my hands on one of those sterilisers in the middle of the night … and you had to do the fluid charts, and my hands were just so sore, and staff nurse had given me some ointment to put on, but it really wasn't doing any good, so I had my hands wrapped in wet paper to keep them cool. And we had to use pen and ink … and some of this water dripping off the paper onto the fluid charts, and blots and things, oh dear, nightmare, nightmare.

In some areas of the hospital the side wards were used for people having implant treatment for cancer in the form of radium needles and vaginal caesium implants. Staff wore badges that monitored the level of radium to which they were exposed.

Helen explains:

we always had radium badges, not that I ever think we had too high a reading … in the side wards … we had a lot of … face needles [for cancer of the tongue] and things like that … we had to be very careful because the biggest side room was next to the patients' sitting room where they had lunch, so you had to try very hard not to have anything in there, and if you did you had to give the younger women, who were pre-menopausal, lunch in bed.

Respect, hierarchy, and humiliation

We all loved … matron, and couldn't understand how she knew who we all were … if you walked past [her] she always said, 'Good morning, good afternoon', and your name as well, I don't know how she knew us all. *Carol*

We had a nice young sister on the gynae ward and I was eating a sandwich with somebody else behind the kitchen door, and we heard the keys jangle and we both … jumped, and she walked in and said, 'You know I'm not very old, I know exactly what you're doing.'… a nice person doing a decent job. *Josephine*

I was very impressed with the way the doctors revered her [ward sister]. She knew her stuff. *Elaine*

some of the old sisters … we were very frightened of … I don't think we were very kindly treated sometimes but … some of them I did respect, they were very strict with us … I think it was a very good sort of traditional training and it stood us in good stead. *Beverley*

Being told off

I remember making hot chocolate on the ward for all the staff one night. This was totally not allowed. As we heard sister's footsteps coming on the ward everyone ran with their cups to a place of safety. Unfortunately I placed mine in the desk drawer where I was filling in the 'Kardex'. The night sister sat at the desk and opened the drawer only to spill the hot chocolate all over important paperwork. Needless to say I had a good telling off. *Veronica*

I remember calling somebody by their Christian name and [sister] let rip, she hauled me over the coals for calling this person by their Christian name. *Beverley*

Jennifer reflects and recalls:

I think sometimes people would demean you and make you feel stupid. … I think I was just lucky I didn't go on those wards … but there was a lot of criticism sometimes which was probably unnecessary because sometimes it was for things that you'd look at now and you'd think was ludicrous. … I think I was on my first night duty, very busy male surgical ward … [off duty] I got called out of my bed because I hadn't put the Vaseline pot from the rectal tray in the warmer to melt the Vaseline … I got pulled out of bed for that … [that night] we were really frantically busy, we had something like six full duties in [patients] … desperate, buttering bread at three in the morning [for patients' breakfasts], clean the steriliser, count the cutlery … and things like that.

Humiliation came in many forms:

one lady … she'd been unconscious for ooh, several days and wasn't expected to live for very long and all of a sudden one morning … she sat up in bed and asked for a drink of orange squash. So sister said to me, 'Go and get this patient a glass of orange squash, nurse.' So I went to the kitchen and we didn't really keep things like that, there was none there, so I brought back a glass of water. Sister looked at it and she said, 'Nurse, if this patient requires orange squash you will find her orange squash, go down to one of the other wards and find a bottle of orange squash!' I felt humiliated and the lady didn't live for very long but she did get her orange squash. *Cynthia*

I was helping serve the lunches … scurrying up and down the ward with the lunch … it was served from a big trolley under the direction of sister or staff nurse, and I forgot somebody…. And it was discussed at the handover after lunch, my name wasn't mentioned but it was so obvious that it was me, and I wanted to die a thousand deaths. *Wendy*

Students were given a helping hand:

the orderlies were marvellous…. They'd always whisper to you, 'Don't do that, sister doesn't like it'. … They were really, really good the ones that I came across early in my career … because often they were older than us and … if they liked you, they looked after you. *Jennifer*

I remember being, not quite told off, but pointed out to me, because there was a medical student who had been doing something, and I rushed forward and took the trolley from him, to clear it up. And I was taken gently aside and told, 'Nurse, you're here in your own right…. That young man is perfectly capable of putting things away…' *Gillian*

When other opportunities arose, as for Diane, deciding to leave was not made easy.

> I thought I'd ... see if I could get into university ... I got a letter saying I'd been offered a place ... to read sociology ... I had to go and see matron, who said, 'Nurse, how can you leave your patients?', and I said, 'Well, I feel I must ... I really feel I must go.' 'Well, you're giving up a wonderful career and I feel you are abandoning your patients...'

Memorable medical staff

> the consultant did his ward round with his entourage, you never dared to speak to the consultants, it was sister's domain or staff nurse's domain who went to do the round with them, you spoke as you went up the ladder to the houseman, and I learnt that very soon on that it was the senior registrar who really knew what was going on. *Wendy*

> the senior consultant ... would carry out a clinic which only happened ... once a month ... patients ... were all rather elderly Caucasian people, and you'd escort the patient in, and they would be greeted ... in a very friendly manner by this consultant, and then having ... made them comfortable, he'd say, 'Shall we begin?' and then they'd take their glasses off, and maybe a nose, or ears, or all, would be attached to their glasses, and it was a leprosy clinic ... they were probably people who worked in the colonial services, maybe been missionaries, obviously been out in tropical climes to have picked up ... this awful illness. ... [T]hey were non-infective at this stage, but it was just ... keeping an eye on them, to their progress. *Hazel*

Never ending nights...

> If, for social reasons or anything, you [wanted to change the nights you worked you] had to arrange it yourself, get approval ... once, I had made that arrangement with somebody, and I overslept, and I slept through the night and the next day, and turned up for night duty when I wasn't due on duty. Because I'd gone through thirty-six hours. *Angela*

Patient care at night included:

> a lot of very young babies and it was literally the routine feeds that we had to get done. ...You made [them] up yourself, occasionally the mother would come in and feed the baby or they would express the milk and we would store it in the fridge ... they were very sick babies, so very difficult to feed. *Cynthia*

> The best night duty was ... the children's ward ... I really enjoyed it but I was absolutely petrified because I was in charge of the ward ... night sister ... was really very supportive ... I remember her saying to me, 'You've had a lot of operations today.... Watch, watch them very carefully, especially the tonsillectomies ... if they keep swallowing then maybe they're bleeding', and I remember seeing this little boy and he was swallowing and in fact he had to go back to theatre ... so a good thing that came of that. *Carol*

particularly on night duty I could see that patients needed somebody to talk to … illness is a very lonely state to be in, particularly if you don't actually know what's wrong with you, and I don't think patients were told an awful lot in those days. So you would have a lot of sleepless patients who clearly needed somebody to talk to, but you shouldn't ever sit down and talk to a patient, you should certainly not sit on their bed. *Diane*

Carol recalls:

I was in charge [of a men's surgical ward] … one evening coming on night duty and the sister had said to me … 'Now many of these men have had ops [operations]…. But I can't get them out of bed … they need to be mobilised…. If you can try and get them up before they go to sleep'… we kept asking people … got the odd one to sit in a chair, then I walked down to the kitchen for some reason and [saw] the television was on in the day room … it was talking to itself, and I went in to switch it off, but actually the announcer said, 'And now the Benny Hill Show…' and I … walked down to the middle of the ward and I just said, 'Ah gentleman, you might like to know the Benny Hill Show is about to start.' Well, we had a mass exodus … they rushed down, drips, drains, catheter bags … the laughter that was coming from that room, and it was then that I realised how important that was as part of the healing process, and they were in a wonderful mood when they came out, not that I approve now of what happened on the Benny Hill Show … they were talking about it the next morning when they woke up.

Night sisters provided support but:

The night sister's ward round always gave cause for concern. One person on the team would be chosen to join her on the round and had to give a detailed history of each patient, usually patient's name and a brief knowledge of the diagnosis. If one had no knowledge of the treatment for the diagnosis a little teaching session followed. I found this one to one session to be very helpful. *Veronica*

Fun at night

On one occasion we received a message from the staff in Casualty saying a patient was on their way to the ward following an RTA [road traffic accident]. This patient had multiple injuries and had a tracheostomy. We rushed to prepare the side room with all the necessary equipment only to find the patient was a giant teddy bear. Other pranks included sending new staff to the Pharmacy for a bottle of TLC or to the X-ray department for a bottle of DXT. *Veronica*

One night when we were not busy I was asked to go to another ward to fetch a bottle containing 'low specific gravity' which had to be carried at a low level just 6 inches above the ground. …. I carried this thing full of liquid [probably water] all the way back to the ward … I felt so important and so responsible. When I got back to the ward I was bundled into the treatment room because night sister was doing the ward round. I realised then that I was the victim of a hoax. Next morning at breakfast … all the nurses heard about it and had a good laugh at my expense. *Florence*

1960s: The Annual Summer Ball was held at the Hilton Hotel. Tickets cost £4 10s. in 1965.

A diverse community

The London was so socially rich … now first of all we served the populations and there was a large Jewish population … quite a large Cantonese, Chinese population, had quite a few Maltese people…. And of course you were in the Whitechapel Road, and so you got to know the stallholders. And they got to know you…. And they'd always give you good fruit, they'd always give you a bit off your stockings, and things like that. *Wendy*

they were the mixture from the East End with all the things that really came from ill health, from smoking in particular because it was very, very prevalent, often the women who'd had multiple pregnancies … it was before the Abortion Act so we still had people coming in … having had backstreet abortions, all very difficult. *Janice*

It was my first exposure to people who were very anxious, who'd been through a lot … mothers who were worriers … they wanted their sons to be married well and we would get ... introduced, 'This is my boy.'... I always remember that, and [they] would call you, 'Dolly' or, 'Doll face'. ... So I learned an awful lot about the Jewish community. ... And they were just so understanding and appreciative. And real characters with stories ... [d]isclosed things. Things they'd been through. And how awful things were. And probably had never told anybody. ... [I've] felt very strongly all my working life about confidence. Not revealing confidences. It's absolutely ingrained. *Gillian*

Our local community was mainly Jewish in those days and ... [sister] expected everybody to come and kneel ... we all just knelt there and she said [Christian] prayers ... I used to go round to the patients and say 'What do you think?' And they would say '...it's absolutely fine, we don't mind, quite nice to see you all on your knees...'. *Carol*

The criminal fraternity were high profile, which did lead to some nurses feeling quite apprehensive:

You were very conscious of it. ... I do remember ... the [Kray's] mum was in and out. Because they lived on Vallance Road. And it was never talked about, you just handled it ... never to resist ... you didn't endanger yourself, your patients or your colleagues. *Gillian*

We had one guy in with a gunshot wound [in a side room] ... two policemen outside, the policeman inside was with him ... [and] ...he was also handcuffed to the bedrail ... when we were nursing him [the policeman] would take the handcuffs off ... he lived to go to prison ... I don't know what he did, we didn't want to know. *Carol*

I did a little bit of time in A&E and I think that's probably where you saw most of them. ... [Y]ou'd stitch them all up, they'd come in on a Friday to have them out, and then they'd be back Saturday [having] beaten themselves up again with somebody else ... so you sort of got to know them. And then when I was a staff nurse I lived out which was very ... adventurous and four of us ... shared a house ... they were terribly protective ... 'they're nurses and they're at The London and they're ours...', in the backstreets of Stepney after a late [duty], I never felt anything other than [safe]. *Janice*

The only time nurses were accosted:

We were revered, particularly in Whitechapel. It was nothing to come off duty and go up the steps of the Luckes [nurses' home] to be accosted by a young man saying, 'Are you busy tonight nurse, you couldn't come and babysit for us?' ... And very often we did, we didn't know them but a couple of us would go off ... you felt safe in Whitechapel. *Cynthia*

I was visiting a patient in a block of flats in Mile End. As I stepped out of the lift on the top floor a man grabbed me by the arm and ushering me into his flat he said, 'Thank you for coming so quickly nurse the baby's head is showing!' He didn't give me time to explain that I was actually visiting the patient next door. Fortunately the district midwife arrived shortly after and the baby was delivered safely. *Veronica*

The 'down and outs'

And there was a large Salvation Army home ... we were able to discharge the tramps who had come in, and sometimes they had lice and things like that, and I learnt the value of having somewhere safe to discharge them, and I've always respected the Salvation Army. *Wendy*

One night in Casualty an old tramp ... came in to sleep. He was a regular customer, often faking chest pain. We encouraged him to leave by offering him some milk and biscuits. On the way out he collected all the newspapers which we presumed were for the street benches. *Veronica*

Learning on the District

I found the district part of my SEN course to be fantastic. I visited places such as Whitechapel, Aldgate, Shoreditch, Stepney, Wapping, Mile End, Bow, Poplar, East Ham and Silvertown. It was great to see patients in their own homes, a different setting altogether. There was a lot of tuberculosis around at that time. My district nurse mentor

1960s: Ward sisters laying an annual commemorative wreath at the Edith Cavell statue in Trafalgar Square. Edith Cavell trained at The London Hospital, and was executed in the First World War.
(Image appears by courtesy of Trudy Wood)

was confident I could see a few patients by myself one day … armed with a nursing bag I would walk to patients' homes. One day I was told to put a dressing on a patient's inguinal hernia. When she answered the door, she was a very small lady, who was very overweight and wore a long dirndl skirt to the floor. Once inside I was shocked to find the inguinal hernia came to her ankle and the reason for the dressing was because it was rubbing on the floor. In all of my career it is the worst I have ever seen. I was later informed the hernia was inoperable due to her heart condition. *Veronica*

Annexes – absolutely loved it – absolutely hated it

I absolutely loved Brentwood … everybody knew everybody … it was just a totally different atmosphere, and I felt really quite at home there. … Such a variety of nursing … I always felt … that I was experiencing nursing that my forebears back in the thirties and forties must have experienced. *Hazel*

I hated Brentwood with a passion…. It was out in the sticks … compared with The London it was bland. *Wendy*

although we did have some CSSD, we didn't have as much as there was available at The London, so there was still a lot of packing of drums for sterilising. We all had the big … water sterilisers in all the wards and departments. … We didn't have piped oxygen, we didn't have piped suction, so…, you were very familiar with changing oxygen bottles and that sort of thing. The call system, bleeping system, was very primitive,…if you wanted a doctor,…you were just ringing round [the wards]. It was so different to The London. *Hazel*

On night duty in 'the sticks'

the night sisters carried bows, big blue bows, quite firm sort of fabric … they would hang their bow outside [a ward], so that if … somebody … was looking for sister, you just looked up 'The Hard', the corridor, and you could see where she was. *Hazel*

we would never call it an ITU [Intensive Therapy Unit] now, attached to one of the wards … there were four beds always filled by … young men who'd come off their motorbikes, and this was the era before helmets were worn. So I did ten … nights … on my own in there with just meal relief, and all four of them were on ventilators, and you'd listen to the respirators … just pray … that it carried on steady and their chests still went up and down … it was all very high anxiety because you were on your own, and night sister came in and would … advise you, but it's a lonely long night. *Helen*

this [patient] died … there were no porters on at night, so I went to get the trolley … and we were taking him to the mortuary … there was a quicker route if you went out the side of the ward … rather than going all down The Hard and all the way round … we were sort of trundling down this path and the trolley had hit something … some sort of stone, the whole thing opens and the body gets tipped out straight into the rose bed. The middle of the night. … Go back and wash him, [then] take him [back] … not that it was with any disrespect or anything, it was just that we were sort of both horrified and convulsed as you are with that sort of black humour *Janice*

The orthopaedic ward … it was huge, I'm sure there were about forty patients in it … the nurse in charge said, 'In order to get all these patients bed panned and washed and their breakfast in front of them before the day staff come on, we've got to wake them up at 6 a.m. officially', we used to wake some up before then … at 6 a.m. those who weren't awake we used to put the radio on, blasting, and it was Tony Blackburn … Radio 1, and I think it was great for us but those poor patients … nobody complained … I think they all appreciated we had to fly around and do all this before the day staff came on which was about 7.30. *Carol*

TB ward

the ward that fascinated me, I enjoyed the most … was the TB ward, and it was mainly a ward of single rooms … and patients would be admitted there from the infected stage, they would all be pulmonary tuberculosis, and we would barrier nurse them, and then eventually once they became non-infective, then they were allowed out, but our patients were with us for a year or more … on night duty … there were a couple of patients who … were now allowed freedom, and they'd found an area beyond the grounds of the hospital where there were apple trees, and so they used to scrump … and because once night sister had done her only round, we would make apple marmalade … the ward had so many lemons available [that were also needed] because that was part of their routine treatment, hot lemon drinks…. And so for breakfast the next day all the patients would get a little container with this produce. But I can't help thinking now, the sisters must have known what was going on, because you know, there's a certain smell to cooking. *Hazel*

Children's ward

We had a lot of hydrocephalic babies and in theatre [the surgeon] was doing some of the first Spitz-Holter valves. *Wendy*

there was a surgeon … who used to do quite heroic surgery on children with brain tumours and things … and sometimes it worked and clearly sometimes it didn't, and so I was sort of pitch forked onto this ward and, you know, children died…. And I do remember really clearly one child who was about four who used to just cry all the time, 'My mummy come', 'cos equally we had all these strict visiting rules around parents, and I found that very, very difficult. Once I'd done that ward I never really wanted to do anything with children again … I used to go off and cry most times, because it was all so sad, and there wasn't any help then. *Janice*

Theatres

there was a great big steriliser nicknamed Confucius … and I can remember having to lay up these trolleys … one morning I …was laying up and I [accidently] dipped my hand and I thought, God, I've desterilised it, and I thought what the hell do I do, and I thought I couldn't live with myself if somebody got an infection, and I had to make the decision whether to confess to sister, or carry on as if nothing had happened. And I thought … I'd never forgive myself … that could be … a relative or me on that table … so I went out to the … senior sister who was a dragon, 'I've just desterilised Confucius'. She said, 'You've done what nurse?' 'I said I put my hand in it,'... she was like thunder and she went into the staff [room], she said, 'We'll be a little late, we've got to boil up Confucius again.' Afterwards though she said to me, 'That took a lot of courage'. *Wendy*

one of the things we used to have to do on a Sunday afternoon ... clean the flea flaps. Now, the flea flaps were metal grids with tiny holes in that used to keep the dust and grime of the street out of the theatres, and it was the nurses' job to clean them. *Angela*

Termination of pregnancy was performed after The Abortion Act (1967) became law in 1968.

I enjoyed scrubbing up, although the first time was for a D&C abortion and I was terribly shocked and upset but tried not to show it. Although I had said that I had no objection to assisting with a termination I didn't know what I was letting myself in for. To suddenly see a tiny eyeball, then a tiny hand, etc being placed on the swabs before me ... I don't know how I carried on. It was horrendous and I never again scrubbed for an abortion even though most were vacuum aspirations. *Carol*

Woodford

Hazel recalls:

I made quite a stunning entrance when I arrived. ... They were two old Edwardian houses... one for women and one was for men, and in the main they were for geriatric convalescence... the entrances to both of them were via a cattle grid outside each of the houses, with a gate either side. I was just so nervous the day I arrived, I couldn't see the gate, so I walked across the cattle grid, got halfway across, fell through the cattle grid, or my legs did...horrendous swellings and bruises.

the student nurses lived in what I suppose were servants' quarters,... up on the very highest floor, with lovely windows that looked out across the countryside. And if you were on a late duty, you could go the day before to the kitchen and lay up a tray, and write down what you wanted for breakfast, and that would be delivered to you by a maid in the morning. ...We were well looked after.

And Carol remembers the light relief:

that's when I developed a love of ducks ... we had Quackers ... the pet duck ... it wasn't a hospital, it was a home for older people and it was ... so different from the acute setting ... and learn about the care of older people ... it was such a different atmosphere. And actually it helped you through your training because you got so stressed at times ... and so you needed that light relief as it were ... to go away from The London ... so I think those annexes were really important.

Banstead

it was a very much more relaxed atmosphere there. All home-grown food, there was a garden and the gardeners produced vegetables. And backing onto woods with nightingales singing. It was a lovely place to be. *Cynthia*

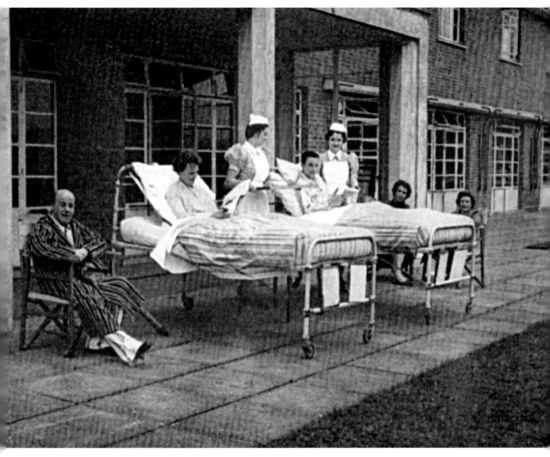

1960s: Patients getting fresh air at Banstead Annexe, Surrey.
(Image appears by courtesy of Liz Day)

One evening we had some children call with a horse with a leg wound. We dressed it and never saw them again. Another evening we had a group of children bring in an injured baby sparrow which we attended throughout the night. The ward report in the morning had an extra patient admitted 'Mrs Edna Sparrow' who managed to fly off by herself. *Veronica*

Diverse learning experiences

I learnt how important a sense of humour is. *Elaine*

A range of different learning approaches is evident, both within the classroom and clinical setting.

Miss X was wonderful. …She gave us a lecture once on sympathy and empathy, and quite a few of the students were a bit sort of what's this all about? … But I've never forgotten…. And there was the one phrase that I carried with me throughout my life … 'You can have all the sympathy in the world, you can be sympathetic to a man drowning in the river, and you can jump in and he'll pull you down and you'll drown together. Or you have empathy and you have [a] sufficient toe in the water that you can help him out, but not so much that he can pull you in to drown,' and I felt that that was so relevant in terms of the groundings for a professional approach. *Gillian*

we used to go to have lectures by the surgeons and one of them gave us a lecture on smoking and various diseases connected with it and as we came out the lecture theatre, he was over the other side lighting up a cigarette. That wasn't very good. *Beverley*

you learnt … from the ward rounds of the consultants … also from the … [ward] report and the Kardex … when the patients rested, some of the staff nurses taught us, sitting at … a table in the ward. *Wendy*

We had one tutor … orthopaedics was her love and we knew this because she used to walk along with a femur tucked under her arm … she'd visit you on the ward, whichever ward you were on, she still walked in with the femur under her arm which she would produce and you would have to name all the different parts of it. *Carol*

However, the best learning aid of all is always the patient as Wendy explains:

It was patients who taught me … I learnt a lot from patients, because if you let patients tell you their needs you can plan your care.

I think one of my best lessons ever taught to me … I was doing the bed pan round in my first ward, and there was a gentleman with cardiac disease, who was on bed rest, and he needed a bed pan, and he wanted to pay me. Because he said it was unpleasant for me, and I learnt … here was somebody who had to have my attention, and my care … but had felt so embarrassed. Here I was a young 18-year-old girl doing the most intimate things and I learnt then how difficult it was for patients, and … the one thing that I had to do was maintain that man's dignity. I learnt a big lesson. … I'll never forget that, and I can still see the bed that man was in too.

the first patient I ever saw with … terminal cancer … I'll never forget that patient, it's these milestones … of your introduction to what disease meant for the patient, the impact of the disease and its process and its treatment…. And I can always remember the perfume she used to this day and I can't stand it. And it's these things that stay with you.

Elaine relates:

my very first case of surgical emphysema. The patient had swallowed a fruit knife … just incredible. I kept going and touching that man's skin, crackle, crackle.

Practice-based learning

Clinical teachers were introduced into The London in 1961 to support students' learning in clinical settings.

clinical teachers were just coming into being when I was at The London…they were brilliant to work alongside you. *Carol*

There was an obvious need, for example:

> my job as a junior nurse was to do the blood pressures … and a lot of the patients needed a blood pressure check every fifteen minutes because they'd had major surgery. …I didn't know what it was, 'Didn't need to know, Nurse, did you', 'Nurse just go and do the blood pressure' … I couldn't do them in fifteen minutes, I couldn't hear them, what was I supposed to be hearing … I was terrified that I'd miss something … tremendous amount of anxiety, 'What if I do it wrong, what if … I don't hear it and, because they [may] need some medical intervention and I've missed it. *Diane*

Not everyone seemed to benefit:

> we had clinical teachers in the ward, but to be honest I don't think they really had any impact. They would come and do things that you had to do [in] your blue book … but that was to fulfil criteria … in terms of our training. *Angela*

Clinical role models

> my role models were people who taught me in practice and it was certainly not, dare I say it, sister tutors. *Wendy*

> a real role model for me … she [night sister] and I helped an old boy sit up in bed … we settled him on two pillows and I gave him a big beam and said are you comfortable? And that was a closed question, and he gave me a big beam and said, 'Yes thank you dear'. And [sister] said, 'How many pillows do you have at home?' [open question]. And he said, 'Six', and I will never ever forget that. *Josephine*

> I learnt from … the student nurse above me and the nursing auxiliaries … and I used to gaze in awe and wonder at the staff nurses and their knowledge … to hear them talking to patients … you think 'I would never have thought of that' … eventually you became a staff nurse and you had that wealth of experience and knowledge and insight and it comes from practice … seeing, observing, hearing … which you can't get in a classroom ever. *Carol*

Making time for a social life

> I used to meet my boyfriend as I came off at ten o'clock, whip in and change and we'd go off to the pub or whatever for an hour, and then I'd come back, and then be up early the next morning. So it was a lot of burning the candle at both ends. *Angela*

> They used to have 'hops' [dances] … I went to a couple and … we had balls in those days … [where we] wore long dresses … there were a couple at The London. *Beverley*

The Three Feathers Club opened in 1968 to enable nurses and many other members of staff to have a club and meeting place of their own.

Attitudes to marriage were relaxing in the hospital:

> One nurse was allowed to finish [her training] and her fiancé was going abroad, he was in the forces, so she was allowed to get married, my gosh! *Wendy*

The social context was still male dominated:

> one actually left to get married at the end of her first year. Her husband didn't want her working, which was sad really for her. *Cynthia*

Work often lead to romance. There were nurse and doctor liaisons, and sometimes with patients:

> [he] was a houseman … it was his second house job. So we met there and ultimately married, and are still married. *Helen*

> First time I saw my husband! He'd just had an operation … he wanted to join the police force and he'd got varicose veins so they made him have the operation. *Cynthia*

> On night duty we got to know each other really well, he asked me out and I did go out for a meal with him but he was married and I decided enough was enough … I kept saying 'We're not supposed to get involved with our patients' which was really a very good reason for not following it up. *Carol*

Finals

Carol remembers:

> We had a [state final] practical in the classroom … I remember being asked to make up a child's feed and I hadn't worked on Buxton Ward for over a year … and [next] I was handed … theatre instruments … three of them I knew, the fourth one … I couldn't recognise at all and as I handed it back I turned it that way … she'd given it to me upside down, yes, it was a tracheal dilator.
>
> Two of my friends didn't pass [the theory exam] first time … they were made to feel inadequate in many ways and I thought that was awful, especially from the head of school … her disapproval was obvious … I mean anyone can fail anything first time.

Wendy recalls her anguish:

> I can remember being asked to lay up [a trolley] for male catheterisation, so I bustled around … the sister tutor who was examining me asked me questions … everything about the trolley and just as the bell went which signalled the end of your examination … she said, 'And where does the urine go nurse?' and I'd forgotten the St Peter's Boat. … I came out in tears, I'd failed … I know I've failed … I shall never ever forget about St Peter's Boat.

On qualifying

> we were given our certificates and our badges by Dame Cicely Saunders … [whom] I really admired … I'm always proud to say I've trained at The London. *Beverley*

> at the end of my training I …worked in the first psychiatric unit opened in a general hospital [at The London] in Rachel Ward … I loved it. *Angela*

I had not done any Casualty during my training … Unfortunately my request was declined 'as SENs were not allowed to work in this department.' I wouldn't take no for an answer and threatened to leave without giving any time back … I was offered the post. This was the best position ever and proved to be invaluable while later working as a lone practitioner district nurse. *Veronica*

While the 1960s was a time of radical change in society, student and pupil nurses remained obedient and compliant. Most newly appointed students and pupils were under 20 years of age and were living away from home for the first time. Senior staff, who taught and managed them, earned their respect. However, as in previous decades, fear and intimidation were still clearly evident. A sense of humour and shared friendships enabled them to 'survive'.

Towards the end of the decade new nurse education courses were introduced and more men were entering general nurse training. Rules were being relaxed: you could stay out until midnight, live out in the second year of training, and even get married.

In 1967 the Salmon Report was published which set out recommendations for developing the senior nursing staff structure and the status of the profession in hospital management. The title and traditional role of the matron was to be abolished. Innovation in health care included: the first UK kidney transplant and the first full hip replacement, and, in South Africa, the world's first heart transplant.

A demonstrable commitment to nursing care and compassion still remains:

several of us actually still go to the Florence Nightingale memorial service at Westminster Abbey so we're doing that this year … and we remember going there as student nurses … it's a really nice service … renewing your dedication to nursing. *Beverley*

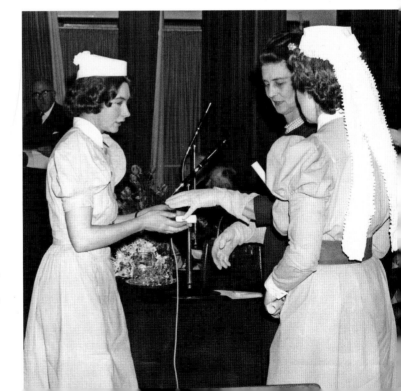

1961: Badge Day: Princess Marina of Kent presents a newly qualified staff nurse with her hospital badge assisted by matron.
(Image appears by courtesy of Trudy Wood)

1970s, Mixed media on canvas, 2017, Paula Day.

Chapter 4

The 1970s – The old and the new

the start of the named nurse and care plans, start of computers supporting care but still good basic nursing care…. Looking after the family of the patient as well as the patient. I remember open heart surgery was fairly in its infancy and being allowed to go up and watch it in the gallery. Amazing technology coming through all the time. … Things that had never been done before and The London always seemed to be at the forefront, we were always there leading the way. Big changes in psychiatry but it was really a social indictment of a previous era. There were the talking therapies, trying to rely less on drugs. *Geraldine*

The 1970s was the decade in which modern computing was developed, Stephen Hawking put forward his theory of black holes, Concorde flew for the first time, and the first cellphone and first microwave oven appeared. It was the decade of decimalisation, David Bowie, punk rock and the beginning of package holidays. An awareness of the importance of the environment, and a concern for its future began to surface at this time.

Alongside this, Britain suffered a long period of economic depression marked by rising unemployment, frequent and widespread strikes, exemplified by the 'winter of discontent', and severe inflation. The IRA had launched a bombing campaign in London, with bombs being left in public places such as on underground trains, or sent in packages in the post.

The role of women in society was altering profoundly. Career opportunities were increasing and more were attending university and living independently. It was becoming more acceptable for women to continue to work after having children.

Early in the decade the Royal College of Nursing (RCN) had led a campaign for increasing nurses' pay which achieved a rise of twenty-two per cent to their income, the largest single increase in the history of nursing. In 1972 the Briggs Report recommended there should be one national, statutory body which should be responsible for setting standards for education and training in nursing. In 1974 there was a substantial reorganisation of the NHS, placing all health services into regional and area health authorities. The number of overseas recruits to nursing was on the increase. In 1977, twelve per cent of student nurses and midwives were from abroad. Of these sixty per cent were from the Caribbean.

At times the industrial unrest during this decade affected The London, with emergency generators in place when the electricity supply might be cut, waiting list admissions cancelled, fewer wards open and volunteers coming from other parts of the hospital to provide essential patient services.

Choosing The London, 'not just a first aid post'

Despite some negativity, there were still a large number of women who wished to become a nurse and recruitment was high with a fair number of nurses in each set, as Julia describes:

but it was quite difficult at school because they kept saying to me 'You could do something better than nursing, you're better than that…'.

there was a waiting list … so you had to apply a long way in advance.

About thirty-five [students] I think, there were six intakes a year at the time.

Family allegiance to The London was still strong:

The London Hospital was the place, the only hospital of any worth, according to my family … the rest were merely, perhaps, first aid posts, and so we had this reverence about The London right from, probably, about the age of three onwards. *Gail*

Many were still coming straight from school, but others had previously worked or studied elsewhere:

I started at The London when I was 21 … I had actually been to university … that made things a little different from those people who started straight from school because I had lived independently for quite some years so that did make a difference … I did English and History and … a bit of Archaeology. *Kathryn*

Being a more mature applicant did not necessarily mean it was straightforward to enter training:

I thought it would be easy, I'd go along and they'd … be grateful to have somebody, and she said to me 'I'm not at all convinced that you are suitable for nursing … if we have an opening I'll take you on probation'… I was like taken aback … I thought to myself … I've been to university, I'm educated and you're telling me I can't be a nurse, how ridiculous. … She said … 'you've had a very glamorous life, how on earth are you … gonna settle down to emptying bedpans … wiping people's bottoms and that sort of thing'. *Lesley*

Nurse training- other avenues

Alongside the general SRN training, other courses were beginning to appear:

[I] started in August 1972 … This was a new integrated SRN/RMN [State Registered Nurse/ Registered Mental Nurse] four year training…. There was a big sense of being special … we were really encouraged to have a broader approach to nursing the whole person, lots of social awareness. *Geraldine*

The first graduate training course began in October 1974, with one intake per year. Sharon recalls:

I had done a degree in English literature so I did a shortened course for graduates, which was an unusual thing in those days, an SRN programme lasting two years three months … I felt very much the need to do something practical after an academic degree. I felt that … something that helped people and helped society was a very important thing to do.

Because we were doing our course in a shorter time our placements were shorter than the norm, but we still had to meet the full GNC requirements. So many and varied experiences – the special care baby unit, the 'clap clinic', medical, surgical, mental health.

There was also a four year course for a degree in nursing, which included clinical training at The London, validated by two London university colleges, Goldsmiths and Queen Mary College.

Living in or out?

Julie remembers the day she arrived to start her training:

> We had to be there the 3rd of January, 1979 … and I … clearly remember it, it was the year … of great social unrest…. There had been heavy snow and the Whitechapel Road was just full of horrible slush, and because there was … a strike, the dustmen, council were on strike, so Whitechapel Road was full of black slush and rubbish and rats from the market, and I can remember … having come up from the seaside thinking …what on earth have I done?

Junior student nurses continued initially to be housed in the Luckes Nurses' Home:

> [the warden at Luckes reception] used to wear a little lace hat … she kept us all in order. *Julia*

> the first day I arrived … I can remember going up … to the … little window [of reception] and … she literally went 'Wait a minute, wait' … I thought 'Oh OK, fine, start as you mean to go on', and I … immediately got the measure of her … so I used to … go out of my way to be nice to her, and she actually became quite a good friend of mine … she used to … rush upstairs to get me if my car was being towed away or something like that … very helpful. *Lesley*

> But I can remember feeling very safe and there was an amazing laundry room where we all did our washing and little sets of two ringed gas burners at the junction of each hallway on each floor … where we had to do any cooking, but most of the time we ate in the canteen. Huge bathtubs …. we did have a washbasin in our room … and we were given meal tickets for the week … different colours for breakfast, lunch and evening meal … I can't remember apart from heating up soup in the nurses' home, we didn't make anything else, we bought a sandwich … or made sandwiches … our … rent was £1.98 a month. *Geraldine*

There were also nurses' homes on other sites such as at St Clements Psychiatric Hospital and Mile End:

> I loved the Roman Road with all its music … different foods on sale and smells … I do remember my bedroom … there was paint sort of peeling off the walls, and I decided … the only thing I could do, I decorated one wall with wallpaper kept up with Blu-Tack. *Karen*

> we were at the nurses' home … at St Clements … you couldn't have men visitors after ten at night …they were kind of oppressive in a way that the universities had kind of abandoned much earlier, so it was like going back in time to … when women were not trusted to look after themselves … so it felt slightly oppressive … from that social point of view that we weren't grown up enough to look after ourselves, and yet, of course we were doing quite frightening things on the ward. *Maria*

Male student nurses were housed separately:

> Four men [in my set] ... I lived in ... [the] Cavell Home, which is where the boys were. *Stephen*

Those that had previously lived independently found it hard to stay in the homes, especially when there were other cheap housing options available:

> I remember ... being dropped off at the Luckes Nurses Home ... it was August '74 ... being allowed visitors ... they weren't allowed in past the white line, [they] had to sit in that little foyer where ... they had to wait ... you sign people in, you sign them out ... having lived a much freer lifestyle ... I didn't actually stay in the Luckes Nurses' Home that long. ... I moved out and I lived in a house in Shoreditch and then ... behind the hospital at Walden Street ... and then I moved out to Hackney later ... but I think it was expected that you would live in the Luckes Home when I started. ... Yes, I escaped. *Kathryn*

> I moved out into a council flat ... it's funny now to think of that it was a flat that three families had already rejected.... So that's why they could offer it to student nurses ... I must say it was better for night duty. *Maria*

> We were mad, when I think back, we had everything done for us, in the nurses' home, but we decided we'd live out for a while. *Gail*

Training: Bunsen burners and men in the back row

The Preliminary Training School (PTS) continued as before:

> we were doing the practical things like learning how to wash somebody.... Passing a naso-gastric tube.... We had to do that on each other and we had to feed each other.... And I remember giving injections ... in an orange. *Sally and Alison.*

Although dipstick testing was becoming available, some wards still used the more old fashioned methods for urinalysis.

> we learnt basics in PTS like bed making, draw sheets, we still had grey plastic draw sheets, testing urine with reagent pills and test tubes.... Oh yes, we had a Bunsen burner. *Geraldine*

In PTS and beyond however, there were challenges in coping with the new mix of students, as Michael remembers:

> there was a lecture on sexual health and the men were asked to sit in the back row in case the girls were embarrassed ... we did a session on bandaging and one ... we had to do was for a mastectomy and I was told that I shouldn't do it on any of the girls ... but a couple of the girls thought this was stupid and actually said, 'Right, here's the bandage, I don't mind ... have a go.' And again the tutors thought actually this is daft as well and in the end it ... changed ... I think we were quite a forward set in that respect.

Other groups had different approaches, such as that of the joint RMN/SRN training:

> As a small group of thirteen in a room ... even with just one tutor ... sometimes we had both the tutors there, it was very much a personal and interactive group

… which really reflected the talking therapies that were just coming into psychiatric nursing and about being in small groups and interacting. *Geraldine*

The uniform and the image

There were contrasting views regarding the uniform:

Don't get me started on the uniform, oh dear, Victorian fancy dress, it was a joke, wasn't it? *Sharon*

Also the London Hospital uniform was always a big pull, it's a beautiful uniform. *Denise*

I was thinking about the … lovely ladies in the sewing room … you got your two old uniforms with your really big sleeves and then your two new uniforms which had less big sleeves, and being told that … in the olden days when smells abounded that you put the smelling salts up your big puffed sleeve and so if you were doing something really difficult as a job you'd … just had a little quick sniff to keep you going. *Karen*

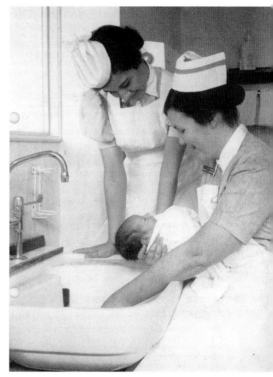

A State Enrolled Nurse (SEN) demonstrating and teaching a student nurse.

I remember … [the tutor] quite clearly, she was tall and rather elegant, rather lovely, and she had the outfit and a long cape and … for some reason, had to lead us from where we were doing some teaching session to somewhere else … we were all following her and we had the purple dresses and short capes and as we patted after her a workman in the garden said, 'quack quack' because we did look so much like her little goslings pattering after her, she had this long cloak and we had these little capes! … I was ashamed at the time 'cos I did feel completely self-conscious in this outfit, it did seem absolutely bizarre. *Maria*

we could smoke [in uniform] when we were having our coffee, and Dunhill were 32p for twenty, and I thought I was really cool because the only people who didn't smoke were either terribly religious or very goody-goody. *Gail*

Social life and marriage

we were warned by [the tutor] right in our first year that most of the doctors just wanted to meet some nice young nurses so to be very careful if they asked you out and don't allow anything to distract you from your main purpose of being there so we were a little bit cautious of the doctors and there were some that were real players so you knew … that you had to steer [clear] of them. *Alison*

Student nurses, mostly coming straight from school, made up a large proportion of the workforce. There was not much time for socialising. With a work pattern following a firmly established rota, it meant only one weekend off each month. However, there were now more opportunities to meet with a wider mix of people at the hospital, as Denise recalls:

> when we started our training The Feathers had just opened up, the social club at the back of the hospital … there weren't any men in our group at all when we were training so it was nice to have a bit of male company and [that] was usually the medical students. I don't think any of us actually married any of those doctors, maybe one or two, but a lot of my set married teachers … I think Goldsmiths College was often invited up to the nurses' balls.

Although it was now becoming more acceptable for nurses to marry during training, rules still had to be observed:

> And even when my husband and I married during my training, having to have separate rooms in John Harrison House … when he came to visit even though we were married…. Couldn't have that sort of thing going on at the nurses' home. *Geraldine*

> I remember one of the PTS Tutors saying that we were … possibly sitting next to the people that we were going to be bridesmaids to, godparents to their children and you'd be friends for years. I suppose you don't appreciate it then, but I've just had my fortieth reunion with five friends that I made at the hospital and I was godmother to all their children and I was bridesmaid to them all so clearly … [the] sort of training that we did back in the seventies, eighties, sixties, whatever, was a training for life and you did make friends for life. *Denise*

Imprinted on the mind

Some of the most poignant memories come from the experiences nurses had on their first ward:

> It was a male medical ward … there was a whole ward full of very old men with acute or chronic bronchitis … I remember asking one or two of them what they could remember … because we were being very much encouraged to talk to the patients while … doing blanket baths or straightening the bed or if you had a spare moment … I talked to someone who startled me very much by saying 'that bastard Churchill', which was gosh … he was a saint in my parents' house so, this was about Gallipoli though, and there was the Russian man … who had the frostbite from the First World War, there was someone else … who'd fought Lenin's forces at Archangel and that seemed just so outrageous that I was talking to him … and giving him cups of tea. *Maria*

> My first ward was down at Mile End Hospital, a men's medical ward, called Wilson…. We had a mixture of patients but many had chronic bronchitis … doing the early morning round with Nelson's inhalers, those pottery things with all the tar, balsam or something, and them all under their towels coughing away … and then us having to do the sputum pots … on the first ward you have that experience of dealing with feeling sick and disgusted by all the sights and smells, and the sputum pots remain probably pretty much the worst. The patients would do their inhalations and then go off and smoke a roll-up on the balcony. *Sharon*

I was introduced to my first ward, Rothschild, which was a renal medical ward ... maybe my first week ... I was asked to go into a side ward to delouse ... someone had been brought in from the streets and he was covered in fleas and things ... he was in a very bad state medically, poor thing. And I remember ... gowning up ... feeling rather out of my comfort zone ... I was sent in there to get rid of his clothes and put them in bags ... and also just to do some general care on him and observations ... I found it quite intimidating because he was ranting rather and I was very new ... he'd been catheterised and he got out of bed and pulled his catheter out ... and I felt ... 'Dear, what do I do here?' And ... he wasn't quite aggressive but ... there was a threat there ... I remember going back to the Luckes Home, getting on the phone to my father and saying, 'I think I've made a terrible mistake,' and weeping and Dad giving me lots of reassurance and, of course, it was ... one bad experience but all part of learning. *Kathryn*

my first ward was Sophia Ward, [sister] was very kind ... but I was scared of her, and ... when she wanted to give an injection to somebody she used to call out 'injection', and I used to find somewhere to hide, preferably with my feet tucked up so she couldn't see my feet under the curtains, but I think she probably realised that was me and she still found me. I didn't like hurting people and I hated giving injections. *Denise*

my first ward was called Goschen [Mile End] which was a female medical ward ... the perfect place to start with proper basic nursing care, full of lovely, little elderly Jewish ladies ... I had never come across any Jewish people, any Bangladeshi people or anything at home, but the patients especially made us feel so welcome. *Julia*

'Quite a weepy affair'

my first experience of somebody dying was on my first ward, he was a young man, he was 21 and he had bowel cancer ... he was very poorly ... he had a young wife ... she was expecting their first child, very, very emotionally charged ... but a decision was made to move him to the side room ... I had that feeling ... he was being tucked away in a side room ... and maybe it was [because] other people were not finding it easy to cope with somebody who was dying, but I had the experience of, obviously supervised because I was a student, giving him his last Diamorphine injection and I won't forget the scream from his wife when he died, and of course I had that feeling of 'I've killed him', but I hadn't ... and that to be the first death, was very traumatic. But the Staff Nurse who was on duty that day was really good and she said to me ... 'Would you like to do the last offices with me or would you like not to?' ... and I decided that I would because I thought if I say 'no' now maybe it's gonna be hard to later. But it was quite a weepy affair. *Deborah*

I remember one nurse telling me when I was a bit frightened about laying out a patient for the first time. 'Just ... come with me and I'll talk to the patient as if they're still alive and we'll say ... I'm going to just turn you over now.' I remember thinking that was a sort of kind thing that she told me there, to ... just do that talking thing. *Kathryn*

Being non-judgemental

Student nurses were to treat patients from a wide variety of backgrounds:

> And having Police, [patients] being handcuffed to the bed ... knowing that you just didn't say certain things, you just accepted, they were a patient and you treated them as everyone else. *Michael*

> a woman who was a tramp, or homeless ... she came in with a very bad cellulitis of one of her legs, and it was huge, this leg, and absolutely weeping and very nasty, and her temperature was through the roof ... you could not put her into the bedsheets because she was so dirty. ... So we were delegated to put her in a bath ... the water was just black ... so we had to refill it and bath her again, and she was very ill, so it was very traumatic for her.... Anyway, we finally got her into the bed in some kind of better state. *Teresa*

> I was very frightened by one of the old men with acute or chronic bronchitis ... he looked like something out of a horror film ... he was really skeletal and he had this mad hair and wild eyes ... and big yellow teeth and I was frightened, and I made myself smile at him and he smiled back and it was so sweet. I've never forgotten the complete change in his face and how I felt kind of ashamed of myself because ... I thought ... 'what are you doing being frightened just 'cos he looks like that'. *Maria*

> I met my first transvestite ever in my life ... this gentleman would walk around ... in a black and red negligee, it seemed perfectly accepted on the ward. *Julia*

Night duty

Working at night, normal sounds could take on a sinister air:

> [working] on ... [the] female orthopaedic ward, and I'd just gone to one of the little bays and coming towards me was one of the patients who'd had a hip operation that day, walking, dragging her drain behind her ... her hip was okay ... but it was the dragging of the drain that alerted me to this noise, it was like ... something out of *Christmas Carol* coming along. *Julia*

> I remember crunching cockroaches on the floor at nights at Mile End as you walked down in the dark with your torch. *Geraldine*

Night sister's ward round continued to cause trepidation:

> I used to pray actually to be truthful, that I wouldn't be picked to do the ward round with night sister, sweaty palms, palpitations, could I be busy in the sluice, could I be testing the urines at midnight, could I be? *Deborah*

With various ploys to avoid being reprimanded:

> always, at night you emptied a drawer out, so that if anyone came through the door, your tea and coffee and anything went in the drawer. *Julie*

There was a cyclical aspect to the work at times as Karen remembers:

> people would wake up and you'd give them a cup of tea because they were awake and then the person next door wanted a cup of tea and then of course three hours

later they were all shouting for bed pans and then you had to do tea all over again ... but actually I loved night duty as well because you had that quality time with people when perhaps they were most vulnerable and less sort of disturbed by ward rounds and other people coming and going.

Despite this some of the memories evoke an atmosphere of calm:

1976 was a very, very hot year ... I was working nights ... I remember ... stepping out onto the veranda ... because it was ... U-shaped at the back of The London you could see the other wards ... and it was very calm ... very hot ... but there were nurses all sitting out on the verandas I think for their meal break ... but there was such a peace about it. It was just ... calm ... the hospital was going on but it was just ... peacefully sleeping ... as much as it could. *Annette*

Working at night however took its toll with both exhaustion and euphoria:

I had a very traumatic night in my second year, at the age of... 19 ... people [nursing staff] ... were off sick right, left and centre ... there were some really sick patients on the ward, and we had one man who was fitting the whole night, he had a brain tumour, and all his family were there ... and in the morning I was so exhausted that I couldn't really give a report, because my brain had locked out. I couldn't even think straight. *Teresa*

I found nights difficult full stop, just even staying awake, that three o'clock, that awful hour ... when you might have your break and you're fighting sleep. ... I never ate and I lost loads of weight when I did nights and I used to ... live on toast and that was about it ... my body didn't feel like any other type of food. *Kathryn*

you ended up eating breakfast all the time. ...You sort of get up and eat breakfast and then I'd never eat during the night and then you'd have breakfast in the morning ... and we were all a bit hyperactive at breakfast I remember ... we all met up in the morning and we'd all discuss what had happened and we'd all get a bit hysterical. *Sally*

The initiation that came with your first night duty as a student nurse continued in this decade:

But I did have my first night duty on Wilson Ward and I was put to 'special' [in a] side room ... there was a man in there who didn't like the lights so he had his blankets up over his head and I had to be very quiet and sit there in pitch dark and just ... count his respirations and of course after a little while I realised that there were no respirations ... when I pulled the blankets back to see if he was still alive that it was only a drip stand in the bed and I'd 'specialed' a drip stand for an hour. *Alison*

and I was down at Mile End when they did things like ... a commode check, would everybody have their commodes to central nursing office by 2 a.m. and you'd go for your meal break and ... [see] ... commodes everywhere. *Karen*

Ward layout, organisation and shifts

> We had three side wards on the right as you came into the ward … three bays of six and then the big end … I remember we had ward clerks and notes trolleys, and consultant's rounds and morning coffee in sister's sitting room, but all the rest of the breaks were in the dining room, the canteen. We were never allowed to eat anything in the ward kitchen…. Ward maids did the patients' lockers and water jugs and the ward cleaners did the mopping and the dusting. Nothing was single use, everything was cleaned and reused … they were only just starting [in] 1973 or for the CSSD at The London, but we still [had] cotton wool balls rolled and bandage rolling at Mile End. *Geraldine*

> So it was almost as if from the vantage point that the sister had … they could see the whole ward and see exactly where the need was … we were really like soldiers being directed. *Sally*

> The shift work … I loved the earlies … because we finished at three which gave you a big chunk of the day and I think we started at eight … and even the lates were OK, half past one until 10…. Although there were times you were catching the bus back quite late at night but … I have to say, I never felt at risk … even though I walked across London Fields by myself, which probably wasn't very sensible, got off the bus to go back to my house in Hackney … I never felt threatened. *Kathryn*

Learning and being assessed

As well as the teaching in study 'blocks' in the classroom, student nurses were supported and taught within the clinical setting:

> And of course we had the clinical nurse tutors in those days as well … they were always in the wards and certainly on day shifts, they were always there … very supportive and working one-on-one a lot of the time. *Stephen*

> you would have little teaching sessions from the house officer in the afternoon … sometimes … follow the teaching round … the whole firm was round the bed, poor patient … really interesting to learn from practice … rather than … in the classroom. *Evelyn*

> I remember being given our blue books … although they were buff coloured, and that was your list of all your duties and things you had to achieve in certain years of your training. *Denise*

Four clinical assessments had to be completed as Deborah recalls:

> my favourite one was Aseptic Technique … it was … back in the days of not metal forceps but plastic forceps to open everything … it's a no-touch technique … whether your barrier is your forceps or it's your gloves … putting your hand in the sterile bag so that you could rearrange stuff on the sterile field.
>
> For the 'Total Care of the Patient' assessment: 'you sort of 'specialed' somebody for the day … actually there was a lot more person-centred care than I think is being given credit for [now].

Michael describes:

> the management [assessment] I did on George Ward … everyone knew you were doing it, all the consultants knew you were going to do it … everyone was on their good behaviour but … I think sometimes people planned to do a few things just to wobble you so you got tested but … you were made to feel this is really important, everyone's behind you, everyone wants you to pass it and there was something about getting it signed off in … the blue books.

There was also a medication assessment.

However, some learning came directly from issues that occurred on the ward:

> I remember going on duty … I think my second ward at Mile End… we were gathered into sister's office for the handover and sister said, 'Before I start nurses would any of you like the toilet?' and we said, 'Oh thank you sister, yes I'd like to go' and she replied 'Well you can't because I've just come onto the ward and Mrs X … [is] in tears because she's asked for a bedpan on numerous occasions and nobody has taken it to her, so you will all now sit with your full bladders and feel exactly what it's like for Mrs X.' *Geraldine*

Nurses generally were encouraged to teach those who were more junior than themselves:

> there was a sort of atmosphere of 'this is a teaching hospital and so if you have an opportunity to do teaching you do it'. *Maria*

Hierarchy, responsibility and stress

The hierarchical attitude was still very evident:

> I was in probably my first … [ward] and there was a ward round and I dared to ask a question of a consultant … and he … just walked on and ignored me and the staff nurse pulled me aside and said, 'You don't speak to consultants, you speak to me, I speak to sister, sister speaks to the doctor and then the doctor will answer your question if he thinks it's a question worth answering.' *Alison*

Despite this, junior student nurses were at times given excessive responsibility:

> on my second ward I was put in charge … just for the lunch break … it was during the day … so everybody was awake and I thought 'It's only my second ward', she [staff nurse] gave me the keys and said, 'No, you'll be alright for an hour', well I wasn't because somebody had a massive haemorrhage … there was no bell, you couldn't ring an alarm or anything so I … ran to the ward next door and got somebody but that was really frightening and I thought … well this is what's happening, this is what I need to do and this is what I did. *Sally*

This led to some struggling to cope at times:

> The responsibility … I'd had Christmas Day off but I was working Boxing Day … I walked onto the ward and a lady had just died in front of me on the ward and I thought I need a break, I can't do this for much longer, I really was at the end. *Julia*

I still found nursing stressful, I found the ward setting stressful, I would worry about going on duty, what I was going to cope with. I can't really describe it … if it was now, knowing what I know now, I would cope much better, but I found it very hard to relax. *Gail*

We were terrified of ringing Matron's Office if we weren't very well because it was certainly not well received to be phoning in sick. … I think that's something that's instilled in nurses generally … we battle on regardless, we don't like to take time off. *Geraldine*

Some are aware of the emotional impact of working professionally:

I think we were taught … that you have to get into professional mode … you have to act as if it's not affecting you, all the time you're having to think clearly, but that doesn't mean that we didn't experience it in the quiet of our own homes at night or in the nursing home because I mean I learned a lot about compassion and I learned a lot about people having a range of illness that actually didn't kill them but made them incredibly handicapped. *Alison*

Working at Christmas

Despite the seasonal festivities, the work still had to be done:

Christmas morning came, I was on an early. Sister said, 'Nurse … you can do the dressings this morning'. Well, I'd never done the dressings, as such, by myself, it was a mammoth task, so I nervously asked the staff nurse … and she said, 'Oh, just look at what comes off and put the same back on'… so off I set, plodding round, eventually getting to the gunshot gentleman … I looked at his tummy wound, and it wasn't too bad, managed … but then he turned over, and I saw the exit wound, which was utterly appalling, and all I could think of, as we'd been told, never let the patient see any sign of disgust, but I was very glad he was not facing me at the time. *Gail*

But there was also, as Karen remembers, a lighter side during that time:

I remember … my first Christmas on the wards … orthopaedics and lots of young lads with their feet in traction, every bedside table was filled with alcohol … it was like one grand party really … because they weren't really sick, they were just stuck in their beds.

visiting the Christmas babies … the first baby boy and the first baby girl had special cots that were … Christmas bedecked and it was normal for nurses on duty that day at some point to go up to the maternity wards to see the Christmas babies.

A demanding role

Some became aware of how demanding it was to be a senior nurse at the time:

But I think they had a very hard time, The London's senior nurses. … It was a very matriarchal set-up, you had all these consultants, some very arrogant men, so these matrons had to be very tough and have their voice at the top table and run this large workforce. … So I think it was difficult for them; they were from a different time, when people felt they had to be upstanding and tough and unsmiling, and they'd kind of descend from on high … it just felt authoritarian, it didn't feel facilitative at all. *Sharon*

And I remember Matron's Office seeming a bit scary, like the nursing officers because they used to come and visit the ward. But I can also remember that they were very skilled and experienced nurses who rolled their sleeves up and pitched in if we were short of staff or there was a crisis. *Geraldine*

East Enders

Many of the nurses were motivated by the attitude of some of their patients:

And particular patients … were really inspiring how they rose above their conditions … I love the pluckiness of the East End character. *Kathryn*

my colleague and I were on nights one night and a gang came in, rampaged through the hospital and went into one of the wards and broke all the windows and I thought 'Oh my goodness, this is what working in the East End is like, I think I'd better go'. But also nice things, some nights some … local tradesmen used to bring us food packages in and it used to be quite odd looking out the window about four o'clock in the morning at Whitechapel Tube Station coming alive and the market starting up. *Denise*

In Mile End … you weren't allocated then to one clinic because it was a smaller set-up, there were different clinics on different days … a fantastic experience and again the long term patients used to come back for … [various] treatments…. The elderly Jewish men with leg ulcers would always bring in cheesecake and apple strudel … it became very friendly, very community orientated. *Julia*

I think I've still got the pages that they gave me which were all of the different religions and cultures with when they had to be buried and how they had to be buried and what the religious observances were. …That's right, yes, because there was a very strict sort of protocol for laying somebody out and you had to look at their culture to make sure you were following what their wishes were. *Alison and Sally*

Lessons for life

I can distinctly remember … I think it was the sister … on Milward … there was somebody that was dying … it was in the big end of the ward and she pulled the curtains, not round completely but two thirds down the side and then she sat and wrote the report next to him … she was just there with him and I just thought that's amazing. *Annette*

probably my second year … and I can remember … [the sister] once … teaching me the value of nursing as opposed to being … a doctor, and how this woman with a chest infection, she said, 'right, if you look after her properly then she'll survive', and I can remember turning this woman and chest suctioning her and doing all this sort of stuff … and she survived and [the sister] said to me 'she survived because of the care you've given'. … That is what good nursing care's all about …you know in the morning she was moribund, in the afternoon she was sitting up having a cup of tea. *Lesley*

we had a young, middle-aged man who … was pretty unable to move and speak but he could grunt … yes and no and various things … I was fairly junior and there was a … staff … nurse … standing one side of the bed and I was the other. … I … [was being shown] how to help feed this patient because … he couldn't manage himself … I can't remember his job now but he was obviously a highly intelligent man and you actually could understand that when you took time with him by just eye contact and his responses and so on, but he couldn't actually speak as such. So … the … nurse was helping feed him and at one stage … our patient was saying, grunting words, trying to, and this … nurse said to him, 'Oh, pretty Polly, pretty Polly.' And I was absolutely horrified. So that stayed with me all my life, how not to do it. This was an intelligent man, he could hear, he could understand, he couldn't express himself and I thought as I stood there that I was horrified and to this day I'm still horrified but it taught me that you never did that. I was so shocked … it did teach me that there were people where compassion was lacking and how never to become so inured to the human condition that you could actually be so crass and cruel as to behave like that with somebody … a patient who can't respond still needs to be spoken to normally and explained to … I think that's been a lesson for life. *Kathryn*

Spheres of nursing

Psychiatric nursing

Psychiatric nursing was a relatively new option in the general SRN training. Most experience was gained at The London Hospital (St Clements), apart from one such ward on the main site:

I was very lucky … I was on Rachel Ward at Whitechapel, a very innovative ward. … We wore our own clothes and were encouraged to talk to patients; the idea was not to drug them up to the eyeballs but to have therapeutic relationships. *Sharon*

We also went to St Clement's Hospital … acute psychiatry… but they were still using Paraldehyde in glass syringes…. Lots of talking therapies just coming in, lots of long-term sedation [with Largactil] with Parkinsonism side-effects. *Geraldine*

It was called [a] psycho-geriatric [ward], and the first day I arrived there I can remember a little old lady who I later found out had manic depression … I was terrified of going … and I can remember walking in very, very quietly … I … just put my head round the door and all of a sudden whack on the head with a stick and this … little old lady was standing on a chair behind the door and ran off down the corridor screaming with laughter … I can remember thinking 'Oh my God, what have I come into'. Anyway, she was a brilliant patient … she was 92 … and she used to come into the therapy session and she would say to the doctors … 'What's on the agenda for today', and they'd say 'Well … what's been happening with you', 'Well, I've been having a marvellous time, who wouldn't have a marvellous time in this lovely hotel'…. But then other days would be … nothing. *Lesley*

Alison describes her memories of that aspect of healthcare:

I mean I saw mental health, how dementia … [was] treated and that was sad and I also had to witness electro [convulsive] therapy which was gruelling … unfortunately in the time that I was on my ward, which was quite an acute ward, there were sixteen deaths and that had never been known … I think I was only there for eight weeks and I nearly left after four weeks because there had been this spate of suicides and they were pretty horrific … jumping under the tube trains and off buildings … it seemed that once one person had done it, it created a trigger. So that was pretty grim and they took me off that ward and sent me down to the psycho-geriatric ward where … they just had … very advanced dementia…. But I saw there a lack of dignity and that stayed with me, the need to ensure that people have dignity whatever happens at any cost.

Well actually one of my abiding memories there was the smoke because everybody smoked … it was awful, it was like a fog and the staff all seemed to stay in the office smoking and the patients were all outside smoking.

Community nursing

The introduction of community nursing as an option in the training could not come too soon for Sharon:

I was very conscious of The London as a rather odd place, doing all this very high-tech, cutting-edge acute care in the middle of this sea of poverty and deprivation, doing leading edge surgery and then sending people back to tower blocks where the lifts didn't work and back to a very unhealthy environment so it was paradoxical, why didn't we do more community-based work?

Michael remembers his experiences:

I was attached to a District Nursing Team in Poplar … I remember the first week I went round with a District Nurse. The second week she said, 'Actually I think you can go and see some patients on your own', so they gave me a pack of dressings, a list of addresses and I used to go round and do dressings. … I remember going in to some of the homes and they were pretty awful and people were offering you cups of tea with condensed milk … you had to think on your feet but I'd be changing someone's dressing, helping taking someone's sutures out and I just learnt that actually if you chat to the people, have some of the tea and do the best you can. …Very diverse [at the] time, there was still a very large Jewish community and having been brought up in the East End of London … I actually was accepted very quickly.

Obstetrics- a step towards midwifery

the nurses [midwives] tended to have very little patience with the mothers in general and ... it must have been very … difficult to have your first child … they spoke to them in a very patronising way, 'Come on mother' … top and tail bowl…. And this is how you do it … and the mums were all in a tiz and we were always waiting for the 'blues' to set in … what was interesting was that we, as student nurses, were showing these new mums how to wash and hold their babies and we'd never done it before. I think the mothers resented us as students telling them how to do things especially if they'd had four or five children … here we are telling them they've got to clean the umbilicus. *Alison and Sally*

it was very interesting doing obstetrics … there were a lot of … [Bangladeshi] young girls having babies very young and that was very traumatic for them because they were having to sort of show Western women their bodies and they just didn't want to do that … so that was quite tricky. There were a lot of West Indian midwives at Mile End. … It was just the beginning of Brick Lane becoming [an] area that the … Bangladeshis … came to … that was reflected in the wards, there was a lot of TB of course … all our side wards tended to have people with TB and they tended to be from that community. So it was a little bit … of East End people feeling … not in a nasty way but saying, 'Oh, look at them, they're all taking up our hospital beds'…. And so, you know, you could see that starting there … the indigenous population. But the East End was always like that … different ethnic groups and then they moved east as they made money … it was just the end of the Jewish community being [there]. *Kathryn*

The Receiving Room (RR)

the one occasion that was probably the most difficult was when I did … an [A&E] placement. … The RR … [the sister] was showing me around and … there was a 'blue call' … it was a cot death and that was my first day experience of A&E … [the sister] was really good … I remember her staying on … just making sure everyone was alright. *Michael*

I also remember another patient in A&E … he was clad in leathers … and I was given the task to undress the gentleman … which I did … I mean I was a very naïve … 20-year-old, and when we took off the leather jacket, underneath the leather jacket were all sorts of straps and all sorts … [bondage] …. And I can remember sort of thinking, oh my goodness. *Julie*

There are fond memories of the nursing officer in the Receiving Room with her direct approach and some unusual requests:

the nursing officer … used to pull you by your puff [sleeve], 'Come here [nurse],' … and [she'd] take you to an X-ray machine where there was an X-ray. 'Right, what do you see?' *Julie*

'Now, nurse', she said, 'Go down the Mile End Road and find the statue of Gandhi'…. She was very into understanding history and having a wider view of things. *Sharon*

The Moorgate crash

A major incident occurred, close to The London, at Moorgate Underground Station where there was a catastrophic train crash on 28 February 1975. The London was one of the main hospitals to which casualties were sent:

I can remember I was working in Mile End and I'd brought a patient up to the scanning department … and waiting in the X-ray department as trolley after trolley of blackened people were being brought in from the disaster … all these people came rushing in first because they all needed X-rays. So that was … a bit scary. *Geraldine*

Annette recalls:

I remember coming on duty for a late that day and walking through the main corridor. It was full of trolleys with people covered in black soot.

The next day, I was asked to work on Cotton Ward, there was a lady there in traction, surrounded by flowers and cards, one of … [the cards] said, 'Thank God you're alive'.

Children's wards

Evidence of social problems and poverty in the surrounding area often became apparent in the children's ward:

at Mile End…. The sad thing there was where we had children who were either victims of abuse or suspected abuse and you'd have a Police Officer guarding … one of the children … it's … not easy on a children's ward. *Deborah*

Karen recalls the difficult cases and the atmosphere on the wards:

I remember a little boy … who was a 'failure to thrive', we'd lots of East End babies with failure to thrive, and he was about 7lbs when he was about a year old, he was minuscule, and we actually sort of tried to teach him to crawl lying him on a little brick trolley and he used to sort of paddle around the ward but he hadn't got the muscle strength.

I sort of love that sense of caring for whole families … so I ended up staffing on Buxton [Ward] with its little red gate through to David Hughes [Ward] on the other side … mixing up all the feeds, and we had great big stainless steel sinks where everything was … 'Miltoned' in the mornings … being elbow deep in water. … I can [also] remember [on night duty] standing in the kitchens with the light just beginning to come through and the birds beginning to sing [whilst] buttering bread.

Theatres

Theatres was not always a popular option, with student nurses being allocated work within a highly specialised field:

they seemed to be cross all the time but I understood it's because their standards were so high and they had a certain way of doing things, we were doing all the autoclaving on site then and everything so it all had to be done just so and it seemed like it worked like well-oiled machinery and then they had to have these blooming student nurses who would come in and take their time up because their lists were always so pressured. *Alison*

I started off in theatre eight, which was neurosurgery, and you would be stuck in there with these operations going on for eight hours at a time, it was almost like something from science fiction … one morning I just couldn't face going on duty at all, so I took myself off, and went on the Underground, and ended up in Westminster Abbey … and then I thought, oh lord, I'd better go back, and so I went in and pretended I thought I was on a late shift, and of course she was very cross with me, but then I told her the truth, I said, 'Actually, Sister, I couldn't face going into theatre eight today, I'm really, really sorry', and she was so kind…. She switched me to the urology theatre. *Gail*

the last … but one, night I worked, somebody had thrown a bomb in one of the pubs in the East End, a petrol bomb … we went on and there were these terribly badly injured, burnt people, all about, and we were sort of waiting half the night … you know some were coming up for tracheostomies … it was so eerie … because we were not doing anything, we were just waiting and then they were going to bring up the first of these patients who needed a trachy [tracheostomy] … I remember, the consultant came up … and he said, 'Girls, have you ever seen anyone badly burnt before?' and we said no, and he said, 'Don't worry, you're going to be fine, you just do what [I say], and again it was another small touch of actually somebody caring about how we might feel. And this patient … he came in and his mouth … because of the oedema … and the burns … and then the anaesthetist gave me a little job to do and you just got … [on] with it. *Gail*

Old and new

The 1970s was a time of great change and transformation for healthcare and nursing.

The convalescent homes linked to The London were being phased out. Banstead Annexe closed in 1977:

Yes. I went to Banstead at the end of my first year … it was a convalescent home…. It was lovely to be out of London … have a bit of sort of countryside … there were horses … in the field outside … I could go on bike rides and things. It was much more relaxed than the hospital…. And we did split shifts there so you'd have … like an afternoon off, you could go out for walks … it was really nice. *Evelyn*

On the wards generally, traditional equipment and treatments were still evident:

everybody had their … thermometer behind their beds … bedpan washers … every patient had a clean sheet every day … I don't ever remember there being shortages of clean linen … people were kept in good beds, and again the thing specific to The London … those canvas backrests … with the leather straps that went round the edge of the beds … they were incredibly comfortable … you always made beds with two of you.

pressure sore care … rubbing with talcum powder. *Karen*

I remember doing dressings and using Eusol … and also I remember patients who were unlucky enough to get bed sores, used to have egg white and oxygen applied … using Spenco mattresses which were like very soft duvet mattresses. *Denise*

New attitudes

Male nurses were able to train at The London from 1969 and were therefore becoming more commonplace, although acceptance of them was not universal, as Michael recalls:

there were some doctors who definitely did not … [think] men should be nurses. During my period there were at least two … I remember one was a consultant … who wouldn't even have male nurses in his theatre … in the seventies male nurses

... were a novelty. ... It was very late coming in [at The London] ... there were one or two sisters who always liked to have male nurses on the ward and actually you had to be careful because you were seen as being the favourite.... And career wise if you were accepted you actually progressed quite rapidly.

The attitudes of the senior nurses towards their students varied, with some encouraging nurses to question and explore their work, and others not at all:

[the charge nurse] ... rolled up his sleeves, did everything with you, whereas some of the sisters in those days really did just stay in the office and not come out. He was friendly and approachable, you could ask him anything and he made the atmosphere a very happy one so it was a good learning environment. It was great that I had him to start with because of his advice and his warning. At the end he gave me a very positive assessment and said, 'You know, I really like having students like you who are curious, who ask questions ... but be careful because not everybody will welcome that'. *Sharon*

Computers

Computers were just being introduced, at first only impacting on some aspects of patient care and management:

I was at The London when we first started using computers and it was really exciting to order a urine sample on the computer or see who you'd got coming into the ward the next day on the computer and they put two games on ... for ... if you're on night duty and you had a space, and one was 'Boxes' ... I don't think we used them very much really ... men in those days came round to sort of see

1970s: A sister and staff nurse using one of the first ward computers.
(Image appears by courtesy of The Royal London Hospital Archives and Museum)

that we all knew how to use the computers, well compared to what we do on computers nowadays it was absolutely nothing, but that was a sort of moment of great revelation in the seventies. *Karen*

The Nursing Process

New approaches that were to transform nursing started to appear such as the Nursing Process in the late 1970s, supported by nurses specifically employed to work in research for the first time:

> I look back and see some of the good things that were starting then … I remember we all sat round solemnly when they told us about the nursing process and I thought, fantastic … thank goodness, at last a framework to make sense of what we're doing, I thought it was the most brilliant thing. *Sharon*

> what I found most difficult [about the nursing process] was if someone else's patient called me and I was supposed to say 'I will get your nurse', now … I don't think I ever managed to say it…. I thought … if I'm walking past and someone says 'Nurse', I'm not going to say 'I will get someone else for you', I'm going to see what it is they want. *Maria*

Reflecting the times, some became involved in the wider issues concerning nursing when they were still a student:

> I joined the RCN, and Unison [public service trade union, NUPE at that time] as well because I wanted both bits of the picture. I was active in the RCN branch [then called a Centre] and that was interesting because you were mixing with a lot of the tutors and more of the hierarchy than you would normally see as a student. I and some other younger ones were very much pushing them for more challenging positions on things, and then I went off to RCN Congress as the branch delegate, so I was getting involved in the wider world of nursing and politics. *Sharon*

The impact of advances in medicine

The first CT scan was conducted in 1972, the first MRI image published in 1973 and the first IVF baby was born in 1978.

> when they were pioneering those [heart surgery] none of those patients survived and it was really hard because you knew that … they weren't going to survive, but they were learning all the time and it was hard looking after them and there was a lot of … reverse barrier nursing. *Sally*

> when I came to The London there were very few chemotherapy drugs being used. … We did the first bone marrow transplant at our hospital [she was] on my ward and it was a risky business, the girl who had the transplant knew it was the first, I do know that she is still alive and doing very well. *Denise*

> I was on Charrington which was a cardiac ward then. It had … like a bay of four beds which was like a coronary care, they were starting to use monitors. *Evelyn*

Renal medicine was advancing fast, with changes in the way the disciplines worked together as Julia remembers:

and it was moving forward at such a pace at that point. We used to have huge machines, lots of things weren't disposable and then it just changed so much.

the Multidisciplinary Team approach I suppose was only just beginning to bed in and in the renal unit that seemed very obvious ... the dietician ... the nursing staff, the dialysis staff, the technicians, it all seemed like one big team together.

Aids and MRSA [Methicillin-resistant Staphylococcus aureus]

Alongside progress, new challenges were beginning to appear for health care. Denise remembers her first awareness of a new disease:

I don't think mental health care was as developed in those days or certainly there weren't the screening tools that are used now for mental health and we had a couple of patients who actually committed suicide or tried to [jump] over the long balconies of the big end, we used to have those balconies open and the patients used to go out and smoke ... because we were on the second floor, they actually took a run and went over the top. A couple of them were successful suicides which was terrible and I remember one person who actually did the same in a very confused state, was one of the first patients that we ever recognised as actually having AIDS and his confusion was as a result of ... [what] was a completely new illness, we knew nothing about it ... and suddenly we were faced with a whole new range of patients ... [who] needed very specialist care.

Bacterial resistance to antibiotics was beginning to emerge:

so I worked on a medical and surgical ward at Mile End and it was when the first outbreak of MRSA came and one of the wards was actually closed as an infection control ... [measure]. *Denise*

The diversity of opportunity on qualifying

On completion of their training nurses were able to become involved in new approaches that were developing at the time, as Deborah found in the care of the elderly:

I staffed on Mercer which was the Care of the Elderly Assessment Ward down at Mile End ... the ward sister there ... she was very keen to listen to ideas and ... [it] sounds a minor thing now but I managed to get paper towels ... but get them in every room so that if we were in the Day Room and somebody spilt their cup of tea you could easily just get ... something quickly.... And I introduced games in the afternoon ... playing Skittles and we'd have armchair exercises to music ... the social element is really important. And we often had people admitted to the ward ... they would come in confused or ... various reasons for being admitted and what very often used to happen, particularly if they'd got a multiplicity of drugs, they would be taken off all their medication, monitored very closely and gradually the doctor would build the medication.... And we had many people who would come in and you were thinking ... 'they're confused ...they're on the downward spiral' and [they] would walk out ... and be well ... for some years.

Nurses were also working on innovations with the doctors:

So my first staffing post was A&E ... it was a time when trauma was starting to become something that needed to be better managed so I was given a project then to actually start to look at how trauma was managed within the A&E Department which was really interesting…. So I did a piece of work … with the neurosurgeons … and again this was pretty leading edge, we converted the Glasgow Coma Scale into a trauma scale which is now the trauma scoring system. *Michael*

After a short spell as a staff nurse, some nurses moved away from the hospital either to gain wider experience or to continue training elsewhere.

Community nursing was developing at a pace:

I started in a rather dilapidated clinic … with one phone … a little bit archaic but then moved to Spitalfields Health Centre in Brick Lane which was state of the art … by that stage, I was leading the District Nursing Team … I climbed the ladder quite quickly … I … obviously did my district nursing training, did that at Southbank … I had a store cupboard, I had a phone, I had a desk, I could link down to the doctors downstairs, I had a filing cabinet with a key … I was quite a pioneer, I was involved in the development of … the documentation for the community … it was great. *Deborah*

After staffing for six months, Evelyn travelled abroad which led to her eventual career choice of midwifery:

Then I went to work in South America in Peru in a little hospital in the jungle just treating anything that came in … I worked on the vaccination programme up and down the rivers…. It was really interesting. … I got the address of the hospital from … one of the house officers who'd done his elective there … so I wrote to that hospital and they said, '… I'[ll] give you board and lodging if you want to just come and work for a bit'… so that's what I did…. Cashed in my superannuation … paid for my tickets … to Peru … I was there for about a year and a half … then because I was having to deal with maternity cases and I didn't know anything about midwifery I came back to do midwifery training … I loved that … although I went abroad again … I stayed in midwifery then for the rest of my career. … Second time I went to The Bahamas which was a job that was advertised in the *Nursing Mirror* and they were recruiting … in England … I did a bit of general nursing to start with and then I went into maternity again…. Very good clinical experience for midwifery there. … I had no equipment really so you were just using Pinards and … clinical skills … no scans at that time of course. … Also going to the outer islands to pick up women [by plane] with obstructed labour and things like that … by the time they would have to call for medical help that woman could be … six hours longer getting to hospital.

Engaging with the person, not just the illness

The nurses reflected on their understanding of the core elements of nursing:

I suppose my messages would be whilst nursing … moved into a kind of more scientific footing … there is a particular art in nursing in about how you relate to patients … I think nursing is a profession, but also it's about being humble, it's about humility and it's about putting patients first and your needs … are secondary. *Michael*

it's … become very … technically orientated, and they need to see that patient as a person … [they perhaps] forget sometimes … but all the things that are attached to them, and the monitors … and all their report writing … just see what that person needs most of all. … Do they need feeding? Do they need to be helped with a drink? Do they need to be made more comfortable? Would their pillows be better a different way? … What would help them to feel better? Because so much of that is … it's the mind. It's not just about what you do to the body, it's about how you make somebody feel, and caring about them. *Teresa*

I did teach kindness and compassion to people, which is something that I so often see completely disregarded … it's teaching people the right words to use … 'What's happening with you today?'… 'How are you feeling?'… 'Do you have any pain at the moment?'… and letting … [them] talk, and also when you're talking to patients, saying things other than just about their medical condition, noticing the fact that the photograph is on the locker of when they were younger … or that they look worried about something, nothing to do with their condition … you have to actually engage with the person, not just the illness. *Lesley*

The 1970s was an exciting time to be working in the NHS and at The London. To an extent the old way of doing things still continued, but new approaches and advances in healthcare were beginning to appear. There were many challenges as people were getting to grips with new technology. Trainees were becoming more diverse, with both more men and more people from different ethnic backgrounds. Nurses were beginning to move beyond the nurses' homes, and live in the local community. While they continued to be proud of their profession, they were also beginning to question the way things were done, which was the beginning of the process of evidence-based practice. This is now key to the way in which nurses practice. It could in some ways be seen as a watershed moment in healthcare.

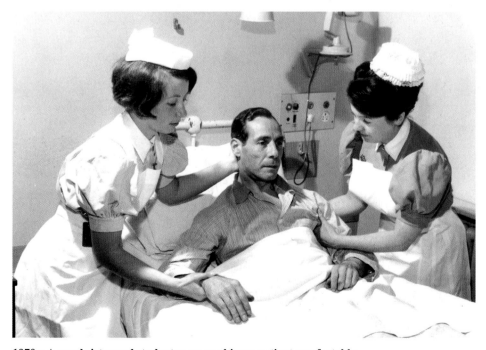

1970s: A ward sister and student nurse making a patient comfortable.
(Image appears by courtesy of The Royal London Hospital Archives and Museum)

1980s, Mixed media on canvas, 2017, Paula Day.

Chapter 5

The 1980s – Transition and turbulence

My message is plain and simple, you are there to care for the patients, never forget the patient with everything else that's going on, whether it be administrative or financial and political shenanigans that go on in this place, you're there for the patient, don't forget them because the patient sometimes does get forgotten. *Andrew*

Ten turbulent years that shaped our country

In this decade Mrs Margaret Thatcher, the first female politician to be elected as Prime Minister in the UK, single handedly altered the way Britain's political, social and economic fortunes were shaped. The 'Iron Lady', as she was known, dominated politics in the UK and was either loved or hated by the public. Her time as Prime Minister saw the power of the unions decline, a long and painful miners' strike and the closure of many mines.

Britain was led into a war against Argentina over sovereignty of the Falkland Islands. The stock market crashed, known as Black Monday, and terrorist threats from the IRA continued and were often in the news.

> I do remember in the eighties when Mrs Thatcher came in … I think that started the fragmentation … of hospitals and care. I think it caused a lot of harm in the hospitals. I do remember there being a big Unison strike because that was when she said we're going to contract out the cleaning services. *Dawn*

> I started my training during one of the strikes, and we ended up with paper sheets on all the beds because [of] the porters' strike. *Joanne*

New computer systems along with mobile phones developed apace. Looking back at this time, it now seems incredible that there were still some people in the East End who didn't have a landline phone. Neighbours' phones were often used to make emergency calls and a tin box was strategically placed near the phone to put money in for the call. Otherwise it was a trip to the nearest telephone box. In an emergency the Police were often sent to the address of a relative.

Mobile phones that did exist were the size of a brick and very expensive [£2,000 at that time]. They were now available to replace the old hospital paging system. In an emergency it was so much easier for the nurses to get hold of a doctor.

> We had no mobile phones in those days and there was perhaps one telephone for the whole of the Luckes Home. *Dawn*

1982: Queen Elizabeth II visited The London Hospital to open the new Alexandra Wing. The Queen talking to staff by Queen Alexandra's statue.
(Image appears by courtesy of Karen Harris)

1982: Queen Elizabeth II meeting a matron and medical staff.
(Image appears by courtesy of Karen Harris)

The Changing Face of the East End

In the 1980s the whole Borough of Tower Hamlets was changing rapidly. Many of the old wharves were being converted into luxury flats and large building projects were underway. Local housing was improving. Renovations were being made to the old terraced houses, with outdoor lavatories being replaced by new bathrooms and indoor toilets. The London Hospital had changed very little in structure although, along the Whitechapel Road, the stall holders were changing as the immigrant population changed, with different fruits and vegetables on offer.

> when I first started there was still quite a sizeable Jewish population in Whitechapel … the old East End girls and boys … say 'Oh you could leave your door open in them days, you could.' *Andrew*

> I do remember my paediatric placement on the Isle of Dogs … mid-eighties … all the tower blocks were starting to go up, but there was still people on the island who hadn't gone off the island all their lives. *Paul*

As a large number of the Jewish population moved out of the East End, more immigrants from the Asian subcontinent came to Whitechapel to fill the void:

> There was new housing developing, and there was … what would appear to be resentment about … large Bangladeshi families being rehoused in accommodation that had a lot of rooms, a lot of bedrooms … there was a certain amount of unspoken friction I sensed in the local community … it was a real mix of different sorts of nationalities and cultures even at that time, as well as [the] good old East End sort. *Paul*

> I felt people were very respectful of other cultures … like what to do when someone dies, that was always observed … I remember Bengali families … cooking their own food [at home and bringing it in]. *Louise*

Why Nursing?

People considering nursing had different reasons to come to The London and now there were more choices about types of training. Many still came for traditional reasons:

> I can't really remember why I wanted to do it, but I can remember why I went to The London because my aunt trained there, one of my cousins was born there. My dad had TB and he was nursed at Brentwood Annexe … so there were strong family connections to The London. So they probably encouraged me to go there, and then all the other things like the nice uniform, being nearer to [home]. *Dawn*

> I think I was about 12 or 13 when I decided to start training. I'd seen a programme on TV, it was actually *Blue Peter* and … one of the presenters, went off to work at Bart's for the day and … it just captured my imagination because nobody in my family had been a nurse … weirdly, years later, I shared an office with someone who had seen the same programme and made the same decision, we couldn't believe it. *Louise*

> it was definitely the right decision and then once I found out that Whitechapel was where Joseph Merrick [the Elephant Man] had been, I thought that's it! Done deal! I'm going! *Lisa*

Other, often more mature students had different reasons for undertaking nurse training:

> I was 24 … so I'd been to university, and I'd studied theology … with a mind to being ordained in the Church of England but felt I wasn't ready, I would like some practical experience and it was that that really got me into nursing, so from university via some nursing auxiliary work I went to The London. *Paul*

> I didn't have a particular desire or vocation … to become a nurse, I'll be quite honest, I have a degree in applied geology … I had a job in geology for six months … I worked for a soils testing company … and one weekend my best … friend's … best friend … came down to see him for the weekend, [she] was a student nurse at The … London Hospital … to be quite honest it was a drunken bet in the Steam Packet Inn in Devonport one night and she said, 'Nursing is very stressful, you couldn't do it', and I said, 'Yeah, I could'. And then it was 'Right 20 quid' and … that is honestly how I became a nurse. … Well I never got the 20 quid. *Andrew*

Others came from a different route from the three year course:

> I did the long training which was the combined BA in social sciences at Goldsmiths College and my RGN [Registered General Training]. *Louise*

> I actually started and undertook my training at Great Ormond Street … it was a combined Adult and Children's Nursing Training, which was run by the School of Nursing there. We completed about 18 months of Children's Training, and before that finished we were presented with a choice of three hospitals that we could go to, to undertake our Adult Nursing Training … [this included] … The London. *Michelle*

Interviews

As in previous decades, arriving in Whitechapel was quite scary for some 18-year-olds who may never have been to the area. Some parents were even more frightened for their children's safety, especially after news of the Kray twins and gang crime in the East End:

> The London invited my parents [to the interview] as well and I remember that they … were very nervous about me going to the East End of London … because of the gangsters and the crime, but actually it was such a clever idea because by inviting them they went and were happy then for me to go plus they could picture where I was going. *Louise*

> I had four interviews and [in] the one at The London, they … [asked] 'What do you think would be the first job in the morning on a ward?' and I said, 'Well, my guess would be toilets and bed pans.' *Rachel*

A new way of life

> It was fairly chaotic, all of us moving into [the] Luckes Home … suitcases everywhere … girls everywhere and the odd boy … all wondering where we were going, what we were going to do next and sort of getting rid of the parents that had brought us up there, and launching out on life. *Rachel*

there ... [were] individual wash basin cubicles that you could ... see round the corner so you could chat and clean your teeth with your friend next door ... the amazing baths ... that were ... [so] deep, that if you filled up you could float ... but because the wall didn't meet at the top you could be chatting to your friend in the bath while you were in the next door bath. *Tina*

Dawn recalls there was a certain amount of climbing involved:

it was a time when we started to have quite a big influx of male nurses ... I remember them climbing up the Princess Alexandra statue on night duty one night in the hospital garden and ... some of them climbing over the hospital gates because they'd been locked out the back entrance.

[M]y friend used to have men climbing up her drainpipe, she had the front of [the] Luckes Home ... halfway up the drainpipe was the bay window of the sitting room so it was quite easy for somebody to shimmy halfway ... I do remember various men coming in that way.

Learning to nurse - the social setting

PTS in the 1980s now included both classroom training as well as the opportunity to get to know the East End:

I do recall that we were sent out in pairs and one of us had to wear ... glasses that were patched over and the other had to guide, so a sort of sensory deprivation exercise ... so we were quite community orientated ... there was that sense that actually where people come from really affects how we look after them, or how we should ... look after them in hospital. *Paul*

Louise remembers the breadth of experience they had at that time:

I think we had a very good PTS ... the emphasis was on getting to know the East End. So our tutor ... was ... very forward thinking ... what she did was she made us walk round the East End in pairs doing projects and actually it was a fantastic way of getting to know your patch ... she made us go up and down in these horrible tower block lifts, stinking of urine. And we went to older peoples' clubs, we went to homeless peoples' clubs which was why I got into volunteering ... really seeing all facets of East End life and I think that was brilliant and again that's very much the sort of social science side of things but I'll never forget it. I remember getting blisters, walking around the East End.

[G]oing round the docklands in the days before it was developed and all those empty docks because it was just at the period that that part of the East End was dying and the new bit hadn't come and the smell of the spices ... in the air ... that really made us think about the different groups we were serving and we did have people who came in to teach us about it, for example, the Bengali community ... as well as people from the Jewish race.

Classrooms, wards and tutors

Basic nursing skills continued to be taught in a classroom setting with increased ward exposure:

I can remember being in a very big classroom. I think there must have been about thirty to forty of us … I do remember all the tutors. … there was a classroom there that was all set up with models of patients, but we did go onto the wards very quickly … you learnt how to make a bed, you learnt how to wash someone in bed, learnt how to do a dressing, and then you went and did it on the wards with one of the tutors. *Dawn*

The Uniform: 'Victorian under-housemaid to feminist'

When they commenced training most of the new students still had to wear unflattering uniforms called 'purple passions'. These were temporary until The London made-to-measure uniforms were ready:

I looked like Orphan Annie. *Rachel*

I was not perhaps temperamentally designed to be a nurse in lots of ways, I was quite rebellious. Used to hate the uniform, though I really quite like it now … I think it has real character … but at the time … being dressed up as a … Victorian under-housemaid … I was quite a feminist. *Donna*

Rachel describes the uniform:

we didn't have all the bits like belts and colours that all the other hospitals had. If you were a student, there was nothing to show what year you were in … nobody's actually bothered what year you were in if you came up to the … job and did the job … you got on.

the battle with the hat every day, the toothbrush to wet the ribbons to pull it through to make it semi-circular, five pleats, no more, put it on your hair, you've just washed your hair, it falls off … the uniform's so starchy it could actually stand around the room, and the collars you had to button on and the buttons you had to pin to your uniform every day … the huge pockets we had which were excellent, hid a multitude of sins.

Lisa points out the uniform's practical uses and the risks taken in the wearing of the hat:

Starched aprons and writing your notes from handover on the flip side which you weren't allowed to do … and going to the blood bank and collecting bags of blood and putting them inside your bib on the walk back to the ward, so that it wasn't fridge cold by the time the patient got it.

We were very rebellious though because you were absolutely forbidden from connecting the … [hats] at the back, it was supposed to be open at the back, five frills, five pleats, but we all closed them at the back with a white Kirby grip and perched them atop, they were completely useless and only decorative but loved it.

By 1988 uniform was beginning to change, first with the exit of the purple passion:

we had a horrible … flarey white dress with a square neck and no shape to it whatsoever that we used to wear … with our natural tights and brown shoes we looked lovely! But we would then go for fittings for our … student ones, so the lilac ones, and we were lucky enough that we still managed to get some of the old,

A student nurses' typical set photo of Set 472 October 1981 wearing their new made to measure uniform before starting on their first ward placement.

well we had like new leg of mutton ones that they made for us … some of us got the actual old leg of mutton ones with the collars that we attached as well and the big buttons that you attached, so the old style, so they were like gold dust when we got those. … Everyone wanted one of those. *Melanie*

we weren't allowed to go out in our uniforms, but you'd see the doctors coming down Whitechapel Road on the buses in their white coats, which used to annoy us…. One of my set got caught, she was trying to hide behind me … she was completely covered, in her coat and she still got spotted by a tutor … [who] was really upset that we were going to have to be seen crossing the road in our uniforms. *Rachel*

First Ward

The emphasis on appearance continued once work commenced on the wards:

on my first ward … there were … ten students, we were on the overlap of the shift …she'd [sister] taken us all into the sluice … and she lined us all up … she said … 'Why I've done this?' and we all looked at each other and shook our heads … she said, 'I've lined you all up in order of scruffiness' and then she just pulled us to pieces. … 'Look at the state of your apron, look at the state of your hat, look at the state of your hair, look at this, look at that' and comparing us to the early shift who'd just been running around bed bathing, making beds … 'I want you all here tomorrow with freshly starched hats, freshly starched aprons, hair in plaits … spick and span' … but we did and we went off and the next day … I think I was late trying to get my hair into a plait. *Melanie*

'At 18 we were quite young'

In the 1980s nurse training was still quite rigid. It was daunting for those young nurses who may have led very sheltered lives to come into nursing and witness many distressing deaths and incidents, these memories remained for many years. Nobody was really prepared for some of the sad and traumatic events that they would experience during their careers:

It actually opened your eyes to the horrific things that can happen to people which were beyond my imagination. *Louise*

I think it was a thirteen-week placement and in that thirteen weeks we saw twelve people die on the ward. *Tina*

I was sent to theatres to bring back a young student, the same age as me, I was on a late shift so I didn't know the story … when I picked him up he was bright yellow and apparently he'd gone down for a Whipples operation which had been unsuccessful because when they opened him up it was too late … I remember the fear of him waking up and obviously him having to be told that … I took out my first stitches on him as well with sister watching and how nice he was to me, but how upsetting it was knowing that he was going to die and he was my age. *Louise*

The … thing that sticks out to me was the first really seriously ill patient I think I'd seen … he was a young man who had been in a motorbike accident and he'd sustained severe injuries, he'd obviously got chest injuries, but he'd also got a severe leg injury and his leg was very, very swollen and … it had been cut and left open … seeing that as a first warder and thinking 'Oh my goodness,' I'd never seen anything like that before … it was the worst thing I suppose to that point that I'd seen. *Andrea*

In at the deep end, it was too much responsibility too soon:

It was male… gastro surgical, and there was I, a first warder … I've shown you once, you do it, a soap and water enema …the wrongs … [I] could have done to that poor patient, even at the time I felt frightened. *Joanne*

Support was 'a bit hit and miss':

in those days there was the idea that someone would keep an eye on you, it wasn't the mentorship … but I think that was a bit hit and miss depending on who they were … the ward sisters were very important in that …sister … was nice but off sick a lot … the times that I was with her, I remember she was kind to me, but … so busy and then not there. *Louise*

It was clear to the nurses how different life was for them when they stepped outside their work:

> and I distinctly remember, because we started our training in October, at Christmas … [I] went home and met up with … school friends who'd gone off to uni who were living the life and [I'd] just spent a few weeks looking after people who were dying … I'd only just seen my grandma die at that age and then … there was no concept then of people going home to die. *Tina*

Ward Routines: Continued prayers, pressure care and bedpan rounds

Despite the East End being a very multi-cultural society, prayers continued to be said on one ward, as Paul remembers:

> [this] was the only ward where … in the mid-eighties … [sister] … had morning prayers every morning and all her staff were required to attend, it was Christian prayers … my sense was that actually it went down very well, I mean perhaps a little bit anachronistic in the eighties, but I think as much as anyone with Muslim patients, I don't think there was any objection to that practice … I take my hat off to her … obviously they're very significant faith differences between the religions … whether it's … prayers on a Friday or individual prayers, or … Christian worship on a Sunday … there's always [a] place for it and I think there's a great deal of tolerance and acceptance as part of our … cultural diversity.

Ward routine was the essence of nursing care. This included bedpan rounds, turning patients every four hours, pressure area care and washes. The patients were seen regularly. If a pressure sore was discovered it was blamed on poor nursing. With new nursing equipment and speedy mobilisation of patients, some of these routines (which definitely might be considered a bit questionable these days), faded away.

> bedpan rounds and pressure sore rounds … we'd go round every couple of hours … offer a bedpan or do a pressure round where we would lift someone, rub their bums and then put them back down again! Now you wouldn't do that because of the friction and everything you were causing, but then you'd religiously go round with your big … trolley of bedpans and your talcum powder, 'cos you'd put that on as well, and give their bottom a nice rub and then reposition them and whatever … so that was something that changed throughout the course of being there, in that airflow mattresses came in and you didn't have to do, although you turned people you didn't rub. *Melanie*

> you had the weekend cleaning book and things like that, but … that made sure that lots of jobs were done and you kept on top of things and it was everybody's responsibility to do it. *Gloria*

Michelle remembers the early responsibility:

> I think we were left far too junior in charge of wards, and that wasn't very good for patients necessarily, but you either sank or swam … and it also sorted out whether you really could cope with it or not.

I remember being one of three on a couple of shifts where the nurse in charge was actually a third year student, and myself, and then there was an Auxiliary. So, very difficult … very busy, and I'm sure there were lots of things that we missed. I think really it was just about getting through the shift and trying to make sure that everybody was alive at the end of it, including us.

Other routine events didn't always go to plan:

when we used to take people to theatres, they used to put poles down the [sides of the] canvas [on which the patient lay] and lift them. I remember one of the porters … back from theatres pulling the pole out of the canvas and … and it went through the fish tank … I do remember all the fish coming out … and dying and flapping all over the floor. *Dawn*

Ward Rounds: 'Had to have knickers on'

Ward rounds with the consultant and their teams occurred weekly. Sometimes it was a very low-key affair, other times it was a bit of a performance. Patients were confined to bed, and were not allowed out to the toilet. Bed sheets had to be untucked at the bottom and folded over the feet. Notes and X-rays had to be on the ward. Woe betide any junior doctor if they were missing:

I do remember on the Orthopaedic Ward worrying … [the consultant] was coming round, and all the patients had to have knickers on for sure, because … [he] would be very angry otherwise. *Michelle*

There was the consultant who did his ward round … once a week, and great homage was always paid to him and ward sister was expected to be on duty and some particular consultant I remember liked the patients to be silent … there was the cleaner hoovering the floor and I can remember him going over and pulling the plug out of her hoover and saying 'I expect silence when I'm doing a ward round.' *Dawn*

Being aware of cultures

Husbands, in some cultures, were very reluctant to have male doctors examine their wives, and male patients were not always happy to have a female doctor. Communication improved as staff became more sensitive about the culture and needs of the local community, as Phyllis recalls:

I hadn't come across them [Bangladeshi people] before and … a lot of the mums didn't speak English. You know, it's amazing what a smile … a little touch and sort of chatter and gesticulation … I always got on OK with them, in fact I got on very well with them.

I had worked with Jewish patients because Queen's [Queen Elizabeth Hospital, Hackney] had quite a high Jewish area … I remember saying to somebody, 'It's so sad, all these … young women who obviously have got cancer.' Somebody said, 'What do you mean?' I said, 'Well all these young girls that are wearing wigs.' Of course I hadn't realised Orthodox Jews wore wigs, and I just thought they were all having chemotherapy, which caused a lot of hilarity.

Gang culture was evident not only in the endemic population as Lisa remembers:

> there had been some gang fighting between Sikhs and Muslims … a whole
> year earlier and this man had been injured … he had been on ITU and
> then came to Rothschild and he was just in a side room, he was breathing
> by himself so he didn't need any ventilator or anything, but he was in a
> persistent vegetative state and his body was contracted. … It was absolutely
> dreadful! … [S]ure enough he died on nights, during my time there and
> we had been told always that if he was to die we needed to call the Police
> because … if he died within the year it would be a murder charge but if it
> was over the year it didn't count.

> My story about the gangsters is away from the wards because I ended up living
> in a flat on Vallance Road which is where the Krays lived.

Night Duty: 'Were we still boiling eggs?'

> I loved bits of my training … the sparrows in the morning on nights when you
> were feeling so tired and ill at five o'clock in the morning. … The dawn chorus,
> and all those sparrows that used to sit on Queen Alexandra ['s statue], and [in] all
> those trees. *Joanne*

Night duty could be extremely busy. In addition to routine work, some wards had patients
being admitted for surgery, coming back from theatres and medical emergencies. There
were usually three nurses per shift and possibly an auxiliary nurse. This would have
included a staff nurse or a senior student nurse plus two other students at different levels
of experience. Sometimes there wasn't a trained nurse on although there was usually one
in the adjoining ward who would be available if necessary. Night duty was either loved
or hated. If you slept well during the day it was fine. but for the insomniacs it could be a
nightmare trying to keep awake all night:

> I have a pathological loathing of doing nights … I couldn't sleep very well during
> the day, I was living in a flat and Whitechapel is busy, I couldn't sleep and it just
> exhausted me and by the end of your either five or sometimes even seven nights,
> I felt absolutely destroyed. *Andrew*

> So when it got to about three o'clock and you were at your tiredest, you
> actually saw the market traders starting to set up because you could see out
> of the window, and that was real nice because that spurred you on … [until]
> morning. *Dawn*

> there was a tradition after night duty that you had to go to the Savoy Hotel for
> breakfast, just one time, so I remember doing that after one night duty. *Andrea*

Ghost stories continued to abound:

> loads of ghost stories…. Like on the children's ward … there was supposed to
> be a puff [sleeve] puller … if [on night duty] you fell asleep feeding a baby
> somebody was supposed to pull your puffs, but there'd be nobody there when
> you looked. *Rachel*

As in previous decades there were the infamous night sisters' ward rounds:

my first night ... [duty] ... never, ever done a night shift ever before ... night sister came up at ten and said she would be back at midnight to do a round ... you were expected to know all your names of your patients, age, diagnosis, what treatments they were on. *Gloria*

the night sisters were very strict and they would expect a high level of ... communication and understanding ... they would come in on your third night and if you couldn't tell them absolutely everything about absolutely every patient, you're for the high jump. And we weren't allowed to write anything down in handover, no notebooks allowed, so we had to know it up here [brain], which is quite a skill. *Rachel*

These nurses had a lot of responsibility to care for and keep patients safe, but they were well supported by night sisters who did ward rounds three times a night and always carried a bleep for emergencies.

quite scary to begin with, really scary ...but you sort of grew into that ... the good thing about that sort of training is that you really did gain experience and confidence. *Donna*

but we ... [had] some ... standard routine things ... you always had to check the CDs [controlled drugs] every night, as close to midnight as you could ... tot up all the fluid chart[s] ... check the resus [resuscitation] trolley ... when I did the neuro[surgical] ward you used to have to sort of get some of the patients washed before the early [shift] started. *Melanie*

Specific procedures happened at night such as on the gynaecological ward with the removal of radioactive implants:

we were told that the night sisters came and removed the radium, and I remember going to clear up ... and wheeling the trolley with the radium back to the sluice, and then being very told off because no one had told me it had ... to stay in the room and be collected by ... Radioisotopes Department. I didn't know that, nobody had said that to me. *Dawn*

Boiling eggs for breakfast was an interesting experience as Andrea found:

We boiled eggs on night duty in the morning ... and asked every patient 'How would you like your egg', and they said, 'Soft boiled' or 'Hard boiled', but every single egg was hard boiled because we used to stick them in a great big pan ... you never had time to stand over them so they were all done about six minutes, so how anybody ever got to eat them I don't know, but it was lovely.

In 1988 Edwina Currie MP announced that eggs were contaminated with Salmonella and at The London Hospital the patients' daily boiled eggs were taken off the menu as well as the scrambled eggs which were often used to tempt an appetite or replace a missed meal.

This practice had to stop as well as the practice of buttering bread in the middle of the night and covering with a damp cloth. Domestic staff took over the breakfast service but nurses continued to serve other meals. All the cleaning and damp dusting was performed by the domestic staff who were part of the ward team and accountable to the ward sister.

Challenging times: Care and compassion for the dying person

> [Nursing is] the most powerful profession that you might ever come across, a good nurse can facilitate a beautiful death so that somebody who thinks that their 18-year-old son who's dying from leukaemia, their world is over, but you can facilitate pain-free dignity. *Lisa*

As the student nurses moved through their training they built up experience and skill in coping with death and dying patients. Andrew recalls one such event:

> it was a Sunday morning and I went in and helped him with a wash and I had to give him some IV antibiotics as well and I had to go, and he called me, he said … 'Can I ask you a question?' I said, 'Yeah, of course you can', and he said, 'Am I dying …?' And I just paused a moment and I said, 'I'm very sorry … yes you are', and he said, 'Come here', and he gave me a hug [sounds upset] and he said, 'Thank you very much, I can deal with it now, I thought I was but my bloody family won't [say]'. … And I said, 'Well I'm not, if anybody asks me that question, I'm not going to lie'… I'm not going to say 'You're going to be fine mate', because he wasn't going to be fine … he was much more at peace with himself after that and I went home and I felt very proud of myself … doing that. *Andrew*

> we always used to stay with people when they were dying if they didn't have a relative, because The London was very hot on that. *Joanne*

Even so there were challenging times, especially when nursing young patients with diseases such as leukaemia:

> we went through a phase then where there … wasn't a shift that went by when one of us didn't break down in tears at the end of it … but you all just pulled together and we socialised quite a lot. *Melanie*

> we used to talk about haematology burnout because when they're the same age as you and they are dropping like that it's very very hard. *Lisa*

> I found it hard … I think some of those experiences were very traumatic and although I think there was a counselling service … I never used it … you just sort of got on with it and didn't really dwell, but actually I must have dwelled a bit because I can still remember and maybe it's no coincidence that I chose to work in older people's care because I found, although it's still sad, it's not as sad as maybe dealing with someone of 19, 20 or children. *Louise*

Sometimes it was too difficult to remain detached:

> I remember being very upset … there was a 12-year-old, and I can still remember her name … she'd been hit by a bus in Epping, and she was first of all taken to St Margaret's at Epping and they were losing her and they brought her here and I remember them doing an abdominal paracentesis and blood came out and they took her to theatre and she had a torn liver, but they lost her on the table. *Andrew*

For some, the experience of coping with death was not just limited to the patients, as Donna found:

> I remember one night we'd just started and the staff nurse … she had a subarachnoid haemorrhage and died … that night … it must have been about my fourth or fifth ward … it was awful…. She just collapsed, I remember I was there in the bay … there was a really good night sister or matron who took charge, and that was impressive … that was shocking, she was a really nice person.
>
> there was another nurse in our Set who committed suicide … that was horrible … horrible … we didn't really talk about it very much, it just sort of happened … I think people kept it quiet, I think they probably didn't want to … rock the boat and upset people.

Further student training and role models

Student nurses were part of the workforce:

> [we were] learning to be a nurse by being a nurse. *Donna*

As such they were often aware of role models that they came across in their time on the wards:

> I really rated her [the ward sister] … people used to think she was a real dragon and she was held in great awe, but … I … really appreciated just her wisdom really, and the old … really sort of old-fashioned sense. …So it was a time of … really powerful women who ran their wards, and how! And you know, there's a lot to be said for it. *Donna*

Andrea remembers one such person:

> There were some good people around, I think I learnt an awful lot from … the charge nurse [on Currie Ward] … every patient was important to him and he … treated every patient as an individual and with a great deal of respect, but with a human touch, he had a great sense of humour, and I learnt from him that, not only is it how we respond to our patients, but it's how we respond to each other and … the environment in which we nurse … is incredibly important and … the standards were high but it was also relaxed … people enjoyed coming to work…. Patients felt safe, patients were cared for…. Staff felt safe and there was a sense of humour on the ward because it could be difficult at times and I think as long as you've got support and happiness with the people that you work with then it's possible to do anything.

Why do you need a degree?

In the 1980s there were different routes to gaining a nursing qualification, with degree nurses, graduate nurses and combined qualification nurses, such as joint SRN/RMN training alongside the general courses, something that continued to influence the nurses of this generation throughout their professional lives:

> I decided I didn't want to do a degree in nursing, although with hindsight I wished I had done because somehow our generation, we were always playing … catch

up.... It just [kept] changing ... in front of us, tantalisingly ... every time I did a qualification, it changed. *Joanne*

There was a stigma attached to being a degree nurse as Louise found:

as soon as we said ... [our set number, indicating a degree set] people would immediately say 'Oh'... lots of negative stuff about being a degree nurse. So that was always quite stressful and I do remember the prejudice against degree nurses quite strongly, although that wasn't from everybody and almost, not lying but being quite economical with the truth in terms of not wanting people to know so that they wouldn't judge us ... we were perceived as being ... well we use the words now, 'Too posh to wash' don't we? That was never used then [in the eighties] but it was almost a bit like well why do you need a degree? There's no need. Because it was really ahead of its time in that respect ... most of my set went ... [on] to become very practical nurses, but there was this perception that we weren't very practical and that we were too clever.

Some people thought the old training was better, but the context of care was changing:

it was proper old-fashioned nursing where you knew your patients, the general nursing care was good, and ... you spoke to people, you knew everything about people. *Phyllis*

the more modern training ... how they train them ... they're so much better prepared.... Because we were pairs of hands, we weren't supernumerary, you were part of the workforce.... And whilst you got excellent experience, and that patient experience won't ever leave you, it, I think, probably led to a lot of stress. *Joanne*

The impact of male nurses

At the same time male student nurses were becoming more widespread. Paul recalls:

I think our set was not atypical, I think ... about 10 per cent of the nurses were male nurses.

I just remember ... being a male nurse was something that some ... especially perhaps more senior ward nurses, some of them found quite challenging.

[S]ome of the senior nurses, nursing officers and so on were male, I mean so it wasn't that there weren't role models.

Even so Paul found there were times when their identity was mistaken:

I do remember some scary things, I remember my first cardiac arrest ... as all the ... male student nurses did at that time, I had a white coat, I do remember I was given the paddles and defibrillator ... I was told to get on with it ... no one quite knew how junior I was ... someone was kind ... enough afterwards to say that the patient had survived ... I mean I think occasionally some quite frightening things did go on ... I don't think we were spared anything but sometimes our supervision could have been closer.

The order of things and challenging authority

The hierarchy on the wards was very evident:

> there was an awful lot of kowtowing to the consultants which … didn't really sit well in my stomach at all. *Lisa*

> I can remember the junior doctors being told off a lot by the consultants … and humiliated in front of the patients and the rest of the team. *Dawn*

Some of the attitudes were beginning to change:

> I think the two key things I remember was always be questioning … never do something because you're told to do it, always say why? … [W]hich we now call that … the whole evidence based practice movement, but that was very, very strong in our set. And … the other thing was having a kind of context in which to work because although … I'm proud of being a nurse, I've always very strongly [felt] that I'm part of a bigger picture and … my colleagues, like doctors, other allied professions, are equally important and we do overlap with each other … I was never overawed by doctors, I always thought of them as colleagues and I think that came from doing my degree actually and studying health policy. *Louise*

As some found, more mature student nurses, such as Donna, felt more confident in questioning offensive attitudes:

> in the School of Nursing … we were being lectured on melanoma by a plastic surgeon … he put up a [mnemonic] … the first letters, so, bleeding, itchiness, and he spelt bitches [B-I-T-C-H-E-S] down … and … I actually said to him, 'Can you tell me why you need to use that word to a set of nurses?' … so offensive, so he got really angry with me … in front of the whole Set for … challenging him … [he] stormed off and got … the Director of the Nursing … she had to smooth things down … my hackles were completely up because of that. … I did come from having … a degree … it really was offensive, and however good the [mnemonic] was, oh! I was so angry, and he got really angry back so it was quite fun really.

HIV/AIDs (human immunodeficiency virus infection and acquired immune deficiency syndrome)

In the 1980s AIDS appeared in the USA and swathes of young men were developing strange conditions in numbers never seen before. These conditions included Kaposi sarcoma, Burkitt's lymphoma and tuberculosis. Many died at a very young age. The majority were homosexuals, but the disease was later discovered to be associated in the heterosexual community with hypodermic use, transmission by infected partners, or by contaminated blood transfusions.

> the other thing I remember most in the eighties was AIDS starting to rear its head … it wasn't there in 1981 when I started, but when I qualified in 1984 I remember we had a lot of young men in the ward with very strange diseases like Kaposi sarcomas, herpes and [en]cephalitis … fit, young, healthy men and I remember

one of the night sisters, who was obviously gay to all of us, coming round and being quite worried and anxious … about 1984 the diagnosis of AIDS came out and suddenly it all made sense what was wrong with all these men … because there were so many of them, they had to actually open a ward specifically for people with AIDS. *Dawn*

I remember … probably in about 1984, looking after some of the first AIDS patients … they were out in the ward with everybody else, as they should be, because they weren't infectious … as long as you followed your precautions, as you would with any patient … Mildmay Mission Hospital … that became an AIDS centre. *Rachel*

Highs and lows of different hospitals- placements

Student nurses were sent to other hospitals in London to obtain experience in other fields of nursing, for example, Queen Charlotte's for obstetric experience and Bethnal Green Hospital for care of the elderly. The majority went to Mile End and St Clements hospitals.

The London Hospital (Mile End)

Mile End continued to be a small and intimate place with a garden, and much quieter than The London, so some nurses enjoyed what was, but not in all ways, a slower pace:

I can remember actually after my first couple of shifts my feet absolutely killing me … I'd get back to my room at Mile End and sit on the bed and they'd be throbbing and just the thought of getting up and walking to the sink on the other side of the room was too much 'cos they were hurting so much! *Melanie*

Louise remembers her positive experience of one ward:

I went to my older people's ward at Mile End, again not really wanting to go there, there was a fantastic sister on that ward and she was so welcoming and so positive about the job and she made students so welcome and did things that I'd never seen before like make us a cup of tea and allow us to drink it in her office, I mean that was quite radical … I remember it was the summer and she bought us all lollipops … on a late when we were hot and she would get the doctors to take us with them on their ward rounds and talk to us which was pretty unusual … because usually ward rounds, you weren't involved or if you were it was in a very observatory, scary capacity. Whereas on that ward the consultants were … very welcoming and talked to us and so I just remember her being brilliant.

And Paul felt he was not excluded from any aspect of nursing care:

my midwifery experience at Mile End … wasn't thwarted in any way, I saw deliveries, and … [took] as full a part I think as any of my female colleagues.

However, not every experience was positive as Joanne found:

I also remember on the gynae ward … there was a young girl bought in who was 11 in theory … no, was she 14? … It was all a bit vague, and I think she may have been raped … but the baby was aborted…. She was in a side room … the baby came out and it was alive and it was moving … I was just told to wheel it to the sluice and leave it covered over, and this little blue thing … I don't know what sex it was, I was, I was just so horrified … I was halfway through my training and … it was awful. *Joanne*

St Clements Hospital: Psychiatry

Historically, The London Hospital (St Clements) was the second workhouse to be built in the Mile End Road, but eventually it was converted into a psychiatric facility.

I didn't want to go, I was terrified but actually … we were all scared, we were all new and the mental health tutors that looked after us were really good, really positive, really encouraging, so much so that I decided I wanted to be an RMN … it was that life changing really having not had any thoughts about psychiatry at all and eventually I did, later on. *Louise*

I did my psychiatric placement there, really enjoyed it, and wondered whether actually I'd made a mistake coming into general rather than psychiatric nursing, not necessarily an easy placement but an interesting one … I found it very, very rewarding really. I remember being assaulted by a patient, and quite shocked by that, I mean just sort of punched down … I … felt quite supported by staff, certainly the nurse in charge, and [also] I think when the other team got to hear about it. *Paul*

I think just listening to patients and beginning to learn some of their experiences and what it really means to be psychotic and how people can be in another world of delusion and you know how very real mental distress is. *Louise*

that was just an amazing experience because I'd had no experience of psychiatric patients and I can still remember all their names … conditions they had … I do think all of them back then needed to be looked after, I can't imagine how they would've coped … there was one girl I remember who was quite young and she used to go down to Mile End Tube Station and for money she'd have sex with men … I don't know what would've happened to her if she'd been completely [out] in the community. *Dawn*

Specialities within training

The student nurses were exposed to working in a great variety of contexts:

theatre ten which was open heart surgery … I found that extremely stressful, very difficult, long intricate operations, not a lot of sort of social contact, quite scary in terms of not just the nature of surgery that was going on, but the teams involved. *Paul*

Bethnal Green was elderly care, also TB … and you could see it was the old workhouse. *Rachel*

Oncology was a developing field at the time and could be intimidating for the student nurse:

Croft was an old Nightingale ward and … it was just the oldest part of the hospital, there was no piped oxygen or anything like that and when you went in the door, you were just faced with two long rows of beds, so that was the men's side and there was just drip stands everywhere and bald heads and ... we knew nothing at the time about cancer ... it looked terrifying and they were so young and so ill and it was heart-breaking and when I realised that I was going there for [a]... placement I thought, oh, how am I ever going to do it? *Lisa*

With regard to termination of pregnancies, student nurses were able to opt out of escorting patients to theatre:

I'd only been say sixteen weeks into my training ... we had women coming in for terminations ... a few women that had septic terminations ... then termination was legal ... I do remember one girl had a termination and she hadn't told her parents it was done at the hospital and her bowel was perforated and she was a very young girl ... and of course then her parents did find out what had happened to her. I remember signing the form to say I didn't want to take people to theatres who were having terminations, but we had to look after them pre- and post-[surgery]. *Dawn*

Working in the district

Once qualified there was the option of working as a district nurse in the community. Joanne recalls:

I remember cycling home from my patch on Limehouse, and I had a bike and I lived out ... by that stage I'd got a little flat in what was the old Brewery Works ... between Stepney and Whitechapel, and ... the male Nurse Manager ... used to check on us to see where we were. And of course in those days we had bleeps, so he'd bleep you and it was like quarter to four, and you'd think, well I'm going home and ... and he used to phone you to see where you were, just to check out.

nursing them in their own house was what I loved because ... you were a guest in their house but you saw them in their entirety. So you didn't just see a scrubbed up little lady in a hospital bed, I mean you saw them with their family's support or not. I mean I remember one little guy with an awful colostomy issue ... when I was at Bow, and he was all on his own. He'd been stuck in this high rise ... even in those days they had bars across their doors for security. Tenth floor up, family lived in Epping, he was a little Jewish gentleman, he'd been left behind. ... And the flat was sparse, and he was just so lonely, and then other ones were real East End, really surrounded by their people, and you could teach them to care for their leg ulcers or whatever. ... But I do remember ... we walked on the district, [but] we did have ... a little old orange Mini, tiny thing, which could cram the commode in if you needed to take a commode to somebody.... And you had only eight or nine visits quite often, and you walked [with] everything on your back in a rucksack or bag.

A lighter side of nursing

Christmas was always an exciting time, despite being rushed off your feet and trying to send patients home, if possible, to be with their families. Decorations were put up with the help of medical students or housemen, although everything had to be removed by the end of Boxing Day. Chocolates and gifts that had been stored up over the year in sister's cupboard were brought out, as well as generous donations from relatives. Father Christmas, and his fairies (usually junior doctors), dressed in fairy costumes with wands, would distribute bunches of violets to the nurses while Santa gave out presents:

> [Sister] … had the side room full of booze … and that was when all the nurses could have a drink and things.
> I didn't get any violets … perhaps I wasn't in the right place at the right time. *Joanne*

The nurses developed an affection for the East End during their training:

> [I] loved Whitechapel. I mean coming out of Whitechapel Tube and just seeing the hospital there, I mean it was in the market … it really did feel vibrant and a really good place to be, so … it was a happy time … I loved the East End. *Donna*

> we used to get bagels … on a Sunday morning … and then go to the flower market on … [Columbia] Road and take flowers home. *Joanne*

Some aspects of East End life were not so popular:

> the fridge full of jellied eels which was the traditional East End thing which I always hated … I remember little labels … which patient's jellied eels they were … and trying it and just thinking urgh. *Louise*

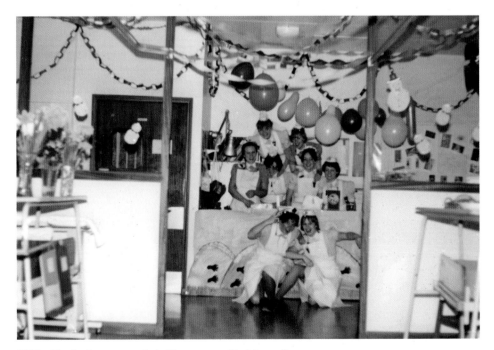

1980s: Student nurses and staff nurses on Christmas Day

1980s: A ward sister preparing the flowers for the Christmas 'fairies' to distribute to staff.

Gloria recalls how there was a choice of how much support was needed:

I think the fact that you had the nurses' homes and you were quite close knit, you could be as close or independent as you wanted to be.

As Joanne found, there were challenges to living out of the nurses' homes in the 1980s:

> I ... felt unhappy in the flat ... it was up a tower rise, and one or two nurses had been attacked. One had been attacked under the corner flat on her way home after a late shift.
>
> I ... made more friends with people from church who were nurses and doctors, but we had something more in common apart from nursing.

But there was a good deal of socialising:

> We drank a lot! ... Good Sams [Good Samaritan pub] on Stepney Way whilst you were a student and The Three Feathers ... each set would organise its own set party at The Feathers but you could easily attend ... somebody else's set party. So they were very well attended by all ... the services ... the Police and the ambulance people ... I didn't particularly drink in the Students' Union ... it was all about Good Sams whilst you were a student, as soon as you qualified you went out the front and you drank in the Grave Maurice or Lord Rodney's Head. *Lisa*

Having a life outside nursing continued to be a challenge:

> I found shift work and being married, it wasn't great really. *Louise*

It was difficult to change your off duty:

> You didn't go on holiday or go to weddings or do anything. You got your rota and that was it and your life was that rota ... it was frowned upon if you wanted to change it. I never did. I think I may have asked once and it was such a formidable experience, you just didn't want to do that again, you knew your place. *Dawn*

Innovations

The Nursing Process: 'On the Cusp of Change'

The Nursing Process began to be introduced at The London in the late 1970s. It changed the basic structure of ward management. It introduced a shift away from the old style of task orientated care to a more reflective, holistic approach. The new system introduced individualised patient care, and nurses were to become more accountable for their own actions. Documentation became more relevant and informative instead of the usual 'slept well' or 'good day' written in the Kardex, progress notes were kept in a separate file next to doctors' notes and individual care plans were written for each patient.

> [over] the three years [training] ... it went from task-based nursing to what was then called care planning and holistic patient care, so that was the change that was sort of foremost but at the very start of my training, so I worked ... with that system ... it developed ... as I was going through my three years ... [the] idea of seeing the patient as a whole and looking after a whole patient rather than just doing 'the dressings'. *Andrea*

As in all things the changes didn't please everyone and many had great difficulty in adapting to this new way of practicing. Dawn recalls:

> I do remember ... coming on ... to do a night duty where I was in charge ... two student nurses, and it being an absolute nightmare trying to get a report and find

out who was going to theatres, who'd come back because you had to go and speak to every member of staff and find out about their individual patients … when you went for a meal break you may be hand[ing] over your patients to somebody else to look after, two lots of patients, but it was a very bad way of managing a ward … then of course you had the problem if you're walking past a patient who isn't your own patient and they say to you 'Nurse', what do you do? Do you say well I'm not looking after you today? Anyway that caused a lot of problems with the night sisters as well, I remember because it was just chaos.

[the old way] was just better for teaching, better for the students, better for the patients' relatives and also, you've got the most senior … qualified person in charge which is right because they have the most knowledge.

BARS: [Behaviour Anchored Rating System] Clinical Assessment
BARS was an evaluation tool which was introduced in the mid-1980s. It continued to contain elements that each student had to pass throughout their training. The students were evaluated by the ward sister, staff nurse or the ward tutor:

it was a little booklet that we took to each ward and we had to get assessed three times during the placement … you would hopefully have the same staff nurse, who was allegedly your mentor, do the three assessments. *Lisa*

The exams the nurses had to sit reflected the new approaches, such as the nursing process, as Lisa remembers:

we just did the one and it was three sections. Section A was health promotion and prevention of illness. Section B was your clinical and Section C was the role of the nurse as a manager. So we came up with mnemonics for each section which meant that it didn't matter what the clinical question was you could apply your nursing process and Roper's Activities of Daily Living, and as long as you met their needs as identified by Roper and kept them alive for the duration of your essay, you were okay!

Computers: New Technology
Ward computers were introduced very early on at The London. The hospital was at that point at the cutting edge of computerisation. The matron at that time was very progressive and a team of people worked together to bring in a very basic program. The computer listed all patients' names on the wards, new admissions and discharges, and lists of patients to be admitted in the future which made bed planning easier. Instead of the doctors writing forms by hand, blood test forms could now be downloaded and printed:

we did have computers which, they surprised me…. So … say we wanted to take a specimen … we could actually print off the form … it was quite a shock to go elsewhere and find they don't have computers. *Rachel*

Clinical Nurse Specialist (CNS)
The eighties saw significant advances and diversification in medicine and surgery (e.g., the introduction of laparoscopic surgery, sophisticated improvements in cancer treatments and drug therapy). To support emerging medical and surgical sub-specialties, new nursing roles were created at The London. These nurses, called clinical nurse specialists, were to

care for groups of patients with specific needs. They worked as part of a team with physicians and surgeons. These nurses were highly skilled and knowledgeable in their area of specialty. Many of the nurses set up their own clinics in conjunction with the medical staff. In 1987 a palliative care service was started. This was later followed by Breast and Stoma Care services and Child Protection. Since then many other nurse-led services have followed:

> the sort of work particularly early on, it was actually very traumatic [in Child Protection]. I thought I was pretty worldly wise, and when I was hearing some of the stuff that I was hearing … you … think, 'God Almighty.' And, you know, the Police aren't the sort of people who can admit that they're having a bad day … but they could to me, which was really nice. *Phyllis*

Conflict and war; emergency services and the first helicopter

The onset of the Falklands war brought much anxiety to the country, although the war did not have as much impact as had been anticipated. The IRA terrorist attacks in the UK continued and The London was regularly put on red alert. Also there were an increasing number of trauma patients seen at The London with the rise in knife crime, accidents and medical and surgical emergencies.

> the rest of the time on A&E … was really short, I was terrified. And then the last day was the day that terrible nail bomb went off in Hyde Park [in 1982] … and all the soldiers and the horses were killed and so they put us on red alert and emptied casualty and I remember just sitting in an empty casualty feeling completely terrified. But then in fact we didn't receive any casualties. *Louise*

To cope with these challenges the Helicopter Emergency Medical Service [HEMS] was initiated in 1989. Funded by charity and later partially funded by the NHS, The London became the only hospital to provide this service. The helicopter covered the whole of London and the surrounding areas within the M25. It enabled patients to be admitted sooner but more importantly, it helped doctors to reach the scene quickly so they were able to provide appropriate and rapid emergency care.

In the early days it caused some amusement when it took off, as papers and other objects were sucked out of open windows, and stall holders across the road had all their stock blown about. These problems were quickly sorted when the helicopter flew out backwards and windows were closed. Lisa remembers:

> I was there [in A&E] for the first helicopter … a little boy had been run over by a lorry and so the expectation was that he was going to be hideously injured and he wasn't … there was barely a scratch on him but the whole building shook when that helicopter landed. And of course it became such a feature of the hospital.
>
> [T]here was … a two-bedded resus room … round the corner from the waiting room when the helicopter first started, but we later got a new resus room that had five bays, four adult and one paediatric. I'm sure it's completely different now but that was the beginning of the trauma call as opposed to just being a cardiac arrest, so you used to get the phone call on the bat phone saying 'adult suspended ten minutes' that all changed to being a trauma call or a cardiac arrest or a respiratory arrest and they put together a trauma response team that was slightly different to

the cardiac arrest team and there was a ward upstairs that had been empty that was made into a four-bedded trauma unit.

Concluding remarks and reflection

Paul remembers the feeling at the time:

> it was Project 2000 that we were all looking ahead to and obviously the professionalisation of nursing … the university based [education] has brought its own challenges … although I learnt a great deal from my ward experience … I think nursing has changed from what I see as an outsider … everything wasn't sweetness and light in my training days and yes while I did learn a lot on the wards, I wouldn't want to say that that is the exclusive way of training and that … nursing nowadays has really gone downhill because I don't believe it has.

Andrea considers the current situation:

> [it] would be to remember that we are there for our patients and that patients always come first … working currently in nursing and working with current student nurses I often hear the phrase 'I've spent all my time doing healthcare assistant things and I want to do nursey things', and that makes me sad because … nursing is all about essential care … with someone who is a role model who will show you that what matters is that our patients are safe, that they are clean … comfortable … pain-free and … not afraid, and that we're there for them and somewhere in doing all the extra things that have come with extending our scope of practice, that doesn't need to be lost.

The London Legacy

> but the main people who have had an impact throughout my whole career have been the patients because the fortitude that they put up with unbelievable indignities and they just do it beautifully and they don't complain and I don't think I've ever … ever known an oncology or a haematology patient to say, 'Why me?'… I really don't. And their families as well and so many of them were young people of my own age, they were in their early twenties. *Lisa*

> you're always a teacher, there's always people who can learn from your knowledge. You have a role with the patients and their relatives and you have a massive role with the people who are coming into nursing now … that is part of your role, not just giving care, but making sure the knowledge base carries on. *Dawn*

> when … I'm asked to talk about The London I'd always say I was proud to train there, I think I had a good … although it was a stressful training … I was always exposed to good practice, very high standards of practice and I'm very grateful for that. *Louise*

> I can only say that The London was an absolutely fabulous place to train, I hold it with the deepest of affection, always look back on my time there with happiness … I don't ever remember any sad times … there must have been difficult times and there must have been sad times but I don't remember them, I only remember

positive things … and that feeling of being linked to tradition, the fact that you were part of an established hospital, an established training school, that extended back for decades and you were part of it. *Andrea*

The end of ten turbulent years, and the beginning of more turbulence in the NHS?

Nursing was facing one of the most difficult transitions as it moved towards professionalisation and the introduction of Project 2000. In education, new teaching courses had to be developed in universities and colleges, subsequently, schools of nursing were later phased out.

The rapid advancement in medicine, surgery and drug therapy encouraged nurses to further develop their careers into specialties, for example, in Oncology nursing, which meant further education in short courses or at degree level.

In 1983, the Griffiths Report was published. The government blamed insufficient management and structure within the NHS for cash problems. Roy Griffiths stated:

> If Florence Nightingale were carrying her lamp through the NHS today she would almost be certainly searching for people in charge.

This report changed the management system in hospitals. The power shifted away from clinicians, and managers were appointed to run hospitals. Health authorities ceased, but were able to purchase health care from different sources in the internal market. Many hospitals later became known as Trusts. Further changes ensued following the Community Care Act which led to the biggest political change in mental health and mass closures of hospitals.

Although the 1980s were turbulent, the next decade would have its own problems with the fallout from the Griffiths Report and subsequent Acts from the government. Prime Minister Margaret Thatcher remained in power until November 1990.

1990s, Mixed media on canvas, 2017, Paula Day.

Chapter 6

The 1990s – From apprentice to graduate nurse

I would like my legacy to be that I always did what I thought was right for my patients and provided them with the highest standards of care and treated them with … compassion … and cared about them and their families and never judged. *Zoe*

This decade saw major milestones at The London Hospital. 1990 was the 250th anniversary of The London Hospital's foundation. This was marked by a visit from Queen Elizabeth II, during which she granted a Royal title on the hospital.

We wore the tails when the Queen came to visit … soon after I started and they pulled names out of a hat [to meet the Queen]. I'm not sure [why] my name was pulled out … I was the black sister…. It was a sign of progression … I had to wear the long sleeves and nicely starched uniform … tails that came out for special occasions only … it was nice. I got quite close to the Queen and that was the only time in my life that I've ever got to meet her…. She visited the wards and we all went to the [Medical College library] … we had a nice tea and it did feel like a special occasion because everybody was in their tails and their long sleeves, it was lovely. In [her speech] she declared that [The London] was going to be called The Royal London. So simple words but it cost the hospital a fortune I'm sure because they had to change all the paperwork, etc … but I think people were very proud to be called The Royal London Hospital. *Kim*

In 1991 Great Britain's population was 58 million. This rise was in part due to immigration, and increasing globalisation, leading to a growing movement of workers from across the European Union and the world. Over the past 200 years this area's population had had a constant, and ever-changing influx of refugees including Huguenots, Jewish and Bengali people. Health care was increasingly affected by the worldwide web providing instant and large quantities of potentially inaccurate information.

The 1990s saw fundamental change in nurse education, as it transitioned from the nurse apprenticeship model which had been started by Florence Nightingale in 1860. Nationally, nurse education moved to Project 2000 (diploma level training) and then degree level entry within the decade. Project 2000 was an attempt by nurse educationalists to radically overhaul the long-established apprenticeship style of nursing training and commenced at The Royal London Hospital in 1992.

The 1990s also witnessed the introduction of the modern matron:

[As a matron] I used to literally visit the patients three times a day in all my wards…. Seven wards at one stage … it was absolutely brilliant and I picked up all kinds of … incidences that could have escalated … it was an objective pair of eyes, seeing what to me are very vulnerable people. *Lesley*

The iconic London Hospital uniform which had been largely unchanged since the 1940s was phased out during this decade. Similarly the 1990s saw the closure of The London Hospital's Princess Alexandra School of Nursing, and its merger with St Bartholomew's School of Nursing.

In 1990 the NHS Community Care Act was enacted, bringing health authorities into the market place, with the ability to purchase goods and services from other suppliers and providers, and manage their own budgets. In 1991 the first NHS trusts were established and The Royal London Hospital merged with Mile End and St Clement's hospitals and local community trusts, to become one of the first NHS Trusts. Later in the decade further amalgamations occurred with St Bartholomew's and The London Chest hospitals.

Why Choose nursing?

Unlike previous decades, far more career choices were now open to women and men, and for some nursing was not their first career choice:

> I'd like to say it was a huge vocation that I wanted to do but…it started off as a back-up plan, because it's not what I intended to do when I left college. *Emma*

> I was getting a bit bored at John Lewis, I liked it and it was a good social life … and it was good fun but I didn't want to be a sales assistant forever and I kind of belonged to the Red Cross at the time … every year, for a week we took disabled people away and I thought, 'Well [if] I can do that, maybe I can do nursing as well', so it sort of led into it that way. *Simon*

> I'd really wanted to be a physiotherapist and I discovered that I didn't like sputum … so I then decided to be [a] nurse … I think really probably I was always going to land up being a nurse but you don't always realise. *Zoe*

> it took me a long time to decide what I wanted to do and I kind of came to the conclusion that I wasn't cut out for office-based nine to five jobs.… I was working in insurance and I hated it. … [T]here was a family history of nursing and family members had said, throughout my life, that I'd make a great nurse and it was a time in Ireland when it was a recession, again, and jobs were very hard to come by and there … [were] always advertisements for nurses, so I thought 'Well if I do my nurse training then I'm pretty much guaranteed of always having a job'. *Victoria*

For some people, such as Kerry, nursing was the only career choice that they considered:

> My brother was very poorly as a baby and he was two years younger than me and was treated at Great Ormond Street and I spent all day, every day that I was there following the nurses around wanting to do what they were doing and at the age of four I decided that I was going to be a children's nurse.

Rebecca recalls:

> I have the photos of me in nurse's uniforms [as a child] and I always always wanted to do nursing … but I unexpectedly did quite well in my GCSEs … I thought, okay, I'll do A Levels, but I still want to do nursing and at the time, I don't know if people remember but there was a TV programme [about a

1992: Six student nurses at the start of their training, all are now wearing the new look uniform.
(Image appears by courtesy of Jules Plumb)

hospital in Leeds] … on the TV and I … loved watching it and I had this vision, I want to go … to basically start my nurse training straight after my A Levels, however, unfortunately quite a significant thing happened in my life in that my Dad died suddenly and I was … actually doing quite well in my A Levels … I had a really really good sociology teacher who said, 'Have you thought about deferring your nursing and going to do a degree and given what's happened to you emotionally it might be a better pathway for you?' … I finished my degree and … I was just doing temping work in London and then I thought, I'm going to do my nursing.

Other interviewees chose nursing while doing voluntary work:

I did some voluntary work in the local hospital and thought, 'My gosh, this is fantastic, really interesting, meeting people, different people, every day, a sense of achievement', and I thought, 'Actually, I'd quite like to do nursing,' and nobody I'd ever known had done nursing, and obviously being a man and wanting to do nursing, people thought I was a bit strange. *Richard*

I was about 16 [when] I actually joined the St John Ambulance. And I used to really enjoy it … and then suddenly we had a guy … it was … the first time that I'd met … a male nurse. … [A]t St John we did first aid but then we also did caring for the sick, it was a module that you used to do, that you used to go in and … learn how to do dressings and do pressure area care, because you could go out into community and look after people who potentially needed respite care and it was from that that I … got into it. And then the superintendent of the [St John Ambulance] division I belonged to became a matron of a private nursing home … and she said to me, 'Do you fancy coming and working for me for a year?' And she said, 'It will do two things, it will either tell you you're doing the right thing or it will tell you you're doing the wrong thing'. … I loved it … I loved the residents … and it was … the patient interaction which actually I [enjoyed] … I remember looking after a woman … who [had] seen the *Titanic* being launched in Belfast … stories that people told you that were just … fascinating back stories. *Christopher*

Why The London Hospital?

I chose the best of my three options, the one I felt comfortable with. *Kerry*

In the 1990s, before schools of nursing were merged into universities, there was a wide choice of hospitals, with their own nurse training school where a student nurse could train. Each hospital and training school had its own particular 'personality':

It was a bit of an accident … [p]in in the book and choose one. Princess Alexandra [School of Nursing at The Royal London Hospital] sounded nice. *Kaleem*

I've always … had lots of memories of coming to visit my great-grandparents at The Royal London and the amazing uniforms. *Emma*

Zoe recalls:

I was advised by a family friend who [worked] … at the Royal College of Nursing to train at a London teaching hospital because he said you can take that training all over the world.

   The London Hospital was the only hospital that offered an open day before the interview day … and you were actively encouraged to bring your parents with you so we went on an open day and the moment I came out of Whitechapel Tube Station and the usual amount of rubbish was all over the place and the usual drunks were stood outside [White]chapel Street … the market stalls and the rather exotic smells … the one thing I do remember is being taken to Luckes Home and being told that this was the worst accommodation they could possibly offer us but … a lot of the accommodation was much better and I don't know what it was about the place but as soon as we left I was very, very sure that that's where I wanted to train.

Even in the 1990s the distinctive London Hospital uniform dictated choice:

[they] were very unlike any other nursing uniforms in any other hospitals, and I suppose as a young girl that appealed. *Emma*

Education: traditional training, diploma or degree?

Potential student nurses had two options at the start of the decade: that of RGN training or waiting until 1992 for the new Project 2000 training.

We were Project 2000, we were the next big thing, that was quite scary. *Kerry*

So when I originally applied I didn't know that the nursing training was about to change, I just thought I was applying for RGN training, but when I came for the interview for here I found out … that it was going to be the new Project 2000 diploma training, and the intake that I was in October '92, we were the first ones ever here … so it was all new. And it's difficult for the students because we had nothing to compare it to so we didn't know any different. *Emma*

they were saying it [Project 2000] was going to be more academic, and a totally different way of being trained with a lot more sort of questioning and reasoning … so I thought, well if that is the way forward I might as well … wait for it and do that. *Simon*

[Initially] it was literally all college based … we did a lot of history of nursing … in that first six months … and learning about the NHS and how it worked and the change[s], because there was a lot of changes going on in the NHS at the time … they also taught us an incredible amount about the history of The Royal London and the history of the nursing in The Royal London, that was good, we certainly enjoyed that and it did make you feel part of something special, we were quite proud to be students at The London 'cos of the history. I certainly didn't have any nostalgia necessarily about my training, but I had a lot of nostalgia for The Royal London Hospital and I still do because of the old building. *Emma*

With the implementation of Project 2000 in 1992, student nurse status changed from being part of the labour force to supernumerary. This led to confusion about their new status from both trained staff and new students:

I think anything new that comes in people will always have their doubts about, people will always have questions … this is the way that the university want[ed] it to be … but I think if you worked hard and actually wanted to learn, I don't think there were any differences, I still learnt how to give an injection, I still learnt … the ways of the ward and I think if you're enthusiastic, supernumerary doesn't mean you sit and do nothing and I think some people do feel, 'Well I'm supernumerary, I can't touch anybody', and we're like 'No, no, no, I want to get in there, I want to do something, I want to learn'. *Kerry*

but a lot of it was how much effort we put in really, or how much common sense we showed to want to learn or to do something. I do remember one girl from my set just sitting down opposite the nurse's station in the first bay, sitting down and reading a magazine … and I certainly didn't have any hesitation to think, well that patient's just been discharged so the bed needs stripping and washing and the linen trolley would need refilling again and it was just … little things like that that weren't particularly let's say hands-on care, but showed the rest of the nursing staff on that ward that actually well maybe he's got a bit of cop on and so

… they were more willing to do things with me or show me things differently … you don't always need to be told to do something. *Simon*

Others starting later in the decade did degrees and experienced student life at various universities:

I did the BSc in Nursing and Human Sciences so it was combined with psychology students at City University, so we had a blended course which was really good. *Victoria*

it was quite exciting because we were doing a lot of our biology and our science subjects at Queen Mary's so we would go into the labs there and do our science practicals and … a lot of time was spent in the university, so I think we felt more like students than nursing students for the first six months. *Emma*

Relating theory to practice:

I learn much more about doing things practically, so they could have told us everything and anything in the classroom, but until I actually do something … and see the patient and put it all in context … does it all pull together. So sometimes it [university] did reflect what we were learning and other times it was way beyond what we had discussed or we hadn't even touched on. *Victoria*

Clinical and university assessments

I think the nineteen exams were enough! *Victoria*

We were all given books for each, I think it was each placement, so people had to sign to say that they'd seen us do the clinical skills … which we'd hand into the university after, or actually the college at the time, to be signed off to say that we'd achieved our hours and achieved the objectives. … [Y]ou couldn't always achieve everything in one placement because the competencies weren't always based in those areas. *Kerry*

The impact of change

Historically St. Bartholomew's Hospital and The London Hospital had very different identities, and the merger in 1993 was a huge culture shock for both sides:

In our group we were very mixed, mixed ages, mixed nationalities … but in the Barts side they were very middle class young ladies, white young ladies mainly. *Simon*

The big thing that happened halfway through our training was we merged with Barts School of Nursing … it was horrendous. … There was a huge animosity … [between] us and them. It was not good, for example you'd go into the lecture theatre 'cos they combined the lectures … the right side of the lecture theatre would be The Royal London students and on this side would be the Barts and nobody mixed, I never ever mixed with the Barts students … it was really quite difficult … because we were very different. The Royal London students were like all ages, so there was youngsters like us … 19-year-olds … people in their 30s …

there were some mothers there, there was people from all walks of life, so a lot of us that lived around in the East End. People from Ireland, people from all parts of the country, there was quite a lot of men … there were some students from Africa. All accents, everything. Unfortunately the Barts students were all young girls, predominantly white, middle class, from private schools … so we were very different. And you just had to look at the lecture theatre and think, oh yeah, that's The London lot, that's the Barts lot, just by looking at people. *Emma*

Initially they were marked differences in approach between the two merged hospitals:

I noticed that level of formality [at St Bartholomew's] and it was, the patients weren't as relaxed and they didn't talk to the patients in the same way, and that again has all changed of course, the culture's completely different now. *Richard*

Capes to cardigans

In the 1990s the old iconic London Hospital uniform was being phased out and replaced with the 'national' uniform, although elements of the old uniform were retained for a while. Emma remembers with sadness:

the first time I was putting the uniform on, bitterly disappointed … because when we became students they took away the old uniform and the hats and the aprons and the puff sleeves, gone.

And your cardigan had to be purple, so they kept some elements of the old colours but it was a modern pink, horrendous dress. The traditional 'modern' uniform, but we had to wear a purple cardigan and flesh-coloured tights and I was really upset. I'm still upset now, that nursing uniform is horrible. Don't take any pride in it, I'd much rather go back thirty years to a proper nurse's uniform.

The male student nurses continued to have made to measure uniform:

all the blokes had to go to Burton's at Cheapside, we were sent up there and we were measured for trousers and they were all individually made for us, grey trousers. So we had the white tunics, and the blokes had the lilac epaulettes, like the old-fashioned ones. *Simon*

The changes in nurse education led also to staff uncertainties about the student's new role, and also theirs:

the staff didn't know anything about us and they didn't know how to deal with us so they just treated us like the old RGN students, and I actually think that was really good, I'm glad they did. … [B]ut the training was very practical based, and you had to get involved, you're here to work, and you're here to do exactly what we're doing with supervision, but you've just got to get on with it, and we were treated like proper members of the team and I think that was a good thing. *Emma*

when we started we did get a lot of kick-back from other students and staff nurses because they thought we were all going to take their jobs, because we were Project 2000 and it seemed to be more academic, which we came out with a diploma rather than just a registration, and I think they thought that we were going to rise up the ranks very quickly and take their jobs, so there was a girl I remember particularly at Mile End Nurse's Home … 'Oh you're going to have our jobs in the old lilac uniform,' … it was just a change, as much of a change for them as it was for us … they were a little bit hostile at the beginning … but because we were the first ones they didn't really know what was coming through. *Simon*

Not only did the iconic uniform cease to be worn, so too did The London Hospital Badge, which had been awarded to nurses qualifying at 'The London' from 1942. The badge was then re-adopted by The Royal London Hospital League of Nurses.

when we passed we had a graduation ceremony at the Guildhall so it was more like a cap and gown situation without the hood because we had a diploma, so we had that, but there was no actual sort of nursing ceremony. We had a certificate, there was no badge giving ceremony, we just collected the badge when you wanted to … everyone that trained between those years will tell you about the badge … because we started at The Royal London we thought we were getting the proper Royal London badge and we didn't, we just got this … it's just like a hexagon thing with … chain links of white and red links, we call it the NatWest badge … that was the most disappointing thing. *Emma*

Care for students became overly cautious:

we were all told that we wouldn't see a live birth because it might upset us, if we saw a traumatic birth it might upset us and so we weren't allowed to see one … some students were in the right place with the right ward sister … they hoiked them in and they were able to see … it's a bit stupid really because you could go on the next placement and … care for somebody dying in a side room. *Simon*

Initial Training

Before Project 2000 was introduced, sets were smaller. Increasingly student nurses were becoming more diverse, with more men, mature students, and people from a diverse ethnic background being attracted to the profession.

We started off with forty … of us, there was ten guys in the set, it was the biggest number of guys they'd ever had in a set, we had mature students, one of the guys … had been a Council road man, digging up roads, and his wife had made a decision to train as a nurse, when she finished her training he decided he wanted to be a nurse. *Zoe*

When Project 2000 commenced in 1992, all students followed a common pathway for the first eighteen months of their education:

we had like what we called a foundation which was the first eighteen months … halfway through your second year, we still didn't really go out on the wards a great deal, you had placements, but you were supernumerary, you were not part of the workforce. *Emma*

Well the first six months … we didn't get on the wards at all … we learned about the healthy person before we even learned about any medical conditions … so we had some very, very bizarre placements. … [F]or the first six months we were going to water treatment centres, I went to Tesco, went to Sainsbury's to see how they did food preparation and food storage, we went to a gym at Tower Hill and had a session there … I think it was so that we knew what a real 'well' person was before we could then develop to see what the conditions were. *Simon*

they did send us out in threes so that was alright, round places like the Ocean Estate and places which were really quite run down … we understood the type of housing that most of our patients were coming in from. *Zoe*

The six-week introductory block before the first placement was undertaken included:

basic nursing skills, so bed making, blood pressure taking, all of those … what we would class as traditional nursing skills … a lot of focus on that … the normal parameters of vital signs and … how to dip a urine. *Victoria*

First Ward placements

Although P2000 students were supernumerary, they still experienced the same fears and apprehensions about their first wards, just as students from other decades had, as Kaleem explains:

We didn't know any different at the time but when you think back,…it was [scary].

I remember doing the temperature on the first week and couldn't read the mercury, how to turn it right.

Due to a lack of placements, a paediatric student's first placement was on an adult ward:

We were allocated wards where our university lecturer/mentor was based which was adult cardiothoracic. [I] didn't want to do adults anyway and I have such vivid memories of walking onto the wards, looking at all these men with … drains and stitching from top to bottom of their chest that I took one look at them, looked at my lecturer, and ran back out. … I thought 'Oh my goodness I cannot do this, this is just not for me at all'… I know I was going to be on an adult ward but I think it was just the shock of it was so busy … there were people in pain … and it was adults. …And my lecturer came out and asked me what had happened … I was just so confused … I wanted to do paediatrics and I know I had to do other things as well but I wasn't prepared for what I saw. And she talked me through it and I went back out there … that was just a taster day and then I actually did a six-week placement on there and by the end of it, I loved it. … [I]t was talking to the patients … they're normal people who need your help. *Kerry*

Other students were more confident and eager to learn:

there … [were] two of us on that ward and we loved it … we were both really keen to sort of do something, even if it was just going to wash a patient … or give them a bed pan. *Simon*

Medical wards often gave more time for students to learn:

they gave you a very good grounding in basic nursing care, and they taught you what care was about really and they taught you it was about basic nursing care, there wasn't anything scientific, I mean in those days they still had a weekly cleaning book on this particular ward … 'weighing the patients' book and … the flowers had to go out of the ward at night into the day room. *Zoe*

Following the eighteen months Common Foundation Course, Project 2000 students split into their chosen specialty and started to learn about the sick person:

> Then we went into our branch … and our placements were a little bit more broad then so they … were at Newham General, at St Andrew's at Bromley-by-Bow, Barts, and The London. *Simon*

Change of culture

In the early 1990s some nurses' homes were still available:

> initially for the first four months I lived at Homerton, the Hackney Nurses' Home there on Homerton High Street and that was a real shocker! … [F]or me, it was a huge culture shock. And then after that I moved to Queen Mary's Nurses' Home at Barts and I lived there for the rest of my training, which was absolutely fantastic! Best location, best address, close to everything, it was great! *Victoria*

As in previous decades living in a nurses' home enabled students to make friends, and provided support in a new environment:

> I didn't know anybody from day one … I actually lived in the [Luckes] Nurses' Home. … and I met a couple of the people down my corridor who were doing the same course but different branches, so day one it was … quite nice walking in with somebody else who I had actually said hello to and it was quite intimidating at first, I got introduced to a lot of people … I'd never been away from home so … I was really, well, very nervous. *Kerry*

The ethnic diversity of the student nurses changed dramatically in this decade from predominantly white women:

> we had people from Commonwealth countries and Africa and in the Caribbean who'd been sponsored, as I understand it, by their governments to come and train at The London as well, with the understanding they then went back home with the skills. *Zoe*

Kerry remembers:

> it wasn't … a particular social class or particular ethnicity, it was mixed, which was appropriate in terms of nursing people in London.
> [E]very nation I think was accounted for. … [T]hat was actually really good because we all brought something different to the table, we all brought our own experiences and we heard about other peoples' countries and the healthcare system and how poor it was and it made us feel quite proud that actually we were going to be working for such an amazing corporation.

The Context of Care

Particular experiences live with nurses, from every decade, long after they have trained. This student witnessed the effects of a drug-dependent mother on a newborn baby:

The first day I was there [Obstetrics] they gave me a baby who was obviously new-born [and] withdrawing from Methadone, and so the cry will never leave me ... they gave me the baby to mind and it just screamed the whole time. *Victoria*

With medical and nursing developments, very premature babies were increasingly being successfully treated, and the student nurse's experience became more intensive in some placements:

I did the special care baby unit here and I think that's the one I felt more nervous about, very fragile babies in boxes ... I actually really did enjoy it, it was heartbreaking at times but I think it taught me that actually if we can get children, babies that small through life then it's a huge achievement. *Kerry*

Some nurses were squeamish about particular aspects of nursing, and despite requesting to avoid certain specialties it was not always possible:

I never wanted to go to theatres ... I wanted to go to ITU and I really asked, 'Can I not go to theatres?' because I'm a bit squeamish. I know I'm a nurse but I don't really like lots of surgery ... I can deal with blood but I can't deal with operations in that sense, and I really asked not to go and then when it [ward allocation] came out I got theatres and it was Royal London Theatres so it was trauma calls. ... [P]art of me thinks they did this on purpose 'cos they knew I was a little bit, oh I don't really want to see that. [One day] ... it was a road traffic accident and the gentleman was very very badly injured and they had to do an above knee amputation and I was already at the wall ... I want to get me out of here ... but they put the limb in a yellow bag to take away, but they put it next to me, against the wall, and I fainted. *Emma*

Mental health placements gave students time to sit with, and listen to patients, giving them valuable insight into mental health and how different cultures approach such problems:

I came away from that placement thinking what an amazing place but half the time you couldn't tell the staff from the patients. ... [I]t was a care of the elderly mental health unit and we kind of integrated by sitting and playing Monopoly with them for days ... we never really did one-to-one because I think the residents didn't feel comfortable enough with us for a while, a new stranger's come in, but the more you got to speak to them, the more you ... realised ... I don't think I really had a great grasp of mental health before then ... but it was quite distressing at some points but you ... got to know the residents quite well. *Kerry*

it's quite interesting to look at other cultures' approaches to mental health as well because certainly in the Asian community if a young girl has mental-health problems the magic man's got her and they will try and get another magic man to get rid of the spirits that are in their body, so it's quite interesting and it's quite a challenge. *Zoe*

Due to advancing techniques and drug therapy, patients admitted to hospitals were now increasingly likely to survive serious illnesses, unlike in previous decades. Modern technology has enabled increased teaching opportunities, while still maintaining the patient's dignity.

I spent most of my time in majors [A&E] because of the helicopter, we used to have some amazing things come in. … [O]n the days that I was in the resus room, we'd never get any emergency calls and then the day I was in minors [minor injuries] we'd have a shooting with a man with an open chest wound. … There used to be a television [screen] in the staff room that was linked to the cameras in resus so the Senior Nurse used to come and get us and say 'Right, this is quite heavy going on in the resus room, can't have you all in there, there's too many people', people used to run from everywhere to watch these amazing things, so he [a senior nurse] used to sit us in the room and talk it through with us. *Kerry*

Developments in patient care, initially in HIV, were the catalyst for changes in the concepts of patient confidentiality and user involvement:

the Grahame Hayton Unit was one of the leaders in the UK of HIV care in the eighties and nineties … mainly at that time, the people we were caring for were young, white gay men, well-educated, and they knew about their condition and they questioned the doctors and nurses, and … we, as professionals, were not used to that level of questioning. Also the element of confidentiality, because of stigma associated and understanding confidentiality, everything from answering the phone to what we wrote, and that's where all the modern concepts of confidentiality and involving the patient came from, from the care of people with HIV. *Richard*

Death and bereavement: 'it's fine to be upset'

Many student nurses witnessed death for the first time during their training, and have lasting memories:

I remember that was the first cardiac arrest I ever saw and … that stayed with me. I did help, yes, I did help. He [arrested] … right in front of me … it was the first time I did CPR [Cardiac Pulmonary Resuscitation]. … [H]e didn't make it, and I had really good support from the staff … I wasn't the only student … there was two of us there at the time and they did really look after us. Yes they did, 'cos we were very upset, I was crying, never seen it before … and they did take us into the office, a couple of them sat with us, debriefed, and said, 'You're absolutely fine, it's fine to be upset'. *Emma*

Even for students who had witnessed death before, it was still a traumatic experience as Kerry found:

my first death was on the cardiothoracic ward … I'd been told it was going to happen, it was still quite a shock … I'd seen family members but I'd never seen just a person I didn't know. And I was quite distressed and … I was with the nurse that was looking after them and the family, but it was kind of just quite sudden … we knew it was expected but it just happened and you think 'Oh is that it?' … That wasn't what I was expecting and I was quite shocked and it was really nice because the nurse that I'd been working with sat down with me and went through it all and explained what was wrong with her and why it had happened and why they didn't resuscitate her and why she had a DNAR [Do Not Attempt Resuscitation Order].

Nurses need to understand other cultures, especially in bereavement, as Emma reflects:

when I was on Mellish Ward particularly 'cos that was acute CCU [Coronary Care Unit] so there was always lots of acute things happening, it was a real adrenalin-fuelled ward … the way that the Bengali community dealt with death which was very very different to anything I'd experienced from our culture. And more public display of grief … in the middle of CCU. I don't think we as a team … knew enough at that stage, we were still learning about other cultures and there was nothing really in place.

She recalls helping with Last Offices for the first time:

the third year … was the first time that I'd helped lay out somebody … but it got easier, it did get easier.

Many remember the lessons learned as students of treating their deceased patient with dignity:

a lovely old lady … passed very peacefully, and I remember the nurse who was helping me do the last offices, she said, 'I always talk to my patients, they're still my patients' and I've taken that with me as something that I always do as well. *Victoria*

Senior Staff Interactions

Despite a relaxation in formality in the 1990s, the old military style disciplinarian ways remained in some areas, as Emma found:

Some of the nurses were scary … and sometimes the things that happened just wouldn't happen now … I remember one of the sisters was behind a curtain with a patient and I just came in 'cos I needed to ask her something and she absolutely screamed at me down the ward, 'The curtains are closed for a reason, what are you doing coming in here, they're closed,' I was terrified … and I thought, God that just wouldn't happen now, well would hope it doesn't happen now. But she did have a point.

Medical staff were always a little bit scary, to be honest as students we didn't have a lot of interaction with the medical staff.

Zoe remembers:

And there was also a hilarious story where I, luckily for me, was rescued by a ward sister before I completely let the side down, I was on Royal Ward and it would have been probably coming up early '93, just before I qualified because it was my last ward and this very distinguished looking gentleman arrived on the ward and started talking to me about a patient and chatting away to the patient and I was just about to go 'Who are you please?' When one of the sisters came along and said … 'Professor X' she said, 'How are you today?' And it was like … because I was just about to say 'I'm really sorry but who are you?' Because I'd never met Professor X, how am I supposed to know?

Late 1990s: The Chief Nurse, Directors of Nursing and a modern matron.

But other senior staff had a more equal relationship:

> the ward manager [senior sister/charge nurse] … was fantastically supportive and really engaging and very interested in the students and making sure that we got the most out of it. *Victoria*

The 'joys' of night duty

Prior to the introduction of Project 2000 in 1992, student nurses, such as Zoe, generally worked seven nights in a row, often working alongside one of the permanent night auxiliary nurses, and benefitting from their experience:

> this patient [on a neurology ward] got out of bed and there was no reasoning with them, they were really, really confused, there was no reasoning about where they were … they just hadn't got a clue, they'd already taken their pyjamas off and … [with] [chest] drains in, I don't know how, and then they decided they'd try and put their pyjama bottoms on as a pyjama top and I was on about night five or six so by this time I was almost getting slightly, I could feel a fit of the giggles coming on and at that point the night auxiliary, I don't know if she'd heard, whether she'd come back from her break or she's heard a noise and before the patient … realised … he was actually back in bed, tucked in, with his pyjamas on, tucked in that tight there was no possible hope of escape again that night and he was asleep already. I didn't even see it happen, I'm still in awe of this lady, I mean the thing you learnt about the night auxiliaries was … as long as you understood when their break was and

you didn't try and interfere with that because if you interfered with that you were guaranteed a night of clattering bedpans, crashing doors and no speaking all night because…. Well they used to meet up with their mates, with their knitting, with the kids photos and catch up with the latest in a day room, you always knew which day room they were going to be so if you did need them you'd be alright.

Some problems did seem worse at night, as Zoe found:

it was a bedpan wash[er] that always used to leak and you just got very creative with creating a dam with a load of, usually the sheet and rolling a sheet up … so it didn't get any further than the sluice room door and the plumber used to come up at night and go 'Oh it's leaking again then nurse, I'll see what I can do with it this time'.

Project 2000 students were not required to do night duty, and only did nights in the third year if they wished.

You can learn an awful lot and I think also you get more time to speak to the staff, I mean nowadays I think the wards are just as busy at night as they are during the day but we used to have periods of time where we could sit down and have some teaching sessions and … it was a little bit more relaxed, people weren't running to theatre every five seconds … the ward was asleep and calm. *Kerry*

I always remember night shifts were always special because you got to know your colleagues as well … and you would do like maybe three or four nights in a row and usually it would be with the same team which was nice … I remember nights were always a focus on eating properly and getting enough sleep…. And I remember making sure I had clean bedclothes because there is nothing worse than doing a set of nights with [dirty sheets] … better make sure I've got a clean duvet and sort of military precision of making sure that I had enough food at home for when I got back … I think you can't beat that feeling … of going home when everyone else is coming to work. *Rebecca*

Many student nurses found it hard to adapt to sleeping in the daytime, particularly in nurses' homes. Despite a polite notice on their bedroom door many resorted to medication:

I used to quite like going back into bed in the daytime 'cos it was a real luxury … I felt like it was a real luxury to be getting into bed at eight o'clock in the morning … [while] the rest of humanity had to work. It wasn't unusual for nurses to get given, or prescribed, sleeping tablets, which I found completely obscure and never took them, 'cos I was afraid that I wouldn't wake up! But, so a lot of people used to avail of that … I slept fine so it didn't bother me in the slightest. *Victoria*

Ward lights were switched off as soon as possible as patients could suffer from sleep deprivation:

on night shift, I had some friends that worked on Mellish and we used to … look from the big end, the big windows into the garden, look across and see that they still had their lights on, we used to ring them up and tell them we were the bed manager, the site manager, 'Can you turn your lights off please, you're on too late,'… so all these lights started going out. *Simon*

Multicultural diversity

Richard reflects on the local population, recalling his first visit to Whitechapel:

> remember coming out of Whitechapel Tube Station thinking, 'My gosh, where am I?' It felt really strange, the population was mainly Muslim, Bangladeshi, I'd not met that population before because you don't find that in West London.

And after working there for some time:

> The London has a very specific cultural identity, and it's probably one of the biggest hospitals in the UK that is embedded in a very diverse, probably the most diverse population in the UK, and so it's culture is very much about ... to understand the local population and help and support them with their health needs. And so our philosophy, I think, as nurses was very much about participating and involving our patients in everything they do.

Kaleem recalls:

> I'll have a patient, a proper cockney that was on Hastings Ward ... he always used to joke so much ... I mean I'd just come from Mauritius, I didn't know anything about cockney rhyme and he always used to tease me, like say, 'I'm going to [the] apple and pears,' and I would say 'What are you saying?' *Kaleem*

> I ... got a bike and was going around ... doing a caseload for the district nursing team, and that's where I really met the Bangladeshi population in their own environment, and really made me understand them, and also, well, Jewish population, but they tended to be isolated elderly Jewish people, and most of their ... children had moved out to the suburbs and they either hadn't gone or weren't given the opportunity to go, or they didn't want to leave, and so they tended to be isolated in flats. *Richard*

> because this hospital is so large we had patients from all over the country ... I don't think it really quite hit me just how different two patients could be in the next beds. One could not have a house and the other one could live in a mansion. *Kerry*

In the 1990s The London Hospital nursing staff were generally treated with respect by 'East Enders':

> one of the things that often stands out is not the patients, it's people in the East End generally that you'd go into Sainsbury's ... you'd be there with your trolley following them and there would be an elderly lady with a loaf of bread and a paper which is obviously what she did every day, oh it's alright dear, you go in front of me, because it was obvious to ... old East Enders that if you were a young person ... a young girl in Whitechapel, the chances are you were one of the nurses and ...we were well respected by people, I never felt fear of walking in Whitechapel at night, never, never, never. *Zoe*

The local community included the criminal fraternity:

> I did care for people who were ... local thugs and minor criminals and they would tell us what they'd been up to. Because of course we had this confidential service,

although we did tell them if they did anything guilty or illegal, we should report it to the Police. *Richard*

Compassionate care

The nursing staff show compassion in many ways, and nurses learned to be adaptable and inventive in all situations:

> I was only thinking today about a child I looked after on David Hughes who had leukaemia who had never seen snow and one of the Staff Nurses went and got him a … bowl … of snow off the balcony so he could play with it until it melted. *Zoe*

This narrative from Kerry shows the compassion and resourcefulness of the staff, when trying to care for an acutely ill man:

> And one of the guys … he hadn't arrested, he had a triple A, so he had like an aortic aneurysm in his abdomen and he was a really lovely sort of traditional sort of working-class chap from the Island, as they call it, the Isle of Dogs … there was a really charismatic, really nice consultant … who was a vascular surgeon and he came down and I always remember he had this beautiful cashmere coat on, like eight o'clock in the morning on New Year's Day and he was really down to earth and he was saying to this gentleman, '…this is what we need to do Sir'. And he [said] … 'can I speak to my wife?' [The consultant said] … 'Of course.' And I [said] … 'Let's try and get her in … and … let's just get her up here'…. And … [the patient said] … 'Oh no, the lift's broken and she's in a wheelchair' and … she's from massive tower block on the island … we didn't have the sort of fancy BT phones or … mobile technology was very new at that time and we sort of managed to wheel the bed up to get him [to a fixed land line phone] to talk to her and I remember … I was really crying because he obviously was going to die either which way and it was just so [sad]. I just remember thinking … it's New Year's Day and this guy's had this really bad news and anyway, he spoke to his wife and she couldn't come in … you've got that knowledge that this isn't going to end very well either which way and anyway he went off to theatre … later on in the afternoon the consultant came down … and he said, 'Oh girls … I just wanted to say that unfortunately you may have heard that the patient didn't survive, but you were all just so nice and I think it meant a lot that we managed to get him [to talk to his wife].' Because it might sound a simple thing moving a patient, but this guy was really ill so we were trying to move like a bed with like drip stands, monitors and he's on the phone when really you want him attached to some sort of monitor that could do something.

Nurses were taught to be non-judgemental in all situations, accepting patient's lifestyle choices and coping strategies:

> you can't get anywhere in Whitechapel without stepping over people who are slumped over from alcohol or drugs, and that was the same then, particularly in sexual health … I always used to think, 'If you're stepping off Whitechapel into a sexual health centre, you're probably quite brave already, because of the stigma associated with it,' and some people would strengthen their resolve by coming in slightly … lubricated to help them … to deal with the stress of coming in. *Richard*

I'm just thinking of a patient in particular who was dying and he had a wife and family, but he also had a mistress and he'd had her for a very long time as well and she was important in his life as well, who was I to deny that man to see his mistress in his dying days … it got a bit challenging and a bit complicated, making sure they never ever met but … I wasn't there to judge, I was just there to care for my patient and make sure that his needs were met. *Zoe*

Communicating in different ways

Increasingly nursing patients who spoke very little, if any English, was an added dimension of communication. A huge number of languages are spoken in the area, necessitating the use of a number of interpreters and advocates:

And … families that don't speak English, I'd never come across anybody I'd had to mime to before or … never used an advocate before and it … makes you realise that actually some of these conversations can be quite difficult and what you say actually can be interpreted in so many different ways and that you have to make sure you're using the right language for people to understand and I still live by that now. *Kerry*

obviously being Whitechapel there was a language issue sometimes but we whittled that out quite quickly because … if I couldn't get through to them then in the [appointment] letter it said that … I was calling and if your first language wasn't English then you could either come up to the hospital for an appointment or if you could have somebody in the house with you who spoke English and you gave them consent to speak to me then we could do it that way. *Christopher*

Nurses learn from their own personal experiences to help care for patients:

we had a patient who was deaf and I have a deaf brother … and I'm not saying I'm particularly good in sign language but I could communicate with him a little bit better, he'd kind of calm down, he had to have security with him, but it was his lack of being able to communicate that was causing … more of a problem. … [W]e had elderly ladies that would come in after having what they thought was a cerebral vascular accident and … I would sit with them and just talk to them because they were so confused and I really enjoyed that. *Kerry*

Role models

Student nurses work alongside qualified nurses and can still recall those nurses who provided excellent care, and became their role models:

there was one senior staff [nurse], when I was a student … and I followed her a lot in my career because she's very inspirational, and she's the nurse that I always wanted to be. *Emma*

I had a really, really wonderful ward manager … who was just dynamic and at the time we wore scrubs on that ward because we were…attached to A&E and she would … come in to do management stuff and then the next minute she'd have her scrubs on and she'd be … doing someone's feet … and it really has stuck with me that whenever you get into nursing leadership roles you have to not be office based ... obviously you've got to get that balance because you can't be doing all that all the time ... I just remember as a very sort of junior staff nurse thinking, I want to be like that when I'm older. *Kerry*

the people I think I learnt the most from was the night auxiliaries, those redoubtable ladies who quite frankly, even these days, would probably still scare me, but they taught me so much ... and again it's about basic patient care ... they were quite compassionate care[rs], they scared me ... I was a student, they're allowed to scare students but they taught me so much about what nursing is about. *Zoe*

for me the greatest feedback I could ever have would be for someone to say, I want to be like [her] ... when I'm a nurse. *Rebecca*

'We work hard but we play hard too'

Peer support is still as essential to nurses in this decade as it was to those who trained in previous decades as Kaleem points out:

we are all in the same boat, we left home and living away from home and we have each other's support, come back from a bad shift, have a chat about it.

I live in a nurses' home and they're always funny, the nurses' home. I mean for a building full of single people and going out, drink[ing], I mean it was good. We work hard but we play hard too.

Zoe recalls:

we had plenty of fun ... the Three Feathers Club was still standing at the time ... we had two Irish girls and obviously a long way from home and didn't know anybody, they hadn't got any family in London and so I can remember us having a surprise birthday party for one of them. I remember us having a toga party at another occasion ... we had some fun.

Balancing family life and nursing

Due to economic pressures, such as the cost of housing, and women's career expectations, more women remain in work. This can create tensions, both in and out of the workplace, as Emma relates:

I think nurses traditionally started young and if you had a family or got married you tended to leave work and not go back, whereas now ... they keep pushing for nurses, 'Oh you can do it any time of your life, if you've got children we'll support you,' but then when you go to a ward you can't work there 'cos of the shifts, they're not family friendly.

my husband said to me when I went on maternity leave, he said ... 'Great, we can finally have a life,' that's what he said, and I went, 'What?' He said ... 'Our lives revolve around your ward,' and I said, 'Don't be ridiculous,' and after I'd been on maternity leave for nine months I said, 'You're absolutely right.'

Rebecca continues:

> I think as well as a profession it's not always been the most family friendly…
> I think in London particularly what's incredibly difficult is you've got the other
> added thing of housing and schooling and so I've had friends that have carried
> on, they've gone off, they've had a baby, they've come back, they tried to make
> it work and then they've got to school age and it's like, do I stay in London or do
> I move out and then people will go on and do other posts.

The London Legacy: '…working in the spit and sawdust…'

The London Hospital has an allure and pulls nurses back after time away:

> I left and moved out of London and I was homesick to a degree because I missed
> that sort of different … ways … I lasted three years and then I've come back …
> it's just always plucked at my heart strings … and it's just a big big part of my
> life really. *Rebecca*

> I went to Australia to work but I didn't stay long, I stayed a couple of months and
> then I came back, missing Whitechapel. … My friends over there couldn't believe it,
> they said, 'How could you?' Because we did a big recruitment with Australian nurses
> so I met them there, and they were, 'I couldn't believe it you are missing this grotty
> little place like Whitechapel and … you're in Adelaide here, nice beach'. *Kaleem*

Some nurses never leave:

> I've never really moved away, because really we [City University] are still The
> London. *Richard*

Rebecca reflects on the importance of The Royal London Hospital for the health provision
for the local community:

> everyone goes on about Barts, but actually this is proper and I think one of the
> things that I love about The London and have always kept with me … is that in
> Whitechapel and in the East End, The London has always been … a significant
> local hospital for local people … The London's in a unique position because
> people recognise it for obviously all its national and international history and
> even now … we've got the pioneering trauma stuff but it's still always retained
> that quite special unique [identity], it's the local hospital for the local people of
> Tower Hamlets and beyond.
>
> Tower Hamlets and the East End has always been a place where people come
> and people move on…the different communities and stuff but there's always been
> an absolute respect for The Royal London, which I don't know if I've seen for
> other hospitals in the East End.
>
> I remember people saying, oh why don't you go and work at Chelsea and
> Westminster and I was like no and it's not to be derogatory but there's something
> about working in the spit and sawdust of here.

There were mixed opinions about the degree pathway. Emma considers:

> My instinct is to say don't do it, but if I sat and thought a little bit beyond that
> I would say think very very carefully before you go into nursing, I don't agree that

nursing should be a degree only programme … I think we needed to go back a few years and change it back to maybe a diploma … or the old training for everybody, and then if you want to do an academic top-up after that's fine, because I think it … stops people who'd be fantastic nurses because they've got the right personality, they've got the right qualities but they maybe haven't got that quite academic [knowledge]…. They can still be nurses, there's a lot of people I've met that have got great academic skills and have done fantastically and got firsts in nursing, but unfortunately they haven't got the right qualities to be a nurse.

Other nurses offer sound advice, reflecting on experience and research:

look after yourselves first, and to make sure that you're confident and happy in what you do and have insight into the impact that you have on other[s], your colleagues and your patients, and…always remember that, because everything that you say, or do, or the way you act, people remember that. *Victoria*

Rebecca reflects:

trust your gut feel[ing] and if something doesn't feel right, keep saying to someone, I know their obs [observations] look right but … assess your patient, learn skills very very quickly that will enable you to get a picture holistically of your patient, so if you are putting up some … medical equipment, say to someone, do you live on your own … and in your mind be thinking about … what do we need to do for this person, what's their set-up, what's their social set-up, what's their emotional support … and don't ever forget about the potentials of doing some quite basic nursing care, which when we say basic it makes it always feel that it's not of any importance because actually it is.

[R]esearch shows us … if you've got a permanent regular team of staff working together that's ultimately going to benefit patients because the staff are going to be more motivated, they're going to be more able to learn from each other as well. … They're a team … your team.

I love every minute of it, well actually, no I'm not going to say I loved every minute of it, there were times where things can be a bit crazy and a bit sad but I love my job, the day I don't love my job is the day I'll leave nursing.

Kerry further considers the importance of working together:

I would never give somebody a job that I wasn't willing to do myself, but sometimes changing of the bed is as important to me as giving chemotherapy because another patient needs to come in but I can't do both, but they [student nurses] can't give the chemo.

Political impact on nursing; internationally, nationally and locally

Government policies directly affect the health service. A lack of trained nurses led to a reliance on the recruitment of overseas nurses.

it's swings and roundabouts with whoever's in power as to what they will provide and what they won't provide so it changes. … [W]hen I first qualified we had a lot of Australian and New Zealand nurses, now we have a lot of Filipino nurses and we've got nurses that are coming from Italy and places like that and you always see a shift…. It's quite seasonal really, it is. *Kerry*

What would I like my legacy to be? … [T]hat I've actually made a difference to patient safety … my role is all about patient safety and I go and I look at things and I just think that is a disaster waiting to happen … I do write lots of policies and … really try and raise the profile of patient safety … and when people say to me 'well that costs money', I say 'well at the end of the day are we here for the patients or are we here to save money?' … [W]e talk about patient-centred care, there's no evidence of it. It's money driven care … because as I'm sure [when] you were trained … [the] patient was at the centre of care and everything revolved around that patient. Now money's the centre of the care and everything else takes money out of that pot, and when that pot's gone what happens? *Christopher*

Making a difference and maintaining professional self-esteem

I think it's when patients and families tell you that you make a difference to their mother or father, and especially in my job where the prognosis is very poor and when relatives come and say … 'Thank you for being there, you've made a difference in my mum,' … [for] the last few months of their life, I think that's very rewarding. *Kaleem*

I think keep going, keep going at it, if you're struggling ask for help, there's help there. Not everyone is as willing but there is help there and it's such a worthwhile profession. I know the politics get in the way but my day-to-day, hands-on nursing, when I ring a family at home to give them a blood result and the child wants to scream down the phone at me and sing happy birthday or random things … it makes my job worthwhile, seeing the end product, whether it's a good or bad product … not all of our patients survive but I've done my best and that's all you can do, is your best, we're humans after all. *Kerry*

Rebecca considers:

I wear glasses and one of my little tricks that I always did was always turning a pillow over, that can make a massive difference if someone feels crap but if you've got a patient … actually look at them and the amount of patients I sometimes see that have got really dirty glasses … you can do those little things which really someone will remember … it's all important but it's about you building up your levels of what you would expect if you were a patient and … the classic one is would I want my mum to be treated like this, would I want my dad to be treated like this?

[N]ever ever ever treat anyone badly, so for me, some of the people that I have had the greatest feedback have been from porters and from the cleaners, so never ever think you're beneath doing something, so always treat people well as you go through your career and that we're all a team.

[N]ursing as a profession is not as attractive as it used to be. … I think that you could earn a lot lot more money sitting in Liverpool Street on a reception, where you can go and have lunch in Pret A Manger and you can do that. I think as a society we've become less altruistic ... I think as a profession we maybe haven't done enough to promote it as something that ... isn't just a dirty job ... you can make a difference ... whenever I've had a bad day and I think well actually, I know I went in and I did something, whether or not I showed someone the way in the hospital or whether or not I held someone's hand or whether or not I did a piece of work with a ward sister or a member of staff or implemented a change in the ward, be it big or small, that I made a difference to someone's life today ... I think we've lost our sense of self-esteem as a profession.

The 1990s saw some of the most dramatic changes to nurse education since the Nightingale nursing reforms of the mid- to late- nineteenth century, with the implementation of Project 2000 and a move towards an all-graduate profession. Alongside these, massive changes in medical treatments had a profound effect on the nursing care. Patients were staying in for less time and more likely to survive serious illnesses during this decade than in previous ones. The iconic London Hospital uniform, which was sometimes cited as a reason for choosing 'The London' was phased out, replaced by the national uniform. Societal and economic attitudes changed towards working mothers, and expectations by women that nursing careers would not be truncated by pregnancy and childbirth have led to tensions. These stresses continue to be exacerbated by employers who desperately require more nurses, but fail to address the stresses and needs of working mothers and fathers. However the hospital still remained as a hospital for local people, set in the heart of the East End of London. Despite these massive changes, safe care and compassion remain the core components of good nursing care:

I'm a firm believer in compassion ... the most important thing is compassion.
Emma

2000s, Mixed media on canvas, 2017, Paula Day.

Chapter 7

The Millennium and beyond

> it was the hardest thing I ever did in my life, training to be a nurse, the most rewarding but the hardest. *Lilian*

The new millennium brought with it major changes to healthcare delivery and nurse education, both nationally, and in the East End of London. Globalisation has led to challenges in modern healthcare for nurses and patients. In 2000 the NHS Plan was introduced; a major ten-year modernisation programme of investment and reform for the NHS, the first since its inception in 1948.

During this period, The Royal London Hospital was part of significant and ongoing mergers and changes. Nurses' homes including the Luckes, Cavell and the Old Home were demolished to make way for a new purpose-built hospital, capable of providing healthcare in the twenty-first century. Construction at Whitechapel began in 2007, and Phase 1 was opened in March 2012, in time for the London 2012 Olympics, which were centred on the Olympic Park in Stratford, East London. Much of the old hospital was demolished, however the Grade II listed original building remains and has been recently purchased by Tower Hamlets Council. Nurses identified with the history of the old hospital building and with those that had nursed in it before them:

> there was something about those wooden steps and putting your palm on [them] … you could see … they'd worn down and you felt like you were following steps … part of history. *Rebecca*

A new hospital building and a sense of loss

> people call The [Royal] London 'the mothership' … I heard that the other day and I don't know if it's the 'mothership' because it sort of looks like some sort of scientific big blue sort of spaceship. *Rebecca*

> we closed our old department [A&E] and moved here … I think leaving the resus room and going in there for the last time was quite poignant because of everything that we had experienced in there … we all had a very emotional attachment to it … in that very small room we had seen life and death and we had … [delivered] babies in that room, so it was very bizarre to be leaving it and drawing an end to it. … [W]e were very excited about coming into a new building…. But there's definitely, for those of us who worked on both sites … there is a … fondness and … you have … your rose … tinted glasses on when you think about it now. *Victoria*

> I always worked in the old hospital and … people miss the corridor conversations and … people miss walking up the steps … there's something around the old

building … it wasn't fit for purpose, you can't do high level, high quality work in a hospital that's old … there was something about that hospital. *Rebecca*

Some of the hospital's history was lost when the new wards were renamed with numbers:

one of the things that did break my heart … was that they made a decision not to keep the ward names … and I [said], 'Why can't they be names…?' Have we asked what the patients want…?' I used to say to them, '… I was a Cambridge [Ward] girl' … but people were defined by their ward name … there was camaraderie, we were the Cambridge girls … whereas I don't know if the generation now are going to have that. … [W]hy can't it be done that we think about bringing back ward names, why don't we ask our patients, they would prefer them. *Rebecca*

Despite the move from the old hospital, nurse tutors weave The London Hospital's history into student nurse education as Richard describes:

we designed a mural … with the history of nursing in relation to Barts and The London, from 1123 to 2012. So there are images of The London and things going on down at Whitechapel, and the students see this every time they're in their laboratories and we tell them this is about their history.

Edith Cavell's statue was moved from the 'old' Princess Alexandra School of Nursing building at Whitechapel to City, University of London:

We also have a statue of Edith Cavell, and we have the Edith Cavell room … we've still retained our pedigree, as I call it, to the students, and I relate our pedigree to The London and Barts. *Richard*

While students no longer get the iconic London Hospital badge on qualifying, they continue to receive one:

they still get a badge that they can wear when they qualify. And it's the badge of the university now because it had to be neutral from the two schools, but the motto in Latin is 'To Serve Mankind', and I thought that was really relevant to nurses. *Richard*

Teething problems

Although it was a state of the art hospital, there were inevitable teething problems with the new infrastructure:

the outpatients [department] … was the first unit that was open in the new building, it was … the first month … and they hadn't quite fine-tuned the lifts … I was in a lift on my own, coming down from … the fourth floor, we crashed past the ground floor and I was thrown to the ground … we were … halfway below the ground level. … I've avoided lifts ever since as much as I can. *Lilian*

Victoria recalls the initial difficulties with the communication systems:

there was definitely teething problems. … [C]ommunications was a real issue 'cos we didn't have a Tannoy, we still don't have a Tannoy, this department is the size of three football pitches and we have DECT [Portable] phones now … we all relied on bleeps and there's dead zones for the phones … wifi doesn't work properly ... there was those issues which ... were fairly basic, were ... a real difficulty. ... [T]here are still ongoing issues, but in the main, working in a newer building that is slightly more fit for purpose ... is certainly far more advantageous to what we had.

The staff now have privacy in their staff room during break times:

> the staff room in the old department ... was right off the main area, so literally any patient could come in and they did, knock on the door and you'd be like 'ah'! Or they could see you when you were sitting having your lunch, they were able to peer in! ... When you look after your staff better ... your patients do better. *Victoria*

Other problems included Barts Health NHS Trust being placed under special measures in 2016 by the Care Quality Commission. Victoria recalls:

> there's a huge organisation and there was a lot of changes when we all amalgamated and the way in which all those change[s] were handled, the staffing, everything, was handled very badly so there was a lot of disgruntled staff across the ... four sites. ... [W]e're now paying the price for it because ... we're in special measures and ... the staffing is wrong ... I think from my point of view, our immediate management team are amazing and fantastically supportive, higher up the organisation it's a bit hit and miss ... it can be quite tricky sometimes!

Not the first direction

For many, nursing was now a second-choice career option, so there were more mature entrants.

> I went in as a mature student ... I left school when I was 16, joined the Merchant Navy and didn't really get on very well in it ... [then] I was working in an office and it was paying quite well ... I was 18 at the time so you know I was quite fortunate to be in such a good job but I was bored out of my mind ... for a couple of years people had been saying to me that I should go into nursing because I like talking to people and helping people so ... I applied ... and then I chickened out. ... I was scared about going from ... a full-time salary to being a poor student living in London. But then about a year later my father passed away ... it was that that made me think, do you know what, you're a long time dead, you might as well just ... [take] the bull by the horns ... which is what I did and reapplied. *Matthew*

> I did always want to [nurse] and then the admin job that I was doing ... they were talking about redundancies and I was talking to ... a friend of my mum ... and I was just saying 'I can't, the thought of going through this for the rest of my life doing admin,' and she said, 'Well what about nursing?' And I said, 'Oh I just don't think I could do it, I don't know if I'd be any good', and she said, 'Well what is it going to cost you if you apply and you get a place and you hate it after three months?' She said, 'Then you've just lost three months, whereas you could spend the rest of your life thinking what if', she said ... 'Go and do three months and if you hate it then [leave]'. *Laura*

For some nurses other life events led them to reflect on their career choices, and change direction. With the end of a mandatory retirement age, student nurses are accepted solely for their potential, irrespective of their age, as Lilian describes:

> Well I'd cared for my parents when both of them were sick and I found that quite tender work, it brought something out of me, but also because I'm a transsexual woman ... when I transitioned in 2009 I'd been a ... headteacher and the education system is really not quite so comfortable with trans teachers and staff as the Health Services, the NHS in fact is incredibly good on diversity issues like that ... so in 2009 I commenced transition ... and decided to explore healthcare and I worked for nearly two years as a Healthcare Assistant ... I found it brilliant, I just loved it and so then I got up the courage to apply to train as a nurse.
>
> I started training at 58 and graduated at 61, which is exceptionally mature, well old, I don't know if I'm mature but it was old ... I thought why will they train me when they could train an 18-year-old who can offer them forty years' service?

There are several universities in London which offer student nurse education:

> I visited City University on a ... visiting day ... when I was working out who to apply for ... I just liked the feel of it and the staff and at the interview they were very, very welcoming.... So I had a positive feel about it from the beginning. *Lilian*

> it's a good teaching hospital, you've ... a ... wide experience of different wards ... different cultures, different medical needs and you've ... a lot of people around you to teach you, not just at uni, but a lot of experienced nurses. *Jessica*

> City has a great reputation ... when I got the offer I really couldn't say no to that. *Priya*

University education

As nurse education moved completely into universities, student nurses' continued to be supernumerary, maintaining the change in status first brought in with Project 2000. However, they still felt part of the establishment and essential to patient care delivery:

> we were told this every day for three years, we were supernumerary, we were not part of the numbers but as we all know how well staffed the NHS is, we were very useful to have around. ... they definitely got their money's worth out of us. *Matthew*

Student nurses now chose specific pathways from the beginning of nurse education, for example adult or paediatric nursing, and shared some of their university lectures. For all nurses who undertake some or all of their placements at The Royal London Hospital, the formal element of nurse education is now completed at City, University of London.

Despite the changes, strict observance of correct uniform continues to this day as Lilian describes:

> it had to be black lace-ups ... the City training was tough and you would be sent off ... if you were being sloppy, if you put a cardigan or something on, over your [uniform], at nights, you could get into trouble ... But I respected that, it's a bit like being in the Army actually.

Student nurses now experienced the advantages of university life:

> Oh, I absolutely enjoy university life. New friends, new environment, a lot more independent and … I think we were supported, and having your friends around you who are also going through the same thing … that also helps you too … go through all that stress. So it makes it less stressful, makes it quite fun. *Priya*

The interviewees, such as Lilian, acknowledged and appreciated the tutors 'firm but fair' attitude towards assessments:

> there was friendship and support I remember but I also remember their toughness and I think they were probably tougher than … quite a lot of other university Health Departments were and it gave us all I think a sense of pride that we were not just walking, sailing through this, they would fail you on tiny things and you'd have to re-sit the whole thing.
>
> if you were being assessed and you forgot to wash your hands at certain points they were very, very stringent in their standards and I respected that.

Laura describes the first year practical exam:

2000s: Sisters standing in front of Queen Alexandra's statue.
(Image appears by courtesy of Paula Day)

> I think when we did our first year OSCE … I think we maybe had a list of ten potential scenarios that we would be tested on from taking your blood pressure to urinalysis…. So you would have to make sure that you understood the rationale for why you would be doing that particular thing, as well as how to actually perform it. … one of our paediatric lecturers was stood there … and making sure I fulfilled all the criteria…. It's terrifying. … I think OSCEs are … a good idea to make sure that actually it's not just the ability to do the task but to understand why you're doing the task.

As Matthew describes, unlike the challenges faced as a 'nurse apprentice' while training in earlier decades, students now have different trials:

> being a student again, juggling placements, school work, I had to take up a job, a weekend job just to pay the bills and things. Even though I got the bursary…. So the challenge was fitting it all in and also a bit of social life and also the fact that I was a mature student and I hadn't studied beyond GCSEs and then all of a sudden I'm studying at university, it was acclimatising to that.

Initial placement

Students now go to an increasingly wide variety of placements, including private hospitals such as The London Clinic, even for their first clinical experience:

> it wasn't exactly a ward, it was an Outpatients Unit with minor surgery involved and I've got really, really fond memories of it because of course when you're a new student, you're dead nervous about your first placement, will they like me? Will I be useless? How will I get on? From day one I enjoyed it. *Lilian*

For some students, such as Priya, who had never been in hospital, the first ward was especially challenging:

> It was in a cardiology ward. So that was my very first time experiencing clinical placement, experiencing hospital, because I have never been in hospital. I have never worked as a healthcare professional before, so I didn't know what to expect. But I was very excited and I think my first placement was perhaps my most difficult placement, just adjusting to … the new environment, the new … responsibilities that were expected of me … what was my role, understanding what I needed to learn, how do I pass this placement … it was the most difficult.
>
> I think, throughout that eight weeks [of a first placement], I probably had a clinical lecturer visit me twice, three times. They were helpful, supportive, but sometimes you just feel as if you couldn't express the difficulties you were going through, personally, like, 'Oh, I'm finding it difficult to adjust to this placement' … I think it's … being surrounded … in a new environment with … very, very unwell people.

Students felt under-prepared by their initial training and had mixed experiences: 'we were kind of just thrown in.'

> I was quite fortunate because I was on a ward … and the team there were brilliant, they were really funny and helpful but … I'd never really set foot in a hospital … on the other side of the barrier. But luckily we were sent into our first placement in pairs, so there were two of us and on our first day they let us work the same shift which was brilliant and … our first patient that we gave a wash to in the morning … one patient took us an hour. … [H]e said to us … he was early nineties … 'Haven't you done this before?' So we didn't tell him that we hadn't actually done it before. But … it was daunting … to be honest with you it felt like we were kind of just thrown in, there was no mollycoddling. *Matthew*

Lilian felt that the old apprenticeship style training would have been more beneficial:

> I personally think we didn't spend nearly enough time actually learning and training on placements so my personal philosophy is I think it would be better if we served apprenticeships in the hospitals.

Laura vividly remembers being left unsupervised for a short while on her first day:

> my first day on placement I will never forget. … I turned up for my early shift and I was allocated to work with X and she was also in charge and we were going to change this young boy … who had sickle cell disease and who'd had a stroke. … [T]he first thing we did was we went in there to go and wash him and change

him for the morning and she got called away because she was in charge so there I was with this child in the bed. The nappy, the pad half off and then this huge explosion. That just hit me. So it was quite funny over the years that I then saw him through my training and I'd always just think 'you pooed on me, that was my very first experience'! … I will never forget my first day.

Whatever the decade, interviewees never forget the first death they witnessed, particularly when it occurred on their first ward as for Priya:

one thing I'll remember from my first placement is, when I first experienced a patient who I had been looking after, passed away, on the second day … just after handover, he was very well, I think it was completely unexpected when he went into cardiac arrest. … [T]hat was my very first experience of cardiac arrest, of … looking after a very sick patient, and of death as well. … [T]hat's something that I don't think I will forget. I think, as a student … nobody ever spoke to me about it … maybe they weren't aware that this was the first time I've experienced it and having a cardiac arrest on the ward can be quite chaotic.

Each ward or placement presented a different style of working:

on our ward we're quite a team. We're quite friendly, we're quite approachable and … that's what it needs to be because they can't learn otherwise. They can't enjoy their placement, you can't learn if you're not enjoying it. *Jessica*

On day duty, students were allowed to choose between the old-style daytime shifts and new twelve-hour shifts:

research-wise they say that long days are better for patients in terms of continuity of care, but I mean it's exhausting when you're just starting your training and you're trying to get your head round how everything works, maybe earlies and lates were quite a good thing. *Laura*

Comparative learning experiences

Compared to previous decades, a lack of placements led to some students not experiencing, for example, any medical nursing before qualification, which could curtail job opportunities and inhibit confidence, as Priya illustrates:

I think at university we could have had a lot of training on looking after patients that are acutely unwell. So a lot more hands-on care … when I came to A&E it took me quite some time to be confident to look after patients in this environment, and it's mainly because … I didn't have [a] medical placement, critical care placement, and at university … you don't have [that] … training. … [T]hat would have helped us a lot.

However, she found the changing emphasis in healthcare gave her greater insight into the causes of disease:

I think being in the community you get to identify a lot of things that you don't consider when you're looking after a patient in the ward, in terms of what their home situation is like and the environment that they live in … I saw patients in Tower Hamlets … who are quite unwell … with a lot of illnesses that were mainly due to lifestyle … it just gives you an insight into … how patients' background can have a significant impact on their health and wellbeing.

[O]n one of my placements I was in a rehab[ilitation] ward … we spent a lot of time sitting with the elderly patients talking to them. A lot of them had dementia … before that placement … I didn't have much knowledge or experience with dementia patients and it … [gave] you a better understanding of … how their thinking is and how are you best communicating with them and get[ting] them settled in the environment.

Priya also felt the need for nurses to be more proactive during training:

I think they should make the most of their clinical placement. … [B]e a lot more … hands-on with your patients … make the most of the placements … be more enthusiastic, so try to take responsibility as much as you can for your patient, because you will have a mentor with you all the time, who will be there to support you, to stop you if you're about to do something wrong.

Others worked alongside hospice staff:

they had time for everybody, you know as yourself as a nurse that time is the richest quality. *Lilian*

Night duty, another dimension of nursing

Unlike previous decades, students now only had to do a few mandatory night duties, but they still felt the pressure of caring for patients at night. The night sister's visits, so often dreaded in previous decades, seem to have become less frightening:

there is always a night sister but I would say visits were fairly infrequent … we were left to our own devices. *Lilian*

Paediatric nursing students were expected to work with adult patients when the need arose:

one night shift [in A&E] there was no paediatric patients so they sent … a couple of us over to adults to give them a hand, which was daunting. So my first adult patient was a man … a big man that was drunk and I was a bit … petrified … being young as well because I went straight from school so I was quite scared, but actually it was fine. *Jessica*

Following the 2013 Francis Public Inquiry Report into the Stafford Hospital scandal, recommendations were made regarding safe staffing levels:

we had one night where we were under staffed, which did happen more regularly than it should … there was myself, we had twenty-four acute gastro [-intestinal patients] … and two nurses. … [B]ecause after Stafford, it was meant to be one for every seven patients we were down to two … we were basically… twelve patients per nurse and one of the … patients went into respiratory arrest and we're … totally stretched, that was a hairy episode. *Lilian.*

Students took the time on night duty to utilise extra learning opportunities:

for some reason night duties always seem much longer than days, even though it's the same hours. And the time passes a lot slower … you're not interacting as much with the patients and the ward is very quiet, so you feel as if things are dragging … after settling the patients, giving the medications, after the ward was settled, you can read a lot more about your patient's care … that was a positive … outcome for me. *Priya*

Nurses often relieve stress and play 'tricks' on each other, as described by Laura, on a paediatric ward:

> because we're a respiratory ward so we have a trache[ostomy] doll for training families … and students…. So Robert the trache doll is invariably found in lots of different situations so he could be found dressed … in a surgical gown in the linen cupboard to jump … for someone to be terrified in the middle of the night, or he could be found sat on the toilet when you go in to use the bathroom. … [O]ne of my favourite memories of Robert was when the day staff came into the handover room in the morning and opened the curtains in the handover room and there was Robert sat out on the balcony in a wheelchair with a cigarette in his trache, which I don't even know where we got [it from] because none of us on the night shift smoked, with a catheter bag full of apple juice hanging over the side of the [chair].

Interactions with medical staff

Sadly in the twenty-first century, student nurses are still made to feel disempowered:

> it needs to be taught that … nurses are capable and to have more confidence in themselves to support each other a lot more and to challenge the status quo …

2012: Doing a 'Usain Bolt', Olympics sisters wearing The London Hospital sister's uniform, as adapted for the London Olympics opening ceremony.
(Image appears by courtesy of Kelly Read)

I had one doctor once, I was doing … a dressing on a leg ulcer … so I was quite busy and the sister came up to me and said that a doctor was … catheterising a male, could I go and assist him, so I frowned a bit and I said, 'Well I can, why does he need any help?' … I stood there for ten minutes while he catheterised this patient and he left the room, he walked out and he said to me, as he left, 'Could you just throw all the stuff away please, just throw it all away', and it's that kind of attitude that … a lot of people still think nurses are just skivvies that doctors can [order around] … that's not the case anymore … nurses should be more autonomous. *Matthew*

This narrative reflects a deeply entrenched patriarchal view of nurses, male or female, which is still held by some medics. Old style attitudes between student nurses and medical staff still remain:

as a student you don't have that confidence … if you weren't sure about something … I certainly didn't have the confidence to ask them [medical staff]. *Priya*

Clinical mentors and role models

Experienced nurses, such as Laura see the benefits of mentorship:

I do think working alongside your mentor you can hopefully try and learn by watching and seeing how … as qualified nurses we communicate with our colleagues and our patients … communication is such an important part of nursing.

I think that it's important to learn how to do things the right way from someone working in that role. I just think if you're just put on a ward and told to get on with it I don't know that you can really provide appropriate care for the patient.

This is sometimes challenging as Laura has found when also managing the ward:

I do enjoy … helping to shape the future of nursing really because that's what you're doing … because I'm very often coordinating the shift on our ward … I find that … quite hard to then mentor the student as well, especially more junior students … really I'd want to work directly alongside them and be showing them … from the basics and if you're in charge and … you've got a million phone calls to make … I do love working with the students but it's … a challenge to try and fit it all in.

And others learnt through reflection with friends who were experienced nurses:

I was friends with a nun who was one of the 'Call the Midwife' nuns … she was in her 90s, and she'd trained and nursed at The Royal London. *Lilian*

Lack of support

Third year student nurses still experienced the same stresses of staff shortages and increased responsibility, as did students from earlier decades, as Priya describes:

Third year I think was, perhaps, stressful, but it was … fun as well. So stressful because it's your final year and you don't want things to go wrong, you don't want to risk … your registration, and there was a lot more expected of you in placement. … Mixed feelings, so nerves as well as excitement, but I definitely enjoyed it. I remember when I was in my final placement and there was a staff shortage, and a bay of patients, there were seven of them. There wasn't a nurse to look after them … I was given that responsibility and that was unsafe. … [T]he shift went well and I was supported by the nurse in charge, so if I needed anything I can go and talk to her and get her support. … [A]t the end of the shift I handed over to a qualified staff and the patients have all been well, no one deteriorated. … [I]t was a good experience for my learning but … that's not how it should be.

Lilian describes the departure of a fellow student:

there was one particular girl in my friendship group … she in her practical placements was the loveliest, loveliest nurse and she was asked to leave in the end because she couldn't cope with the academic essays and English wasn't her first language and I just felt, it was a real shame because we lost somebody who … was very good with patients.

On qualifying

After qualification, some interviewees found it easier than others to transition to the staff nurse role:

once you're registered … you're going to be learning every shift … there was never a shift when I haven't learnt something. *Lilian*

the transition from being a student to a staff nurse, I found that quite easy … because I took a lot of responsibility when I was here as a final placement student. *Jessica*

Others felt that they needed more clinical experience before qualification:

I think all of us to be honest, were saying we didn't want to graduate when we did, we felt very unprepared to be going out into the big wide world as accountable nurses. … I think we needed more clinical time … again because of the shortage of staff there wasn't always time to teach us all the clinical stuff on placements so … a lot of us didn't feel ready for the big wide world. *Matthew*

it was very scary. … [T]he more experience I had, the more confident I became to delegate tasks, or even ask for help and say, 'I'm struggling with this, can you allocate someone else to give me a hand with this'. *Priya*

On-going care and compassion

Despite many of the challenges of nursing patients in a modern healthcare system nurses remain committed, compassionate and caring:

it's all privilege basically you're dealing with people at their point of need, at a critical stage in their life and you have the privilege of being there with them, it's so special. *Lilian*

I love nursing, I think it's an absolute privilege being a nurse and I love building a relationship with my patients … I love bringing a smile to patients. *Matthew*

A selection of badges awarded to nurses who trained at The London Hospital from 1941 until the present day.

Challenges of diversity

The thing is with nursing you get the whole cross-section of society. *Lilian*

In an increasingly global healthcare system, nurses and patients are from all faiths, cultures and social classes which may lead to tensions, as described by Lilian, during a training placement in a private hospital:

> there was a very wealthy man who flew into the country for some minor surgery … and he started speaking in [another language] to his family who were there in the room and I came in as a student to help and they started laughing their heads off and they obviously saw that I was trans and I thought they were just joking away and it went on and on and they were hilarious … I went out of my way to be really helpful because that's my mindset and then my mentor took me out and spoke to me and said, 'I'm afraid they were laughing at you' and at that point I burst into floods of tears and I felt devastated and I felt belittled. And my mentor was great at that point because although she was kind … she said, 'You're going to go back in there and give them the same quality service…. You're going to get other stuff like this, you've got to be stronger than them'. And I did, and for the next week I gave them quality service and at the end, I think that somebody may have had a word with him, but he actually wrote a letter praising my work so it seemed like I actually won that one over.

The 2005 London terrorist attacks

On 7 July 2005 staff of The Royal London Hospital played a major part in the emergency. Once again in a major incident the hospital's location was pivotal to getting prompt care to the victims. Many people will recall the fear for loved ones who were in London during these atrocities, and the concern when unable to contact them by mobile phone. These narratives from interviewees who were working then highlight the care and compassion staff gave, despite the anxieties that they had about their own relatives, as Rebecca relates:

> I went onto Cambridge [Ward] because … that was turned into sort of a receiving place from A&E and … I [said], 'Look I don't mind ringing people up to let them know their relatives are here.' … [A]ll the phone lines went down and for some reason my [mobile] network was still going … I remember ringing a gentleman whose wife had been brought round and she'd sustained quite severe lower limb injuries but she was alive…. She was clearly going for surgery for an amputation and she was aware of that but it was just the smell, it was like burning … and I remember ringing her husband and he said, 'I'll never forget you, thank you so much, I've been ringing round [all the hospitals].'
>
> I think there was a lot of people that were working that day that we didn't know where our friends and relatives were so there was a point, particularly I know my sister-in-law, we weren't able to get in touch with her and she took a route on one of the tubes that was involved and I couldn't get hold of one of my brothers … I was getting messages from people saying, are you alright? … I managed to speak to my mum to say I was okay but it was a difficult day because we were all … part of it as well as looking after the people.

Staff showed great compassion and team spirit, gaining support from each other. Rebecca describes:

> a double-decker bus turned up from Aldgate full of [patients] … I remember being outside with a colleague at the time and I was [thinking], 'This is surreal,' it was just this … double-decker turned up outside the … main entrance of A&E … and … they'd set up a … pastoral relatives [area], [for] the walking wounded … the people that were like shocked [were], wandering around … and there was a lovely chaplain … and he was there with the chaplaincy…. You saw so much compassion and so much people just did…. And then it was a bit strange because it … all happened and then it all calmed down really quickly and I remember good old Sam's, the pub, was a bit of a point for people to … go and I remember … being a bit dazed and I remember London feeling very strange because obviously people couldn't use any public transport so it … had a weird feel about it.

Some patients appreciated nurses being honest with them about the full extent of their injuries, no matter how life changing they were:

> we opened up the Trauma Ward the day that the 7/7 bombs went off … and a lot of work after that with the patients who'd been affected … that was an area that I was always very interested in, in post-traumatic stress … I think I provided some of what wasn't there … dealing with the people who had literally life-changing trauma and so few nurses are able to talk to patients at grassroots about … dying, about massive injury, consequences … there was a girl there who'd got … amputations … and I said to her 'OK', I said, 'So how are you', she went, 'Oh I'm OK', so I said … 'So how do you feel about the amputation', and she just broke down, and she said to me 'You're the first person who's asked me about that', she said … 'People are sort of almost like, acting like it doesn't exist'. *Lesley*

As Lesley goes on to describe, sometimes nurses do become involved and show their emotions:

> that was … another thing I think I learnt in nursing 'don't not say things because you're upset'…. 'Say what you think the patient wants'…. Because if you try and constantly hide from your own feelings, even if people say to you 'don't get involved', you have to be involved to be a nurse, it's ridiculous… .Don't lose control if you can … and sometimes you will and that's not a crime … to me, being professional is about knowing what's happening to you, is knowing perhaps what your limitations are but also being able to turn round to people and say that I did it … often you're crying because you can't cope with the situation you're doing.

Following the bombings members of the local Bangladeshi population feared censure, but offered practical support:

> I remember some of the Bangladeshi patients … particularly a man holding my hand crying, saying, 'This isn't my fault, please don't blame me', because obviously people were, there was already feelings that it was … [a terrorist attack] and I remember … lots of people, the local community coming to the hospital wanting to donate blood and do stuff. *Rebecca*

A change in culture?

Lilian considers the future:

> Kindness and care … backed up by a government that empowers you to do that properly and well because what distresses me as a nurse is that it's so easy to de-humanise your interactions with patients because of pressure of time or because of under staffing or because of the extent of tasks that you're expected to carry out. … [P]art of being a nurse is being soft and being hard, you've got to have a hard shell as a nurse but you must never lose that kindness … we need to stop treating people as if they're commodities on an industrial scale. *Lilian*

The following narrative is from Matthew, who having trained as a nurse, decided to train as a doctor, therefore experiencing nursing from two angles:

> Obviously having seen both sides now … I mean with no disrespect to all the nurses that I've worked with … nurses just don't seem to support each other … as soon as anything goes wrong they're the first to point the finger. Whereas with doctors they all support each other, there's a lot more support from their medical union, the BMA.

He feels nurses are increasingly taking on far wider roles, but sadly, often continue to feel unsupported, and afraid of potential sanctions which could be imposed by their professional body:

> I really think nurses are, or can be, very highly skilled. I once had a doctor request bloods for a patient and I asked him to do it and he said, 'No, you do it far more often so I'd prefer it if you took the bloods', and I think examples like that … prove that … nurses are capable and with the right training they can be capable of doing absolutely anything. I think there just needs to be a change in culture.

The seventeen years of this new millennium have seen many changes at The Royal London Hospital. The apprenticeship model style of training which was started at The London Hospital in 1880 has moved to a graduate education programme. Patients are now cared for in the new twenty-first century 'fit for purpose' hospital which was opened in time for the London 2012 Olympics. While some nurses felt a sense of loss on moving out of the old hospital buildings, the new building has given nurses and patients more space and privacy. The hospital continues to serve the local community and constantly adapts to the diversity of its patients. Since the Millennium the rapid pace of modern technological development continues with its constant impact on healthcare delivery. This coupled with ever changing political responses towards the provision of healthcare has led to ever increasing demands being placed on a finite resource, along with changes in society. The new hospital was built to meet those changing health care needs of patients, and the staff continue to serve the local community, and constantly adapt to the diversity of its patients.

Chapter 8

Moving on

the thing that nursing does for you, it gives you a basis … to do so much, travel … different jobs, become a specialist. I think … one of the good things about now … you can stay clinical. *Janice*

While previous chapters have included events after training, this chapter is entirely dedicated to 'what next'? As in all walks of life, some nurses opted to remain in clinical practice in hospital or to work in their local community. Others decided to move into management, education, research, government, or a combination of these; some rose through the ranks to become 'high fliers'. Some left The Royal London never to return, others could not wait to come back!

Diverse opportunities

I wanted to do emergency nursing … I went to A&E at [another hospital] … stayed there for six months, I did like it but it was a bit dull, so I came back … I couldn't be doing with [the people], they'd be giving out if they lost a pashmina and you're like, really, this man is having a heart attack, you're giving out to me about your pashmina … it was very frustrating. So I came back to The London … to 'real' people. *Victoria*

A spiritual calling:

I got married just as I was finishing [my training], and I'd already been selected to go forward for training for the church. *Donna*

Some recognised a need for change:

I was a bit fed up with hospitals … so … I went into a children's home … for children under 5 … I had a lot of newborn babies which I loved. *Irene*

I staffed on Sophia Ward for almost a year, then … [I saw an] ad for Pontins in Sardinia … they wanted a hotel nurse for the summer … I … met Fred Pontin there…. He said, 'I'm absolutely delighted to meet you … because you're from The London Hospital', because he funded the new theatre [at The London] when I was there. *Carol*

Seeing the world, flying high

I took time out … [to work for] BOAC. … In those days glamour was an air stewardess or a model … I'd always fancied air stewardessing … the first [flight] I was on was New York back and forth, and then they opened up the Far East [route] … to Australia [which] took about … fifteen days, and we were called 'British Overdue Airways', always delayed going east … always refuelling … I would do the Far Eastern and I was on the first trip where we were all invited … big cocktail parties, very wealthy people in Hong Kong, and it was there that the stewards were enrolled with all the gold smuggling…. And I was on one flight with a guy that obviously … they had these padded waistcoats with the gold bars and of course the money they were making, and we were going into Delhi and the skipper warned him … BOAC could do nothing … so of course he ended up … in an Indian jail. *Iris*

For some, such as Winifred, marriage had to wait:

a medical student who became a doctor just as I was leaving [The London] … asked my father could he have my hand in marriage … I liked him … but then I said I wanted to see the world … so I joined the Princess Mary's Royal Air Force Nursing Service as a … flying officer … I then decided … to go to Canada and so I [later] joined the Royal Canadian Air Force. I had to go to London to put my hand on the bible to swear to serve the Queen of Canada, and I thought 'she's my Queen you know.' Anyway, I flew to … Ontario, had three months at Officer School there…. So off I go to Newfoundland … I'm the only female on the whole station … and then I learnt to fly, I used to take on-call through the control tower … because it was Air Search and Rescue, so you had to be on-call all the time, I had five staff … in the end I was so bored I volunteered to help in the Sunshine Camp for Crippled Children for Eskimos and Indian children. *Winifred*

Others, such as Jennifer, chose to gain experience in America. Here she describes challenging the ward culture in the 1960s:

New York … they asked me to run a ward that had been a problem ward and the problem was that there was a racial issue … the black nurses and the white nurses didn't talk to each other, the black nurses used to come in with gloves on to wash a white patient, you wouldn't really believe this, and … the white nurses were doing the same for the black ones…. So I put down guidelines, I was not having that, I didn't want any gloves … and I wanted them to look after all patients as they would look after their own family, and it did get better.

'Into Blue'

Going 'into blue' was a significant achievement in whichever decade you trained:

I was summoned to Matron's Office and offered a relief sister post … and I said, 'No, I was really happy in Upper Wards, I've only been there five months and I'd like to stay,' and she said, and I remember this very clearly, 'Let me put it this way staff nurse, you can either do relief duties in a purple dress or you can do relief duties in a blue dress'. *Helen*

I was [a] black sister on the wards at that time … a lot of the people just around the hospital got to know me quite well, and you know, there were a few black workers that were really proud to see a black sister, and they were like, you know, 'Wow,' you know. It was something that they obviously hadn't seen. I think some of the other sisters didn't quite know how to accept me, initially. Some of them had been there a long time … they didn't quite know how to take to me, which is a huge contrast to the way the hospital is now. I mean, we have BME networks … they want to see black and minority ethnic workers progress. But back then, I think it was a bit of a shock to the system for me to be suddenly in the midst. So it wasn't always easy, but it wasn't all bad, either. *Kim*

after two years … I became sister on the ward … the most prestigious moment of my career … that's all I'd ever wanted to be was a sister on a ward … a really big moment. *Emma*

Increasing bureaucracy:

I went to outpatients, where I stayed for twenty-four years … it was so much easier to get things done … I even got … my clinic decorated, just through talking to the staff, but it's very, very different now. I mean, you've got to go through rounds of emails and paperwork to get anything done … everything has to be costed, but back then it was … very informal and on a more personal level. *Kim*

Challenging times included:

when you were the sister of the ward, if you were on duty at Mile End, you were very often in charge of the hospital as well as looking after your own ward, so it was not easy. *Lesley*

Hazel found:

there was an opportunity to become a relief sister … I was sent to … Devonshire Ward, covering [for] one of the sisters … I shadowed her for a few days … we'd got the Dialysis Unit then, which was fairly new [opened in 1968], and they'd only recently started doing kidney transplants, and I remember her parting words, 'Don't worry about transplants, we haven't had any for ages,' and I went on duty the next day and there were two!

And from being a relief sister to becoming a ward sister:

I became the ward sister [for a different ward] … the consultants took private patients … some of them easier to work with than others … I've nursed … lovely people, you never ever felt uncomfortable with them, but then equally you would get … oh, I suppose you'd call them the nouveau riche, who thought they absolutely owned you, and expected you to be skivvies.

Becoming a ward sister did not always protect you from deprecating remarks, as Gladys found:

my first day as sister [this consultant] said to me, 'How is Mr X?'… I said, Oh I think he's had a slightly better day, and he said, 'I don't want you to think anything, I want it to either be yes it is or no it's not, but not I think so,' and that lived with me all my life. I still feel bad if I say I think so!

At night, Gillian found her care and compassion extended to the junior medical staff:

[I] became a night sister. I enjoyed it ... and we had opportunities to act up, you know, take turns in running the hospital ... we did the ward rounds ... we did most of the checking of the drugs. So you were on your feet all night ... to give the IV drugs, to take radium out ... covered the [Dialysis] Unit ... very good preparation for me ... in my later life as a nurse practitioner, and taking autonomy, taking responsibility, and of course whether or not to get the doctors up, sometimes just so dog tired you'd literally have to pull them out of bed and get them dressed ... they did such long hours, and they were all quite young, junior, and if they were on for a whole weekend and part of that weekend was a Bank Holiday, they were like zombies ... I remember one had an epileptic fit ... it was just through sheer exhaustion ... and they daren't say anything because they were so lucky to have a job at The London ... and also we kept them safe ... clinically.

There was 'light' relief for some, as Michael describes:

at the end of seven nights the night sisters would have a gin party. ... So we'd go to the Tower Hotel in London or to Spitalfields Market where some of the places were open early in the morning, have breakfast with quite a lot of gin and then you got seven days off ... a lot of [the market traders] ... they would buy you drinks and it ... was unwinding from the seven nights.

Beyond 'blue'; on becoming matron:

I became assistant matron, deputy matron, matron ... it was an easier job to run the hospital than it was to run [a ward]. Yes, it was straightforward ... it wasn't such a worrying job as the clinical bits! *Gladys*

When I walked up the steps my first morning at The London [as matron] and the old tramps were sitting there or the alcoholics. As I walked in they said, 'Good morning ma'am', and I thought, 'I've come home', because that's what we remembered it as, and they were still there. *Brenda*

Passionate About Public Health Nursing

Improving public health should be part of all nursing and midwifery roles. Over the past 150 years the role of the health visitor has evolved in response to the priorities for health promotion.

Somebody said, 'Why don't you do health visiting?'... I thoroughly enjoyed it ... and then I went to London University ... to do the Diploma in Health Education before I became Health Education Officer ... I got an MBE. *Joan*

Iris remembers:

at the end of the staff year ... [sister] said to me, 'Get out of this place ... you can always come back ... explore the world ... The London's always going to be here,' and that was incredible advice ... we all hitch-hiked in those days ... hitch-hiked around Italy for a couple of months ... a girl that I trained with and myself, and then I went back and did midwifery.

And after some years she worked as a health visitor:

> I went to the South Bank … it was the new Faculty of Nursing at the South Bank and we were the first entrants to do this Diploma in Health Visiting … I loved health visiting, loved it.

Winfred recalls the needs of one new mother in her care:

> I'm absolutely passionate about health visiting … all the experience I've had with life made me a better health visitor…. It was on the thirteenth [floor of a] tower block and I went to see this young mum with her baby and she looked very nice and the baby was fine, we had a long chat, and then I said something about being a mother … and it was something … she said … made me worried, a thirteenth floor, husband away working in … the Falklands, her grandmother whom she loved very much had just died, she'd no mother and father … then I had a telephone call from the NSPCC and they said [they had a phone call] from somebody [about someone] who wants to kill her baby and she lives on the thirteenth floor on this block…. And then I had another telephone call from somebody else who said that the neighbours are complaining 'cos the baby's always crying at night … went to my boss and said I'll have to see this lady very frequently'. She said, 'Sorry but you've got the most [clients]'. I had all these tall high-rise blocks … and there were loads of new babies. 'You won't be able to manage it'. I thought, 'What can I do?'… so I said to this young mother 'I'm gonna ask you a favour … I always have a lot to do in this area so I always sit in the car and eat my sandwiches and I usually use the toilets down below but now they're all broken … so would you mind very much if I used your toilet every day?' She said, 'Well why don't you bring your sandwiches up here and eat them with me … it would be company'. So of course in my lunch hour I saw her every day and of course we talked, we didn't talk about babies, we just talked about clothes and make-up and life in general.
>
> …it was the end of the second week and she said, 'I've got something to tell you but you won't like me if I tell you this … I want to kill my baby … I know that sounds terrible but I can't cope with looking after him … I go to the kitchen, I get a wooden spoon, I wrap it round with cotton wool and then I hit him over the head with it' … so then she started to cry and I said, 'Now look the baby's fine, the baby will survive come what may, but you're the one I'm worried about … I'm not worried about the baby,' although of course … naturally I was concerned, but I said, 'You need looking after don't you?'… So I said, 'Well I'm going out now to phone the … social worker and ask them to take your baby, now when you're better you'll get your baby back so don't worry about that…'. In those days you didn't have a mobile, so I had to go to the phone box. I phoned the Child Protection Officer, 'You have to come immediately to take this baby', I said. 'It's no good doing it in two hours or tomorrow, you've got to do it now otherwise I take no responsibility…'. I had a good relationship with them and they did come right away and take the baby … and then I told her doctor … she was admitted for a short time [to the local psychiatric hospital], and they brought the husband home from the Falklands…. It was the mother, and nowadays they don't seem to care about the mothers.

Public health nursing also attracted those such as Kathleen, who initially wished to travel, and then gave much of her life to caring for those living in Africa:

> We decided, before we got too old, we were both 28 at that time, that we would like to go abroad. So we went to ... the province of Alberta, as public health nurses.... For the first time in my life I had some money ... a big car ... you perhaps covered 200 miles a day.... Also, we were responsible for the health in schools, and ... Ukrainian settlements.
>
> [T]hen ... I decided I'd like to enter religious life ... I made my first vows ... worked for one year ... in a major seminary ... and then I was assigned to Africa, where I spent the next thirty-seven years ... preventing illness ... most of those years ... were spent in remote areas where we trained the person, chosen by that local community, to be their community health worker.... She, it was often a woman, had brought up her own family... [was] experienced in living already, and we took a group of them together from the various little communities around, and we gave them very basic skills, but with those skills they could save lives. You know, the simple one of what to do when ... a baby has diarrhoea....They did wonders for their people, and their people didn't have money but they could help them by cultivating their land for them. If they delivered a baby then, if they were very fortunate, they'd give them a chicken or something like that, you see. They were paid in kind ... money didn't really come into it.

Norma remembers:

> when I left school ... I was head [girl] ... you were meant to go on to Oxford and Cambridge and so on but I said, 'No, I'm doing nursing,' and they were horrified.... What on earth are you doing nursing for?' And I never regret it, it's a wonderful preparation for life ... I did my degree as a part-time evening student ... I wanted the social context of healthcare and so I did social sciences.... Now I do a lot of humanitarian aid work abroad and it really takes me back to where I began, that nursing is a wonderful preparation for ... healthcare that takes place around the world, especially in developing countries ... it is in relatively rural areas and nursing is at the front line and the basics don't change, rehydration for diarrhoea ... prevent malaria rather than treat it.

District nursing

The District Nursing service is now over 150 years old, providing an invaluable service to individuals, families and communities. Tina relates her experiences:

> I did the community in '87.... Initially I worked in Bow... all around the Roman Road and Mile End ... I can remember when it snowed, couldn't get my car out so ... everyone put their wellies on ... and got around, and patients being very grateful that you actually had come out.
>
> [O]ne lady ... had a really dirty house and she was infested with lots of interesting things and we had to go in and give her a bath, but to give her a bath we had to clear the mouse poo out of the bath, clean the bath ... help her in, she wasn't particularly mobile or cooperative I seem to remember ... and then we had

this antiseptic … it was because she had fleas and head lice … quite a military operation to get this done.

I remember there was a couple I used to visit … they didn't have a bathroom, they … used to wash in the kitchen sink and that lady had quite extensive leg ulcers…. But … you went through the kitchen and the toilet area out onto a little balcony and then you could look out all over the back of the tenements.

[T]he Police Station in Arbour Square was used as a Court on Thursdays … they used to have quite high security prisoners arrive and they would seal off either end of the road. They would have armed policemen on the roof … but they allowed the District Nurse through to give the insulin … so that was always quite an adventure.

[O]ne of the reasons for coming out of uniform was the fact that, when you were in uniform, you were advertising to the world … that your patients were vulnerable … I can remember … we were visiting a young guy who was HIV positive and dying of AIDS … he wouldn't have wanted uniforms. Why would he want to advertise it? … [W]hen I subsequently went to work in [south-east London] and the nurses came out of uniform there was a lot of people against it, but actually … you are making your patients vulnerable and it is security.

Dawn feels there is less job satisfaction now:

I find nowadays, I would honestly say seventy per cent of my time is taken up with various templates, documenting what I've done, and I spend thirty per cent of my day with patients … I don't feel that's what I trained to do, and this obsession with documentation which is not improving care because you're rushing your visits, because you know how long [it's] going to take you to document. It's barmy!

Midwifery

The history of midwifery is complex. In the UK, its origins can be traced back to Anglo-Saxon times. It was not until the 1902 Midwives Act that there was legal recognition, compulsory training and regulation of midwifery.

I did my eighteen-month post registered midwifery [training]. I did nine months at Homerton Hospital, and nine months at the Whitechapel site. I mean The Homerton was the same hospital group but a very different hospital to Whitechapel … Homerton was very modern, purpose built [in 1986]…. The London Hospital had not changed at all. *Dawn*

A delivery in the community, in the 1960s, became a challenging experience for Pauline:

when I decided to leave midwifery it was probably [because of] a bad experience because I did love it but … when I was doing the district [as] a pupil midwife … my midwife [supervisor] used to send me ahead to assess a situation before she got there…. I got to this house and it was the woman's fourth baby and when I got there she was about to deliver … and she delivered fine, but then the placenta wasn't coming away … so I tried to rub up a contraction and when I gave a push, my goodness, at least two pints of blood came whooshing out and she was saying to me, 'Ooh, I feel a bit dizzy' and we used to carry a little card … for the Flying

Squad, and you just had to write the address and a simple message so I put PPH [postpartum haemorrhage] … I said to [her husband], 'Run to the nearest phone box, dial this number…', and I thought, 'Where is my midwife?' The woman was almost unconscious and we did carry … ergometrine…. The Flying Squad got there very, very quickly … and of course midwife arrives now! They put up O-neg [blood] and pumped it in with the old-fashioned Martin's pump … with the wheel … it was like a red rubber tube … that went into a cannula in the patient's arm … and you had to wind the wheel to push the blood in. Anyway, she obviously was taken off to hospital and I was absolutely distraught because … I thought she was going to die. I went to see her … I said to her, 'All your notes had said normal pregnancy … have you had problems before?' And she wasn't the brightest spark in the box, anyway she said, 'Oh yes, I've always had to have the afterbirth removed because it didn't come away but I thought if I told them that they'd make me to go to hospital to have the baby, and I wanted to have the baby at home.'

For those who remained in midwifery:

I went up to Inverness and worked as a health visitor up there. But during that time I realised you needed to be a midwife. All the nurses up there were triple duty – district nurse, health visitor, midwife – and I felt very much left out and lacking a lot of knowledge because I wasn't a midwife and I did miss The London a lot. So I applied to do … my midwifery at The London … I think in my whole nursing career I've enjoyed midwifery the most. *Dawn*

I'm a midwife … a coordinator, or sister in old money, on the delivery suite…. Work mostly nights, which I've done for, gosh, about fifteen years now. *Gloria*

Career paths and progression

A career in nursing can be so diverse. Marina combined clinical progression with academic study:

in 1961 I did the … sister's course … worked for six months in Rothschild Ward … [then] sent to … Brentwood [Annexe] … I returned to The London as night superintendent … [then] I took the Diploma in Nursing at the Royal College of Nursing. I was allowed to go back on duty an hour late … it was the only way because it was an evening course … [I then] went to Bristol … and worked as an assistant matron there … in 1967 I returned to The London for two years, to do the … Sister Tutor Diploma Course, which was at the Royal College of Nursing … we did a lot of physiology and science studies with the Medical College at the Middlesex Hospital, including our visits to the post-mortem rooms for dissections and that type of thing.

Rachel used her specialist knowledge:

I wanted to specialise in nursing the physically disabled and so I moved to the … then Royal Hospital and Home for Incurables in Putney, now known as the Royal Hospital and Home … they did a post-registration course … and then staffed there … I can remember one young man. I think he was only 17, and he was on the Rehab Unit and he'd collapsed ... in the hospital he was attending, and nobody knew whether it was a spontaneous brain haemorrhage ... or whether he had a seizure, fell and banged his head, but whatever, he [was transferred] to us labelled as being in a vegetative state. We took him to the speech therapist and within half an hour he was able to spell things out on a board, because nobody actually bothered to look at how he could communicate.... And we had another lady who was an anaesthetic disaster, strangely enough from The London, and she'd been in there for two years.... She came to Putney and within a couple of weeks the tracheostomy was out, feeding tube was out, just think what we could have done if we'd had her two years earlier.

The introduction of new nursing roles was also rewarding as Louise found:

I had a friend who was a GP, who I met through my voluntary work with homeless people, and he'd just got his own practice and was very keen to have a practice nurse which was a new thing at the time [in the 1990s] ... I loved it, absolutely loved it, just around the corner from The London.

Some interviewees reflected on the way experience in one role, together with transferable skills, can lead to ongoing career opportunities. Marina recalls:

in 1974, I ... was very fortunate in getting a Florence Nightingale Scholarship to the United States, and I travelled ... I was visiting hospitals, colleges and universities, both for nursing, medical and dentistry, and looking at their ... learning techniques and the whole emphasis was ... looking at how the application of theory to practice was perceived and taught, and what methods they were using.

I went back to the London, and I was there then until 1975 ... I became involved with the Diploma in Nursing Course and setting that up at The London.

Marina describes her later involvement in the development of Project 2000:

[I then] went to work at the Department of Health ... briefing a succession of Secretaries of State ... [later] I looked after the education division for the whole of the UK ... it was the time when they were setting up Project 2000, very, very difficult for me because I did not agree with it ... but I couldn't say so because it was government policy ... but I did make sure that I appointed somebody who I knew was ... capable of being able to cope with that remarkably well. I just felt it was being pushed through too hurriedly ... I didn't disagree with the university background ... what worried me was ... not being prepared in the right way ... they needed more practical [experience], and they also needed to prepare the trained staff in the ward for the different type of training ... unfortunately, it clashed with all the managerial reorganisation in the hospitals where they had removed a lot of experienced people from the wards.

Stephen remembers:

I did a Masters in Medical Education ... because I've always been interested in education but I never wanted to be a tutor ... but I've used it to develop leadership, decision making skills and also used it to educate multi-professional teams because that's one of the good things in the Army ... you do get to lead multi-professional teams, so you have doctors and dentists and physios on the command not only nurses.

Michael recalls how his career developed:

it was [sister] who said to me, 'Look, if you're going to get on in nursing you need to spread your wings and you need to do something probably in a District General Hospital and see a different experience'. So a post came up ... a nursing officer post for trauma ... and orthopaedics and I hadn't done orthopaedics but, typical man, I thought I'd give it a go and I got the job.

[then] it was a big leap, it was the Assistant Chief Nurse job working at the District Health Authority ... manpower planning, capital developments, all the workforce staff and also the start of Project 2000.

and describes his progression:

I [then] became the Director of Policy and Standards for the UKCC when it was just about to merge with the NMC, and I was the first non-educationalist to be appointed to the UKCC ... [then] a job came up at NHS Direct ... they wanted a Clinical Director to manage ... New Media ... their website television services.

Career paths beyond nursing

I left the NHS and went to the 'dark side' and worked for one of the company's supplying the [stoma] pouches and things, but I still kept my nursing registration ... basically I see nurses that do the job that I did ... it's good for me 'cos it keeps my hand in, and you can swap information and ideas of practices between them. *Simon*

And then I jetted off to ... Malta and I worked in a hospital there ... even though I'd never done a placement [as a student] in haemodialysis, they put me on the haemodialysis unit ... the Maltese government is struggling just as much as any country to find nurses and they place you wherever they desperately need [staff] ... after a year there I loved it, it was really interesting ... not all the patients spoke English so there was a bit of a communication barrier. I picked up some Maltese eventually.... And then whilst I was out there I applied for medicine ... I've wanted to do medicine since [I was] a kid ... I left school at 16. I thought that was the end of the road for medicine because I didn't do my A Levels and I wasn't aware that there were alternative routes into medicine ... on [one of the] wards there was a junior doctor ... she was one of the best doctors I've ever worked with. She had such a caring manner with the patients.... There was one patient [with] pancreatic cancer ... he was End of Life care and ... he used to lie in his bed all day, obviously he was really down and a recluse, and any other doctor who saw him just ... didn't bother about him.... But she took the initiative to talk to him and suggest ... antidepressants even though ... he'd only got a few weeks ... I started speaking to her about medicine ... and that was it, the spark had been ignited. *Matthew*

Sharon recalls:

> The core of what I do has always been nursing.
>
> [B]y the time I'd finished being a Staff Nurse ... I never went back full-time to any clinical nursing ... life just takes you in different directions. Because I'd been doing the writing I was then offered a wonderful opportunity to work on *Nursing Mirror* doing journalism training. I was so impatient for change ... it always felt that change had to come from top down rather than 'Why can't we get together and do it ourselves?' which the work I led at the King's Fund was doing. Because all the wisdom is there in the team.... Ask the frontline staff, they'll tell you ... the core of what I do has always been nursing and I've just tried to help it along in different ways, in different roles and I've had a very interesting and unusual career doing that.

And for Paul:

> I [now] practice as a hospital chaplain ... the challenges that I see ... for nurses who give a lot of themselves ... I don't see nurses today are any better looking after themselves or looking for support ... being a good nurse is not just about knowledge and professionalism, it's also about being true to yourself.

Educating past, current and future generations

Over the decades the nursing curriculum evolved from a training programme to degree level education. Initially, schools of nursing were based in hospitals:

> I became a tutor. I always made quite a thing about the importance of doing ... last offices, and how one should do it with the greatest dignity possible.... And, interestingly, years later, when I was [in] hospital ... one of the nurses said, 'I know you, you were my tutor, and I particularly remember you teaching us last offices'... it was a great thing to say to me just as I was going down [for]surgery! *Marina*

Some, such as Norma, ventured further afield but returned to nurse education:

> And then I worked in the academic world at a rough tough time, teaching sociology, where the majority of staff were hard-line communists ... written a book about that ... I then was appointed to be Director of the Nursing Education Research Unit ... University of London.

The phasing out of roles included that of the clinical teacher. Teaching in a dynamic clinical area, as opposed to a controlled classroom setting, requires experience, flexibility and ingenuity. However, in the late 1980s, it appeared that the application of theory in practice, skill development at the bedside, and role modelling were undervalued compared to classroom learning.

> I became a ward sister and then a clinical teacher ... which I loved because you work partly in the school, partly in practice, you work with a student on a one-to-one basis, what could be better than that? ... But then the profession in its wisdom phased out clinical teachers ... there was ... no clinical progression, and we were all expected to be tutors, nurse teachers, lecturers, whatever you now want to call us, I thought that was so short sighted. *Carol*

Another nursing role that was phased out, this time during the 1990s, after the restructuring of nurse education under Project 2000, was the role of the SEN:

> I loved my training as an SEN, but reluctantly converted to RGN through peer pressure. I later became a specialist nurse in bladder and bowel [care]. *Veronica*

An integral part of the role of a registered nurse is supporting student nurses in their learning. Sound advice includes:

> Constantly acquiring new knowledge, and applying what you've learnt, and realising ... that you've got student nurses who rely on you so much. *Hazel*

Veronica emphasises the need to:

> be a good mentor to the students and pass on your experiences. Students will always remember a kind, thoughtful and considerate 'teacher' who taught them well.

But nowadays this can be challenging:

> according to the NMC the students have to work at least forty per cent of their shift with their mentors.... It's quite hard having to make sure that their shifts always match up with their mentor. *Laura*

Other challenges include:

> so I've got regional responsibilities now with Marie Curie [charity] as a practice development facilitator. ... [I]t's a big job. It consumes more than the hours that I'm paid for ... and I still make sure I do one night a month because I want to be current in my practice. *Deborah*

Role modelling is a powerful teaching strategy as Rachel has found:

> I've been working in a specialist dementia unit nursing home ... I have managed to change their attitude to one of the women in the side room ... she was violent, noisy and aggressive and I said I'd go and help change her ... we came out ten minutes later and the ward manager actually said to us, 'Why haven't you changed her?' We said, 'We have changed her.' She said, 'But I didn't hear her scream.' We said, 'Why should you hear her scream? We treated her with respect ... explained everything we were doing and actually there was no need for her to scream.' One of the carers actually said to me, 'I'm a "Dementia Champion", but ... I've been going in there like a bull in a china shop. I need to talk to her.'... I want everybody to treat the patients as individuals, not just as a diagnosis or a case history.

There is no substitute for the patient as the best teaching and learning aid:

> the patients are your tutors...all they ask of you is that you walk alongside and do what you can, and bring your skills and knowledge to their care. *Wendy*

Gillian remembers the sage advice she received back in her training and the need to keep an open mind:

> I took away from him [the paediatrician], something which I have never forgotten, 'That little human being before you. Anything you want to know

about him or her, you ask the mother. Nobody else in this world … will know as much about that little person … your responsibility is to make sure that you … unlock the information that she has. That … you listen to her, but also you ask the right questions which will glean the information you need.' That has been a real thing for me to hang onto over many years. And especially when I was a nurse practitioner, when I had sole responsibility. And people were rushed through the door, I always remembered, 'Ask the mother.' And the other thing was be wary of a child who rushes up and cuddles everyone. Not a nice, quiet little child. Start asking a few more questions.

I came across … a retired nurse, and she'd been in [hospital] for some time … they just [couldn't] find anything wrong with this woman…. 'Oh, well [they said] before we send her home, perhaps we'll just get the psychiatrist to see her', because she was just obsessed with this pain … within … an hour … of the … [psychiatrist] seeing her … she was whipped off to theatres, and she had a tumour. I was sent [to bring her] back to the ward … and she was saying, 'You have no idea the relief it is to be believed.'… [A] message I took … with me. How important it is … to listen to the patient and not jump to your own conclusion. In fact, as we got more senior, [also] not to allow doctors to jump to conclusions.

Norma emphasises the value of personal experience:

I had the best nursing education anyone could possibly have which was six months as a patient with renal tuberculosis…. You can tell a definitively good nurse and not a good nurse the minute you become a patient.

The 1990s chapter referred to the merger of the schools of nursing as Richard describes:

I kept being invited to the Princess Alexandra [College of Nursing] to teach about HIV, because there were very few nurses in the UK at that time that had any experience to teach nursing students, and … they asked me if I would … develop a degree in sexual health and a programme on HIV, which I did, it was the second one in the UK and then [I became] a lecturer practitioner … and within a year we'd merged with Barts.

we all applied for our jobs … it should have been an equal relationship because it was two major schools … Princess Alexandra [School of Nursing] is five years older than Barts School of Nursing, which we like to tell them, although of course their hospital is much older than ours…. Eventually it changed, but it just felt more hierarchical, more formal and more distant from the population.

and I became a lecturer, and then we were incorporated, in '95, into City University where I work now … [in a senior role] … I'm [also] a link lecturer … so I go every couple of weeks solely to see students at The London … preparing the nurses of the future.

Lifelong learning

I wouldn't say I'm an 'expert' because it always changes, care changes, treatment changes, protocols change, but I love what I do and I'm enthusiastic to keep learning. *Kerry*

[The] Open University only take your credits from fifteen years … I said don't you realise you're missing out on a whole group of people that trained in '92 to '95? They changed the rules, so they will take now anyone that did a diploma from '92 onwards … so I'm finally doing [the degree] … it's been challenging, but relevant … it's just hard – working, family and studying. *Emma*

For Lilian, a recent, mature, graduate in nursing, the profession has opened up new avenues:

I left [The Royal London] … very quickly managed to find a job at a care home … I have a care home with forty-four elderly, frail people, and I love my relationships with them, and I love them and I'm not ashamed to say that … every shift is rewarding, tiring but rewarding, and that's what's been given to me, by being given the chance at the age of 58 to train as a nurse. *Lilian*

Pioneers

Nurses are often among the first people to identify the need for change, develop a new service, and support innovation in practice as Sharon describes:

When I think about my experience at The London, it fired me up, a lot of it was very positive but a lot of it wasn't, and it made me very passionate about wanting to change the system, partly the system of education but also the system of care and the whole nature of the health system. So it lit a fire in me that still burns. The experiences were so powerful that it fuelled me to do the things I've done since then in my very varied career, so it was a gift, in a paradoxical way.

Wendy highlights how she developed the breast cancer nursing specialism:

in 1978 I'd been doing health visiting for two to three years … and I sat on the edge of my seat [at a conference], listening to these speakers who were nurses … and I got the 'ah [ha] syndrome' because I could see what could be done…. And I set up and developed that service on the health visiting model. I visited newly diagnosed women with breast cancer in their own homes, and I attended the clinics … and it was incredible. And that's where it evolved, a specialist nurse role … what I was doing in that job was giving information, practical help, and emotional support. And those are the three foundations of clinical nurse specialism … I did the first Master's degree that was set up for cancer nursing at the University of Surrey … I managed to get a grant to set up a breast cancer nursing course with the [then] English National Board … we got a grant from government … we did it through a consensus conference … all the other disciplines were allowed twenty minutes to state their case, radiologists, surgeons and that, nursing got ten minutes, I've never spoken so fast in my life … we set the course up and the rest is history.

Jennifer relates her move and the opportunities that came with becoming a clinical specialist nurse:

a brand-new post, the specialist had just started and they wanted somebody to start a breast care service and a stoma care service … I knew I thought a lot about stoma care because this was also the ward I had in America … they used to have, in the early days, terrible skin problems.... With the merger ... Barts was going to have the breast care and The London was having the stoma care and I wanted to do the stoma care ... I got encouraged to talk at the School of Nursing, I then got asked to talk in Eastern Europe ... in Hungary and the Czech Republic ... Poland and Turkey.

Denise describes the beginning of Palliative Care services:

myself and another nurse from Hackney Hospital set up the Macmillan Palliative Team as a nursing only service and that's, well, nearly thirty years ago ... it's grown dramatically. We started off with two nurses in a small room at The London to now seventeen people in a much bigger office suite at Bart's Hospital.

Services for children:

When I first started ... it was just officers from the Child Protection Team and then their role changed and so I ended up working with the CID, the community safety units who dealt with all the rape, non-family rapes ... I worked with murder teams, I worked with a massive broad spectrum of police officers which was good, and I was very, very proud because when I retired I was given a commendation by Tower Hamlets Police. *Phyllis*

coming back here [to The Royal London] and setting up the shared care service [for children]. [A colleague] and I worked really, really hard and brought all of our expertise and skills, along with the locum consultant at the time, and I'm very proud to say that we did this. *Kerry*

Helen recalls her experience of beginning to use research to underpin patients' needs:

Quality Assurance was new, there were books written about it, but mainly from America ... I spent the first month or two reading in the library and then I interviewed lots of senior people ... and I focused on outcomes, and I started off doing point prevalence scores for pressure sores ... I did The Royal London, Mile End and the Community. So I did a lot of visiting ... and the most shocking thing was the Community had practically no aids at all. So they'd got quadriplegics nursed at home, sleeping in ... a double bed with their spouse with a Grade 4 pressure sore ... I did quite a lot of ... fundraising ... we were buying aids ... and then of course it became a specialism, Tissue Viability.

One matron in particular spearheaded the use of computers at The London, chairing the first conference on computers in nursing and writing several books. Dawn remembers:

I know The London Hospital ... was one of the first hospitals to have a computer system.

New role development:

I'm quite proud of the work I did on medication errors ... there is now a Medicine Safety Nurse ... the other thing I did ... when it became apparent that people in more specialist roles were doing things and that they weren't always very clearly described what they were doing, and it wasn't always the case that their employer was very clear about what they were doing ... so we had a project of scoping what everyone was doing. *Helen*

Back to Nursing

Many interviewees returned to nursing after 'time out' for a family:

> when my youngest child was about two or three … I was really terrified of going back 'cos I thought, I don't know anything … it's been so long…and there was a tiny advert … asking for nurses … for night duty in the community … where I lived … so anyway this person, who's now a great friend of mine … was the nursing officer for night duty … said, 'Oh, you'd be absolutely perfect, when can you start?'… [S]o we laugh about it now but she always says … 'I wasn't really bothered about how up-to-date your clinical skills were 'cos I knew we could do something about those … I was looking for somebody that would fit in with the team.'… So I went back into nursing and I was a district nurse and I fell into community by accident and I loved it. *Janice*

> had my children and then worked in nursing homes … I was matron of a nursing home … I really enjoyed looking after the elderly … I always think that my basic nursing training at The London … stood me in good stead for that sort of care. *Beverley*

However, some, such as Kathryn, felt undervalued at first:

> At one stage I had to do a 'Return to Nursing' course and I was a little disillusioned by the content of the course, the way it was managed and the fact that … I was quite a senior nurse by then, had a lot of experience and … I felt really undervalued. All the things I'd done to date didn't seem to count for very much which was a little sad.

Despite this, she has continued her career:

> I did midwifery for several years … I also did home deliveries…. So then I had my family, four children … I did go back to work … when my youngest son was quite small … early nineties probably … I went back and started doing part-time practice nursing … because that fits in so well with family life … very much enjoyed my practice nursing. I worked in several different practices … always increasing my hours as the family got older. I did lots of specialist training in asthma, diabetes … travel medicine and cardiac courses … I became specialist in asthma and diabetes chiefly, but I did all aspects of practice nursing from treatment room, bandaging and dressings to … running my own clinics … very interesting.

For Hazel, primary care also provided an ideal opportunity to develop her skills:

> I saw an advertisement for an occupational health nurse … eventually I left to have a family. Had my two kids, did a bit of work as a care assistant in a local authority elderly persons' home. Absolutely hated it, because they didn't take any account of my qualification, and I saw too many things I didn't like, and then, hey presto, a local GP advertised. So that was 1990, when another government change came, and they all needed practice nurses…. Acquired more skills, did my family planning course, became a diabetic nurse, oh, did all sorts of things.

Who knows where nursing may take you?

I really enjoyed The London because … my interest in diversity was broadened … I can remember when I went on to be President at the RCN, diversity was very, very important … you learnt how rich it was and how it enriched life. *Wendy*

[The London] gave me that foundation and, even though I didn't realise it at the time, gave me the direction, which is the reason why I'm where I am now … the most senior nurse in the … [military]. *Stephen*

I acted as the Chief Exec [for an NHS Trust]. … I did it for a year and it was fantastic, but I said …, 'I think … I shall lose my nursing, I don't want to do that.' … Then the Chief Nurse job came up … it's been a fantastic career. *Janice*

Mayoral duties:

it's all about raising the profile of nurses, and when I was Mayor, we did the Remembrance Day service all around Edith Cavell. *Gillian*

I started to become involved with local politics and then … they were like … you could be a councillor, people would love you, you're a nurse, you work at The London.… I got elected in 2010 … [then] we need someone to be deputy mayor … I remember sort of just being overwhelmed … and so I ended up … the Deputy Mayor of Tower Hamlets. And the Trust loved it.… And so for me … The London is intrinsically linked with my love for the local area as well. *Rebecca*

For services to nursing:

My greatest achievement in my career was meeting the Queen Mother, who was patron for the Queens Institute of District Nursing, and receiving a long service award. *Veronica*

when I met the Queen … I said to her, I don't deserve to be here. I can think of hundreds of people I've met in my life who should be standing here in front of you. *Gillian*

This chapter has provided further insight into life after nurse training. The opportunities, challenges, rewards and diversity of practice are clearly evident. This snapshot of career pathways represents only a small sample of the thousands of nurses who have trained at The Royal London Hospital across the decades. It is inspiring to see how, for many, following the discipline and rigidity of basic training, they continued to reach their potential. The chapter also paves the way for current and future nurses. Previous generations have shared their wisdom, care and compassion and the opportunities they had for career progression. Most would no doubt agree that no matter which nursing journey is undertaken:

I'd just like to be remembered … for doing the best that I could, for being supportive to the staff, and giving the best care I possibly could to the patients. *Kim*

Chapter 9

How things have changed

[I]t always changes, care changes, treatment changes, protocols change. *Kerry*

the basis of nursing, which is compassion, empathy, understanding and all the sciences … that's all still there. *Richard*

All nurses are used to constant change in their working life, brought about through global technology, nursing, medical and pharmaceutical research and development and a rapidly ageing population.

it's very easy to look back and think it was all marvellous when it wasn't … when I led on all the reduction in healthcare associated infections, people used to say to me … 'well in your day … it wasn't like this', and I used to say, 'I had no idea, we never measured infection, we didn't know' … there are some fantastic things about now… newly-qualified nurses who are just fantastic. *Janice*

At this stage, during the second decade of the twenty-first century, it is a good time to reflect on how nursing has changed. These changes, coupled with numerous political decisions on how to adapt the NHS to cope with increasingly expensive treatments on limited resources, has led to interviewees from across all the decades expressing opinions on the changing face of health care. Many are now seeing the NHS from 'the other side of the blanket', albeit for friends, family or themselves. As can be seen from previous chapters, several of the nurses interviewed have continued in nursing throughout their lives, while others returned after taking a break to have a family. Over their careers they have seen many changes in nursing, its role in society and the role and skills required of a professional nurse.

The nurse's role

Economic and societal changes have had a huge impact on the role of nurses over the years. Over the past eight decades nursing has had to integrate the art of nursing and the science of treatment.

I think that obviously [there has] been significant changes in treatment … human beings are human beings [the] world over, and the art of caring is quite different from the science of treatment. *Paul*

Overall there has been a much greater breadth to the nurses' role, such as is found in primary care, and with the advent of nurse practitioners and nurse prescribing. Innovation and advances in pharmacology and medicine have impacted on, and changed nursing care:

now, as a nurse practitioner, we prescribe PPI tablets for people with dyspepsia and things, there was nothing like that … it was all big surgery, gastric surgery, vagotomies, pyloroplasties, tubes and drips, huge operations for what we can now prevent by putting somebody on a tablet to cut the acid mechanism. *Gail*

the treatments have improved enormously. As far as nursing is concerned I think they've tried to make us quasi-doctors too much so the basic nursing care is [lost]. *Rita*

Nurses have increasingly taken on a wider role, as Stephen describes:

There's so many nurses in advanced practice now.... They're not substituting doctors.... You can demonstrate now improvements in patient care and that's really what we've been championing here … demonstrating the requirement for advanced practice and for specialists but because when you're on your own, when you are autonomous or you're in remote and rural [areas] and you're either in charge of a small team or again you're practicing alone, you've got to have that decision advantage or decision superiority to make the right clinical decision the first time and that's very important.

Diversity

As patients menus change to reflect the diverse cultures of the hospital's patients, some can feel 'left-out' as Brenda relates:

I was doing a round one day and … I was talking to the patients and I saw this old gentleman who was a real cockney, who when I first said good morning to him he said, 'Oh who are you?' So I said, 'Well I'm the Director of Nursing', so he said, 'Bring back the bleeding matron', and I said, 'I am she'. He said, 'Sit down and I'll tell you a few things. … Get rid of these bleeding curries and give me some fish and chips'… I said, 'Oh, I'll see what I can do', and he was fine but those kind of things stick with you don't they? [On] … the elderly unit down at Mile End, the nurses said, 'Oh they wouldn't eat that and they wouldn't eat this', I said, 'Go out and get them fish and chips one night as a special treat, you can have the money' … and they did and they said, 'Well they did enjoy it', so I said, 'Yes, because it's what they're used to'.

Increasingly, nurses are of all nationalities and ethnicities, are both male and female, and of all sexual orientations, reflecting today's society. Over the decades some patients have often found this difficult.

Lilian describes the pain and discomfort of experiencing sexual discrimination:

those are the only incidents which I'd describe as transphobic where people seemed to be prejudiced against you. Because the great thing in healthcare is if you're actually meeting peoples' needs … and if you're a good team player with your colleagues, that's what they're looking for. And most people that you work with, as a transsexual nurse, the first shift, they may do a double take and they may not be sure what to make of you because they may not have ever met somebody who's trans before, or they may have … confused me with somebody who's transvestite … but actually … after you start working with them or in the case of a patient/client view, after you've gone in the second time … they just … start to think of you as a person.

Changes in nurse training and education

Some nurses feel that students no longer have a sound foundation in 'basic nursing care' at the start of their training:

> I think PTS was a very good start because we were very protected, but we dealt with real people, so I think that's something that's lacking in today's training … that first six weeks' grounding. Because I get students now who really don't know one end of a patient from the other…. They can tell you all about the anatomy and the physiology and all the psychological things and everything, but give them an actual person and they're not very good. *Rachel*

> they're now bringing back practical classrooms and getting people to learn the basics of nursing before they actually start the degree courses … somebody has picked up on the fact that they were missing out on the introductions and principles of it. *Marina*

Millennial interviewees also shared their concern, as Laura explains:

> people who trained at a similar time to myself are always saying that they don't feel that students have enough clinical experience these days. And talking to the students … they were saying that … in their first year there weren't enough paediatric placements … so they were actually child branch [paediatric students] but having adult placements, so placements at The London Chest or an adult ward at The London. … [T]hey're now wanting to cut the student nurse bursary with the aim … that more students can come and be … student nurses but actually there already aren't enough student placements, certainly for paediatrics, not entirely sure how that rationale … holds up. But we'll leave that to the government!

Emma adds:

> the clinical ward teachers are much missed and much needed, although mentorship has taken over and everyone is expected to be a mentor which is right.

Dawn provides the perspective of the supervisor with regard to current nurse training:

> it's so onerous having a student nurse [to supervise] now because there's so much paperwork, so many objectives … assessments, that all the joy of having a student working with you is being taken away because it becomes very much a task. Who's going to do her formative assessment and spend two or three hours sitting there, going through that? I think it's become too formalised.

Laura reflects on the difference between now and then:

> from … hearing about nurse training fifty years ago it sounds very different, in fact my boss talks about being left in charge … of the ward on a night shift as a student and she thinks student nurs[es] these days have it easy.

Kim, who trained in the 1980s, acknowledges the value of evidence based nursing care, with the patient at the centre:

> nursing was very task-orientated back in the sixties, seventies, and that changed … the era that I was brought up in … was a good era to come into, where you

did question things, it was evidence-based, as opposed to just doing something because that's the way it was [always] done ... I think that was good care that we were giving, good, basic care, it's about communicating, about treating the patient as a whole, all of that still applies.

Others feel that a combination of 'hands on care' coupled with a degree level education is essential:

We were a pair of hands, we were used and abused.... And of course the training now is far more expensive being degree trained nurses ... but you do need that knowledge, you do need that insight, but you need that hands-on as well. *Carol*

Student nurses no longer train solely in one hospital, and have placements within the numerous hospital and community settings in the Barts Health NHS Trust area. This often results in students not identifying with and 'belonging' to a particular hospital as Sharon relates:

Our training was hard as well but I suppose what's lacking, the thing that's changed, is that there was something about being a student nurse at The London Hospital, for all its faults, where you felt you were part of a community, both within the nursing body of the hospital and within the wider hospital and indeed within the social community.

[B]ut one of the unintended consequences of what I think was the right thing, to move nursing into university, is that the nursing students don't quite know where they belong, and because of the enormous turnover ... it's like a sausage machine ... so they don't even get to know each other that well, they travel immense distances ... they don't really have any relationship with the community in which the institution is and I suppose it's also part of the changes in society ... I don't feel my students, intelligent, well-intentioned people, have that sense of belonging anywhere.

Changes in the clinical setting

Trained staff also identify with a lack of belonging, in part due to the contracting out of many ancillary roles:

I do remember all the other staff that the hospital employed, like porters ... they had accommodation, they were fed ... ward maids from the Philippines that all lived on site ... that was the very nice thing about The London, it was a real community ... now, everything [is] being contracted out ... I think people do work better together when they're supported by other members of the team ... but contracting everything out, I think has been very, very detrimental to [the] overall ethos of any hospital and has contributed to very bad morale because you just don't feel you belong to anything. *Dawn*

And it was teamwork ... because you had your ward orderlies or kitchen maids ... and they took pride in their work as well and they were a respected member of the team, whereas now everything is contracted out and they want the most work for the least amount of money, and although those people work hard, the sort of personal pride element in it has gone because if they're short somewhere else ...

they'll just be pulled once they've done a certain amount of work to then go and help out wherever, and they're not particularly valued like they used to be. *Gloria*

Lesley describes one way of helping to make staff feel part of a team:

I think … the most important thing to me was to get the staff to work together, to be happy together, so … every Thursday night we'll be meeting in the pub across the road, and I have to say, it worked brilliantly, and I can remember … one of the senior people saying … 'How do you manage to maintain your recruitment?'.

Some things remain unchanged as Jessica, a 2000s trained nurse, indicates:

We made beds and … clean. Clean and make beds.

And Sandra, a 1960s' nurse, describing the current situation:

And targets, and targets, to rush through things.

Kim, who trained in the 1980s, adds:

I think it was good care that we were giving on the wards … there are some things that have changed, we don't whip out egg white … to put on wounds anymore but your approach to caring for a patient, that hasn't changed.

Gillian describes how emergency care has evolved:

The London [Hospital was] … at the forefront of the development of emergency care as it is now … I remember being sent to the Whitechapel Road … to get the lightest, softest suitcases I could … [for] a maternity … grab bag. So that you were able to go out to people [quickly]. … [W]e now talk about the golden hour in emergency care … how quickly you can get to your patient. … I look up and I hear the helicopter and I think that's how it started small with those couple of suitcases from the Whitechapel Market.

Many people felt that changes, including the loss of old style management roles such as ward sister, impacted on patient care:

I find it very sad that the ward sister doesn't know all the patients, you cannot run a place without a Captain of a ship. *Brenda*

I saw nurses like Sister X and really powerful women who just knew their jobs, and were managing people, and … I think about the NHS … there's just so much change … I think over the last thirty, forty years the NHS has just lost its way, and one of the reasons is we don't have [old style] matrons anymore. *Donna*

Nursing today

good quality, basic nursing care, it's fundamental to everything … I want clean sheets on the bed, I want the rubbish taken out of the room … if you give someone a drink, it's in a place where they can reach, you turn the water jug with the handle towards them, it is just such basic stuff that is sadly missing from a lot of nursing care today … I might be a sister [now], but if … the rubbish needs doing or someone needs taking to the loo, I will do it rather than walk round and round looking for the person involved with that patient to do it ... and they say, 'Oh, but you're a Band 7', I say, 'Yeah, I am a Band 7, but I can still make a bed.' *Gloria.*

There is a feeling that some nurses have lost their compassion:

I think ... people have lost the compassion ... [y]es, coming down in the lift just now there was two nurses talking and one of them was saying, 'Oh I bet ... [X] keeps asking me for a cup of tea,' and the other one just went, 'Make a really bad cup of tea, he won't ask you for it again!' I mean that shows you how the compassion is. *Kaleem*

It is a sad reflection that interviewees who trained in recent decades feel that current working conditions could lead them to lose their nurse's registration.

there's a lot of fear around [of] ... losing your PIN [NMC Personal Identification Number]. *Matthew.*

Kim describes how communication about health and safety information has changed:

there's more uniformity ... in the old days, I don't recall ever going to a safety huddle [meeting]. Now ... there's representation from every ward and department at nine o'clock every morning. And we talk about any issues going on in the wards, or departments, and ... if there's anything Trust-wide that needs to be disseminated then that's discussed ... it might be revalidation, consent ... infection control [and], 'Are we okay for staffing today, tonight?' ... it's a uniform approach rather than individual departments just doing their own thing. ... [A]nything serious that's happened, anything that needs to be discussed...that's where they do it, and they'll repeat it over a few days ... and then the information is emailed around to you, as well ... I think that's a huge improvement, you know what's going on in the wider Trust ... you can then bring it back to your teams.

As society has become more informal, so too have some nurses stopped calling patients by their title and surnames:

when I talk to patients I say 'How would you like to be called? Can I call you by your first name? What would you prefer?' *Carol*

I think some of the problem is with Christian names and a lot of patients don't want to be called by their Christian names ... it's about respect isn't it for your patients? *Brenda*

Hazel, who trained in the 1960s, highlights that, despite an increase in informality, confidentiality has improved:

in the Outpatients' department ... half the seats were facing in one direction, which would be medical outpatients, and in the other half, the chairs were facing the opposite direction, which was surgical outpatients, and at each end, there was the most enormous weighing scale. ... [A] porter would be allocated to stand at each of those scales and your name would be called out, and you'd have to stand on the scales, the dial of which was so enormous that no one could ... [help] seeing how much you weighed, the porter would then call out your weight to the nurse who was standing some distance away from him ... she would write it in the notes. ... [T]hat would be breaking confidentiality rules now, wouldn't it?

A change in public expectations is now reflected in how all health care professionals are treated by some patients, and patients and their families have become more vocal about their 'rights' as Christopher explains:

I think doctors have experienced the same thing as well ... nobody would ever swear at a doctor, answer them back, whereas you hear stand up arguments in some of the wards sometimes with doctors now and patients ... there's definitely a cultural change of respect.

[C]ertainly people of younger generations are definitely ... 'I've paid my National Insurance, I want this, get it for me or I'm going to put a complaint in about you' ... it's the expectation is that ... you're there to do as they tell you to do and you should be thankful that you've got a job because of them ... that has really changed.

Time

The most noticeable change is the length of time that many patients stay in hospital:

if a patient had a simple operation like a hernia they were in hospital for two weeks, now they're day cases ... big major changes in treatment. *Pauline*

a lot of things that are done by day care surgery ... people used to have to be inpatients for a long time ... that's exactly the same as it is with cancer care and haematology that there are many more advances, people spend a lot more time at home and they come in for day therapies. ... [M]any medical advances which have an impact on nursing care. *Denise*

people would come in for more resting than they do these days ... and then may even have gone off to a convalescent home. *Cynthia*

Recently it has been suggested that convalescent homes are reintroduced, in order to address the issue of 'bed-blocking' patients, and those who are rapidly readmitted after a premature discharge. Phyllis considers:

they're always saying ... things go round in circles ... they got rid of all the convalescent homes ... and of course what's happening now is that they kick patients out, and the next thing they're going [back in]. ... [J]ust before I retired ... I get a phone call, 'The BBC would like to speak to you on the radio,'... they did say to me ... 'How have things changed ... since you started nursing?' And I said, 'Well one of the things is that patients are thrown out of hospital much more quickly, in the old days there would be convalescent homes,' ... I said. ... 'My mother, for instance, had kidney surgery and then spent ... about ten days in a convalescent home where you ... get used to ... getting back to ... normal,'... and I said, 'This doesn't happen these days, people have major, major surgery and they're thrown out very, very quickly.'

These perspectives are from interviewees who have themselves become patients, or have witnessed how a lack of time may impact on the care currently given:

I'm not saying that nurses don't care now, they often don't have time, their workload is so different to ours. *Cynthia*

they don't seem to have time to talk to the patients or the people and that was a big part of it all … you knew your patients, they don't have time to. *Brenda*

Changes in working practice

Today, staff to patient ratios are part of safe working practice, while in the past these did not exist:

I think the major challenge sometimes is staffing and being expected to take more patients than you've really got the staffing capacity for … anecdotally people have said to me, 'Oh … back in the day we would just … have to take them', they wouldn't even be able to try and argue their corner to not take them. *Laura*

Interviewees identified a reduction in personal care for patients and increase in paperwork. Jennifer describes:

I mean we used to wash people probably four times a day we used to give them early morning [wash], blanket bath, afternoon wash and a late wash in the evening … that's totally gone out now, you don't get any washes at all.

[M]y friends that are still nursing, talk about the enormous amount of paperwork, covering your back really.

Over the decades nursing has changed, partly in response to changes in society:

you can't really build a relationship up when patients are only in for one or two days…. The whole ethos of nursing has changed and I think you can never go back to what it was, in some ways you shouldn't go back to … cleaning the sterilisers and counting the cutlery, we don't want to go back to those days. *Jennifer*

Political influences

The NHS is facing increasing challenges, and nurses feel unsupported by politicians, as Lilian explains:

the Health Service is under huge pressure, ageing population, chronic illnesses, increasing multiple needs and Trusts that seem to be, across the country, under … huge financial strain and pressure and considering the humanity and compassion that I saw … from nurses … and going away and doing two jobs to try and … provide for their families and yet they would give cheerful humanity to them and you can't put a price on that but you can exploit it and take advantage of it … most people, if you ask them about the NHS, if they've had personal experience … will say they were very touched and impressed by the staff themselves but the system is under such huge pressure so I don't feel that we're supported politically.

The removal of the bursary from 2017 is of concern to current nurses, and the financial impact that its loss will have on recruitment of future student nurses. It is thought to have already affected application numbers for nursing degree places, which at the time of writing continues to decline. Gloria describes:

We were salaried, not a lot, but … we didn't come out with the debt that they've got now.

[N]ow that student nurses and midwives are going to have to pay fees, just like you do in any other degrees which will cripple them … they get a limited bursary, it's not a lot of money, so they're still reliant on parents to support them, to live, and lots of them will do auxiliary work, and … in their holidays they'll do bank auxiliary work to top their money up. … [T]hat's hard, because the academic expectation is so great, they don't really have that much spare time.

Student nurses today now face a large student loan to pay their fees:

if you need nurses it's difficult to say that someone will go to university and build up … at least £30,000 worth of debt to work twelve-hour shifts with no lunch break. *Matthew*

Currently there are about 40,000 nursing vacancies in the UK:

in the old days, you know, you advertised a post and you'd have twenty applicants who'd all turn up for interview. Now, it's not like that at all. So recruitment has been a long, slow process … we're using a lot of agency staff to plug the gaps while we've got this rolling recruitment programme, and we're getting there, but it's a slow process. *Kim*

With a growing shortage of nursing, and caring being underfunded and devalued (Bunting 2016), a controversial solution appears to be the increasing use of robots. Ford (2017) reports on an international study, led by the UK, into the use of robots to support the care of older people. This use of artificial intelligence to support the work of nurses may be of benefit to society. Yet, there are many practical and ethical challenges. One example by Read (2016), in her play set in a hospital ward, demonstrates how patient care can be severely compromised by a 'nurse' who, it is eventually revealed, is actually a robot. However, for the present, to address the growing shortage of nurses, strong political leadership, including in nursing, is required.

The nature of nursing and the status of caring

the problem still is for some policymakers and sometimes for people who harp back in the profession … people need to be kind and compassionate and caring 'cos that's what you remember when you're sick … but actually it's very dangerous to have somebody who's kind, loving and compassionate and doesn't know what they're doing … I mean I don't want somebody driving along the road who's caring, kind and compassionate and doesn't know how to drive a car. *Janice*

Increasingly nurses can feel undervalued by politicians, yet recent research shows how more registered nurses can improve the patient experience:

I've worked on all these commissions, the Prime Minister's Commission [2010], the Willis Commission [2012], and I'm now working for a parliamentary group that's looking at global nursing development [APPG 2016] and it's the same issues over and over again, and we write the reports and they come up with all these recommendations…. And they are not implemented. Because it's too tricky and too intractable and society is still not ready to acknowledge the importance of caring, to acknowledge the value … to give it the status it needs. There's still the idea that you can replace registered nurses with less qualified people to save money…. Absolutely crazy, when for the first time we're amassing all the evidence, like the RN4CAST work, a huge EU-wide study … and they started … outcomes, comparing hospital outcomes related to the concentration of RNs in the workforce and guess what, the environments with the higher concentration of RNs have fewer deaths, fewer infections, more patient satisfaction. It is as plain as day and that's a massive, robust study, so this study is dynamite, you talk about safe staffing, well here is the evidence and still they think they can save money by watering down the skill mix, oh and let's train up more people to be enrolled nurses or care assistants, well hang on, why is that going to … how is that going to help? So there's a lot to do. *Sharon*

Recognition and appreciation of good nursing does occur across the generations as Vera, a 1940s' trained nurse, recalls:

my husband had to go to A&E … I was sitting there while he was being attended to and this young man, I thought 'Oooh wow, what a super nurse he is, quiet, methodical' … and a doctor came wandering past and I called him over and said, 'Excuse me, you know that gentleman over there, Staff Nurse, do you know how good he is', 'Yes' he said … that's good, because to be appreciated is so important.

Change for the better?

Interviewees had witnessed or experienced both good and poor nursing practice, and many accepted that the changes they witnessed in nurse education were for the better. Generally they felt that nurses should have a more in-depth basic training, before starting their degree programmes. Equally some felt that there was an important place for apprenticeships in nursing: some students made superb practical nurses, but struggled academically. Ironically the role of the Associate Nurse is being reintroduced, thirty years after the State Enrolled Nurses role was phased out.

Richard's thoughts conclude this chapter:

it's not just nursing has moved on, society moved on, and society itself wanted a different type of service … people … [are] living longer, and the longer they live, the more complex their health conditions become because they become multi-layered. … the patients that my students now care for would not be alive when I was an equivalent student … because we didn't have the knowledge, the technologies and the treatments that are available to us now.

[W]e are measured differently by the commissioners, Health Education England, the general public and the hospital Trust themselves. … [T]he media, I think, have stained the character of nursing because of a few disasters, terrible things that have happened. But out of the … 500,000 nurses on the register … a handful of people … should never have been nurses…. The majority of nurses are hardworking, they don't watch the clock, they work well above the hours that they're paid for. There are nurses in London who will qualify and get £25,000 working shifts, weekends, nights, like we did, but they can't afford to live in Zone 1 or Zone 2 or even Zone 3, where the hospitals are, so their expenses in travelling to work are great, it means that they have to get up at the middle of the night … to get into work here, into the Trusts … we lived near where we worked most of the time.'

Nursing could be on the edge of a precipice or it could be on the road to greatness, we don't know … we still teach compassion as the basis of where we are, the essential [skills] … these are absolutely the basis of nurse education in the twenty-first century … they might have changed slightly how we teach them, but those skills are still taught today, because that is the role of a nurse.

Conclusion

[T]here's this fabulous quote I've heard from Eva Luckes that says 'The London expects the impossible and gets the impossible', and I think what The London taught me was … you can deal with anything, you might sometimes have to take a step back and think about it for a moment but you can deal with it. *Zoe*

We hope that this book will have triggered many memories for those who trained and worked at the hospital. Seen through the lens of oral history, the text is dominated by the participants' voices, providing a glimpse into the visible, and not so visible, lives of nurses across the decades. For current and future students, it will have provided insight into what life was like to nurse within a particular decade. For all readers it is hoped that the book provided enjoyable reading, enabling comparisons to be made across the decades of what has changed in nursing and in society as a whole.

Nursing has developed and evolved. It has changed from the 1940s, when training required tasks to be undertaken according to rote instruction, to the current situation of individual professional autonomy, which encourages enquiry and the use of evidence-based practice. The phrase 'the patient comes first', and the need for safe care and compassion, however, has resonated throughout all the decades. Being compassionate, which cannot be measured, rationed or costed, as Bradshaw (2004) points out, is fundamental to the needs of all patients.

Many threads have emerged across the decades in the nurses' accounts. The vast majority of nurses who trained in the earlier decades came to the East End at the young age of 18. Their accounts reveal a rich seam of memories of how it felt when they first arrived, the details of their living conditions, the friends they made, and how often they became 'friends for life'. They also reveal their fears and anxieties, particularly when embarking on their first ward experience. Questions arose as they continued in their training, as to whether they had 'too much responsibility too soon'. Many described their experience of seeing their first death when working on their first ward. Some indicated that the memory of these events has stayed strongly with them throughout their lives. These stresses continued to be felt across the decades, with differences in how student nurses have coped. For example in earlier times, it was felt that living in a nurses' home along with your 'set' helped students 'survive'. More recently reference is made to how helpful a supportive sister or mentor can be, although this depends on the time such a person has to fulfil this role, alongside their other responsibilities.

Despite these pressures, there emerges clear elements of identity, pride and loyalty. This came with being part of The London Hospital and working with the people of the East End. There were evocative memories of seeing the market stalls beginning to be set up in the early hours of the morning, when the nurses were working on night duty. There was reference to the 'pluckiness of character' of those whom the nurses cared for and whose roots were in this part of London, and many memories of the 'never-forgotten patient'. Also, very evident was a respect for the diversity, and a love of the East End and its population.

Pride was displayed particularly in the earlier decades, in the descriptions of wearing the unique uniform. The nurses' accounts demonstrate feeling a sense of dismay dressed at first in a 'purple passion', pride when being fitted for their first student uniform, a feeling of achievement when becoming a staff nurse, and the lofty status of moving 'into blue' on gaining the title of 'sister'. Conversely, a sense of loss of identity came with the change to a national uniform, changes in the badges, and with the coming of the new hospital whose wards were no longer named, but numbered. These names had, until then, reflected the history of the hospital, identifying those who had been so important to its existence, before the establishment of the NHS.

It is interesting to see the changing work demands there have been for nurses across the decades, and therefore their changing roles. From the 1940s the gradual change is described, from fastidious cleaning routines, counting of cutlery and bedpan rounds, through the various approaches such as the Nursing Process, where there is more focus on individual patient care. At the same time, the obligatory residence in a nurses' home while training, with its strict rules and discipline, came to be replaced. Nurses first moved out at some point during their training to live independently in flats or shared houses in the local area. Currently, nurses have the same level of independence as anyone undertaking higher education.

Many referred to how much they learnt from the patient, and were all aware of the impact good nursing care had on the wellbeing of those for whom they were responsible. The change in the type of diseases and conditions nurses worked with over the years is clear, from caring for the many who suffered with pulmonary TB shortly after the war, to the severe respiratory diseases that resulted from the smogs that were to blight London before the Clean Air Act of 1956. Later with the advances in surgery and medicine, corresponding nursing skills were developed, such as within renal medicine, intensive care and emergency medicine. AIDS in the 1980s is referred to, as is the rise of microbes such as MRSA that are resistant to antibiotics. Nowadays, nurses rarely work with patients in hospital over a long convalescence which had been the norm in the past, particularly in some of The London Hospital annexes. The accounts of the more recently trained nurses reflect this, when sometimes it may not be possible to get to know your patients due to their stay in hospital being so short, perhaps no longer than a few hours.

Across the accounts there are descriptions of the introduction of nursing degrees, the training of more mature women and men, moving eventually to Project 2000 and the current training of all nurses to degree level. Overall it seemed there were losses and gains in nurse education over the years. Those most recently trained felt they had insufficient clinical experience before they qualified as a nurse.

The nurses' stories showed also a strong sense of fun, from the initiation of those student nurses working their first night, to the practical jokes played on some of the medical staff. The unauthorised entrances used after hours when the nurses' homes were locked, were often known to the senior nurses, used by them in the years before.

The accounts of the nurses moved through their training to beyond, and provide an insight into the depth and wealth of expertise into the variety of fields they have pursued. Some specialised by moving into midwifery, community nursing and health visiting to name a few. Many stayed to achieve senior positions within the hospital. Many travelled and worked abroad. The range of experience is vast. Many have become leaders in their field within the UK and others have striven to improve the lives of those in other countries. Some have moved to other disciplines, but always there appears a recognition of the value of the training they received at The London Hospital.

There are seismic changes currently unfolding in the recruitment and retention of nurses, with the loss of bursaries, and the resultant effect of university fees on recruitment. This is coupled with a loss of nurse recruits from overseas such as from the EU.

There is a fundamental need for society to continue to have people to care for them at times of need, but will the profession of nursing still continue? The evidence is there for the better outcomes in patient care where there is a larger proportion of registered nurses, but will nursing exist in the future, or be replaced by a cheaper, less autonomous workforce? With the progress of Artificial Intelligence, what role will robots play in patient care in the future?

Whatever the future may hold, the affection that is felt by those who were interviewed is clear:

> I think The London is a special place. A lot of us say that if you train at The London it's somewhere that never leaves your heart. *Laura*

Glossary

Activities of Daily Living: A model of nursing which incorporates the activities of daily living as described by Nancy Roper, Winifred Logan and Alison Tierney Model of Nursing.

All-Party Parliamentary Group on Global Health [APPG 2016]: reported on how developing nursing will improve health, promote gender equality and support economic growth.

Aneurysm: A bulge in a weak area in the wall of the artery.

Archangel: One of the main Russian ports used by Allied troops in the First World War to aid the Russians during the civil war which occurred after the 1918 uprising. The main port used by the Royal Navy during the artic convoys in the Second World War.

Bat Phone: Phone connected directly from A&E to the ambulance service, used in the 1980s.

Blue/white book: A procedure manual, given to every student nurse at the start of training as a practical achievement record. E.g., taking temperatures and blood pressure readings. The manual had to be completed before final exams.

Blue Board: Prescriptions for medicines written on blue paper pinned onto a board, usually on a rail at the foot of a patient's bed.

BME networks: Black minorities and ethnic workers community.

Bone marrow transplant: A medical procedure to replace bone marrow which has been damaged by disease or chemotherapy.

Bronchoscopy: An endoscopic technique using a small camera which enables visualising the inside of the airways for diagnostic and therapeutic purposes.

Catheterisation (urinary): Insertion of a small tube into the bladder to allow drainage, measurement and testing of urine.

Cheyne Stokes respiration: Abnormal pattern of breathing characterised by periods of progressively deeper and sometimes faster breathing, followed by a gradual decrease that results in a temporary stop in breathing. Usually seen towards the end of life.

Clap Clinic: Clap, slang word for Gonorrhoea, also refers to genito urinary medicine sexually transmitted disease clinic (STD).

Clean Air Act of 1956: Government plan to reduce pollution by introducing smoke free zones where only smokeless fuel could be used e.g., gas, electricity and coalite.

Colostomy: A surgical procedure where part of the large bowel is brought out onto the surface of the abdomen through which faeces pass into a disposable pouch.

CT scan: A scan that uses X-rays and a computer to create detailed images of the inside of the body. Combines series of X-rays to create cross-sectional images.

D&C: Dilatation & Curettage: A surgical procedure in which the cervix is dilated and the uterine lining is scraped.

Dipstick testing: A means of testing urine using a manufactured strip of colour codes which can immediately record any abnormalities in the urine.

Dix Bottle: Chest drainage bottle, developed by Professor Dix, consultant urologist to The London Hospital.

Draw sheet: Long half sheet often placed over a rubber mackintosh. The sheet can be pulled through following pressure area care to provide a clean, crease free area to lie or sit on.

DXT: Deep X-ray therapy.

Elephant Man: Joseph Carey Merrick was an English man, born in 1862, with very severe deformities that were first exhibited in a freak show as the 'Elephant Man'. He then went to live at The London Hospital after he met Sir Frederick Treeves, so becoming well known in London society.

Ergometrine: A medication causing contractions of the uterus used prophylactically to prevent heavy bleeding after childbirth.

EUSOL: Edinburgh University solution of lime was used for cleaning wounds.

Gallipoli: Peninsular in the southern part of Ottoman Turkey, famous for the Gallipoli campaign, one of the Allies' greatest disasters in the First World War with a loss of 58,000 men.

Glasgow trauma scoring: A neurological scale which aims to give a reliable and objective way to record the state of consciousness of a person. Scoring system later revised.

Haemodialysis: Usage of a kidney machine to remove fluid and waste and to correct electrolyte imbalance.

Hop picking: Known as the East Enders summer holiday in Kent. Where hops were picked to flavour and stabilise beer.

Hydrocephalus: A build-up of fluid on the brain which can increase pressure and can cause brain damage if untreated. The condition can be congenital or acquired.

Infra Dig: Abbreviation of Latin *Infra dignitatem*, 'beneath (ones) dignity'.

Inguinal Hernia: A protrusion of abdominal cavity contents through the inguinal canal.

Kardex: The brand name of a filing system used to record handwritten summaries of patients' condition and treatment, which was updated each shift.

Last Offices/laying out: Preparation given to a person following death.

Lupus Vulgaris: Chronic infection of the skin with tuberculosis.

MRI: Magnetic resonance imaging. A type of scan that uses strong magnetic fields and radio waves to produce detailed images of the inside of the body.

MRSA: Methicillin resistant staphylococcus aureus. A type of bacteria that is resistant to several widely used antibiotics. This means infections with MRSA can be harder to treat than other bacterial infections. Also called a 'superbug'.

Nelsons Inhaler: Double valve ceramic steam inhaler used to treat chest infection.

Nightingale Ward: One large open plan ward with beds arranged along both sides with a nurse's station.

Many tailed binder: Scultetus binder of many tails applied in an overlapping fashion over the trunk to hold dressings in place or for abdominal support.

Mastectomy: Surgical procedure to partially or completely remove one breast or both for the treatment of breast cancer in men and women.

Metastatic growths: Cancer which has spread from the primary site to another area in the body.

Milton: Sterilising fluid.

NMC: Nursing and Midwifery Council. The regulator for nursing and midwifery professions in the UK. The NMC maintains a register of all nurses, midwives and specialist community public health nurses eligible to practise within the UK. It sets and reviews standards for their education, training, conduct and performance. It also investigates allegations of impaired fitness to practise.

OSCE: Objective structured clinical examination, designed to test clinical and competency skills.

Palliative Care: An approach that improves the quality of life of patients and their families facing the problems associated with terminal illness.

PAS: Para-amino salicylic acid (PAS) is an antibiotic primarily used to treat tuberculosis, first used clinically in 1944.

Pinard Horn: A type of stethoscope used to monitor the heartbeat of a foetus.

PPI: Protein pump inhibitor: Tablets (e.g., Omeprazole) that reduce acid secreted by the stomach.

Prime Minister's Commission [2010] 'Front Line Care'. A report by the Prime Minister's Commission into the future of Nursing and Midwifery in England. The Commission was established in March 2009 to explore how the nursing and midwifery professions could take a central role in the design and delivery of twenty-first-century services in England.

Pyloroplasty: A surgical procedure which widens the lower part of the stomach, (pylorus) so stomach contents can empty into the small intestine. Operation is usually combined with a vagotomy.

RN4CAST: was initiated in 2009 using European funding. It examined how organisational features of hospital care impacted on patient outcomes, nurse recruitment and nurse retention, both in European countries and across the world.

Samaritan Society: Marie Celeste Samaritan Benevolent Society was founded by Sir William Blizzard. In 1903 James Hora made a magnificent gift to the society in memory of his wife Marie Celeste, provided the name changed in perpetuity. The Society administers relief aid for patients who have been discharged from The London Hospital (e.g., for convalescence).

Sickle Cell disease: A group of blood disorders typically inherited from parents. Commonly found in families with black origins (e.g., Black Africans, black Caribbean, black British). The disease is also found in India, the Middle East and Eastern Mediterranean.

Sluice: Room for dirty procedures and waste.

Specialing: One nurse caring solely for one very ill patient.

Spenco Mattress: Brand name for a mattress used for the prevention and treatment of pressure sores.

Spitz-holter valve: One way valve shunt used to drain cerebro-spinal fluid in order to control hydrocephalus.

Streptomycin: Streptomycin was discovered in 1943 and was the first antibiotic that was effective against tuberculosis (TB). The major side effect of this drug was deafness.

Stridor: Abnormal noisy breathing due to an obstruction in the airway.

Stoma Care: Care of a patient who has a colostomy, ileostomy or urinary diversion.

St Peter's Boat: Receptacle for accurate measurement of urine.

Surgical Emphysema: Gas or air in a layer under the skin which has a distinctive crackling sound when touched.

'Tails': Part of the sister's uniform only worn on special occasions, e.g., Christmas. Tails are two lengths of goffered cotton clipped to hair under a cap secured with grips.

The Review: League magazine sent out to all members of The Royal London Hospital League of Nurses.

The Willis Commission Report 'Quality with compassion: the future of nursing education' [2012]: examined and reported on the future of nursing education in the United Kingdom.

Thoracoplasty: A surgical procedure originally designed to permanently collapse the cavities of pulmonary tuberculosis by removing ribs from the chest.

TLC: Tender loving care.

'To Dress': A period where nurses were sent off the wards to collect and change into a clean apron after serving breakfast to the patients.

The Hard: Central corridor in Brentwood Annexe.

Tracheostomy: Formation of a direct airway through an incision into the trachea or windpipe to allow a patient to breathe without the use of the nose and mouth, a tube is inserted to keep the windpipe open.

Tracheal Dilators: Surgical instrument may be used temporarily to keep the tracheostomy open during tube change.

Tuberculosis: TB. Is caused by bacterial infection. Myobactrum tuberculosis, usually affects lungs but can damage other parts of the body, spread through inhaling droplets from cough and sneezes of an infected patient.

UKCC: United Kingdom Central Council for Nursing, Midwifery and Health Visiting.

Vagotomy: Is usually performed in conjunction with a pyloroplasty in which the nerves that stimulate the stomach acid and gastric mobility are cut.

Ventilator: An appliance for artificial respiration (respirator).

Whipples: Complex operation to remove part of the pancreas, small intestine and gall bladder, often used to treat cancer at the head of the pancreas.

Windrush 1948: One of the first boats bringing migrants from the Caribbean to the UK.

Bibliography

Abel-Smith, Brian, *A History of the Nursing Profession* (London: Heinemann, 1960).

Abrams, Lynn, *Oral History Theory* (Abingdon: Routledge, 2010).

Anthony, Grainne, *Distinctness of Idea and Firmness of Purpose. The Career of Eva Luckes; A Victorian Hospital Matron* (Unpublished Master of Arts dissertation, London Metropolitan University, 2011).

Baly, Monica, *Nursing and Social Change* (3rd edn, London: Routledge,1995).

Bornat, Joanna, 'Oral History and Qualitative Research', *Timescapes Methods Guides Series* (http://www.timescapes.leeds.ac.uk/assets/files/methods-guides/timescapes-bornat-oral-history.pdf, accessed 8 March 2017).

Bornat, Joanna, Robert Perks, Paul Thompson and Jan Walmsley (eds.) *Oral History, Health and Welfare* (London: Routledge, 2000).

Borsay, Anne, 'Nursing History: An Irrelevance for Nursing Practice?' (*Nursing History Review*, 2009): 14-27.

Boyd, Andrew, *Baroness Cox: A Voice For The Voiceless* (Oxford: Lion, 1988).

Bradshaw, Ann, 'Compassion in nursing history: attending to the patient's basic human needs with kindness', in Shea, Sue, Robin Wynyard and Christos Lionis, (eds.), *Providing Compassionate Healthcare: Challenges in Policy and Practice* (Abingdon: Routledge, 2014): 21-32.

Bradshaw, Ann, *The Nurse Apprentice, 1860-1977* (Aldershot: Ashgate Publishing Ltd., 2001).

Brindle, David, 'Nursing makes all the difference in healthcare: how the job has changed', *The Guardian* (https://www.theguardian.com/healthcare-network/2017/feb/28/nursing-makes-difference-healthcare-job-changed) [accessed 9 March 2017].

Broadley, Margaret E., *Patients Come First* (Tunbridge Wells, Pitman Medical Ltd.,1980).

Brooks, Jane, "The geriatric hospital felt like a backwater': aspects of older people's nursing in Britain, 1955–1980', *Journal of Clinical Nursing*, 18, 19, (2009): 2764–2772.

Bunting, Madeleine, 'Who cares: the emotional labour of an undervalued, underpaid workforce', https://www.theguardian.com/society/2016/mar/15/care-workers-undervalued-underpaid-radio-3, [accessed 7 March 2017].

Clark-Kennedy, Archibald, E., *The London A study in the Voluntary Hospital System, Volume Two, 1840–1948* (London: Pitman Medical Ltd, 1963).

Clark-Kennedy, Archibald, E., *London pride, the Story of a Voluntary Hospital* (London: Hutchinson Benham Ltd., 1979).

Davies, Celia (ed.), *Rewriting Nursing History* (London: Croom Helm,1980).

Daunton, Claire (ed.), *The London Hospital Illustrated, 250 Years* (London: Batsford,1990).

Fishman, William J., *The streets of East London* (London: Duckworth, 1979).

Ford, Steve, 30 January 2017 'Robots could 'revolutionise' care of older patients' (www.nursingtimes.net/news/research-and-innovation/robots-could-revolutionise-care-of-older-patients/7015226.article) [accessed 7 June 2017].

Graham, Margaret and Jean Orr, (eds.), *Nurses' voices from the Northern Ireland troubles: personal accounts from the front line* (London: RCN Publishing, 2013).

Grant, Linda, *The Dark Circle* (London: Virago, 2017).

Hallett, Christine, 'Researching nursing's history: Historical texts: factors affecting their interpretation', *Nurse Researcher,* 5, 2 (Winter 1997/98): 61-71.

Helm, Toby, 'Recruitment crisis hits NHS with one in nine posts currently vacant', *The Guardian* (https://www.theguardian.com/society/2017/may/13/royal-college-nursing-nhs-recruitment-crisis) [accessed 27 July 2017].

Heritage Lottery Fund, *Oral History: Good-practice guidance*, available via: https://www.hlf.org.uk/oral-history, (2014) [accessed 1 July 2017].

Jones, Kerry, Alison Warren and Alison Davies, 'Mind the gap. Exploring the needs of early career nurses and midwives in the workplace', (*Health Education England*, 2015) (http://www.nhsemployers.org/news/2015/08/mind-the-gap-exploring-the-needs-of-early-career-nurses-and-midwives) [accessed 9 March 2018].

Kirby, Stephanie, 'The resurgence of oral history and the new issues it raises' *Nurse Researcher*, 5 (2) (1997/98): 45-58.

Leap, Nicky and Billie Hunter, *The Midwife's Tale. An Oral History from Handywoman to Professional Midwife* (2nd edn. Barnsley: Pen and Sword, 2013).

Lewenson, Sandra B., and Eleanor Krohn Hermann, (eds.), *Capturing Nursing History. A Guide to Historical Methods in Research* (New York: Stringer, 2008).

Lost Hospitals of London, http://ezitis.myzen.co.uk/index.html. [accessed 3 August 2017].

Mackay, Nancy, *Curating Oral Histories: From Interview to Archive* (Walnut Creek: Left Coast Press, 2006).

Maggs, Christopher (ed.), *Nursing History: The State of the Art* (Beckenham: Croom Helm,1987).

Maggs, Christopher J., *The Origins of General Nursing* (London: Croom Helm, 1983).

Mann Wall, Barbara, Nancy E. Edwards and Marjorie L. Porter: 'Textual analysis of retired nurses' oral histories'. *Nursing Inquiry*, 14 (4) (2007): 279-288.

McCubbin, Carol, *Nurse's Voices: Memories of Nursing at St. George's Hospital London 1930 – 1990* (Kingston University, Faculty of Health and Social Care Sciences, 2010).

Mears, Carolyn Lunsford, *Interviewing for Education and Social Science Research: The Gateway Approach* (New York: Palgrave Macmillan, 2009).

Menzies, Lyth I., 'Social Systems as a Defense Against Anxiety. An Empirical Study of the Nursing Service of a General Hospital' *Human Relations,* 13 (1960): 95-121.

Merrifield, Nicola, 'Nursing degree applicants still down 23% amid fresh concerns over mature students' The *Nursing Times*, [Online, available from: https://www.nursingtimes.net/news/education/figures-show-nursing-degree-applicants-still-down-by-23/7017136.article, accessed 26 June 2017].

Miller-Rosser, Kolleen, Suzanne Robinson-Malt, Ysanne Chapman and Karen Francis, 'Analysing oral history: A new approach when linking method to methodology' *International Journal of Nursing Practice* 15 (2009): 475-480.

Mortimer, Barbara and Susan McGann, (eds.), *New Directions in the History of Nursing: International Perspectives*' (Oxford: Routledge, 2005).

Neuenschwander, John A., *A Guide to Oral History and the Law* (New York: Oxford University Press, 2014).

NHS Management Inquiry. Griffiths, R. Department of Health & Social Security. London 1983.

Nicholson, Virginia, *Millions Like Us. Women's Lives in War and Peace 1939–1949* (London: Penguin, 2011).

Nicholson, Virginia, *Perfect wives in ideal homes – the story of women in the 1950s* (London: Penguin, 2015).

Parker, Edith R. and Sheila M. Collins, *Learning to Care. A history of nursing and midwifery education at The Royal London Hospital, 1740–1993* (Orpington, Bishops Print, 1998).

Perks, Robert, *Oral History: Good-practice guidance* (Heritage Lottery Fund, 2014). [Accessed via http://closedprogrammes.hlf.org.uk/HowToApply/goodpractice/Documents/OralHistorygoodpracticeguidance.pdf on 7 July 2017].

Perks, Robert and Alistair Thomson, (eds.), *The Oral History Reader* (New York: Routledge, 2006).

Read, Kelly, 'Within Required Parameters' (2014), www.lazybeescripts.co.uk/Scripts/script.aspx?iSS=2216

Ritchie, Donald A., *Doing Oral History, a practical guide* (Oxford: Oxford University Press, 2003).

Ritchie, Donald A. (ed.), *The Oxford Handbook of Oral History* (Oxford: Oxford University Press, 2011).

Rowbotham, Sheila, *Hidden from History, 300 Years of Women's Oppression and the Fight Against It* (London: Pluto Press, 1973).

Salvage, Jane, *The Politics of Nursing* (London: Heinemann, 1985).

Terry, Louise M. (ed.), *Because We Care: Poetry and Values of Health and Social Care* (London South Bank University, 2010).

The Mid Staffordshire NHS Foundation Trust Inquiry, Francis Report. London: The Stationery Office, 2013.

The Oral History Association. Principles for Oral History and Best Practices for Oral History. (2009): [Accessed via: http://www.oralhistory.org/about/principles-and-practices on 7 July 2017].

The Royal London Hospital Archives and Museum, RLHLH/N/6/76, Official Ward Book, 2 January 1943 – 30 December 1944, 5 August 1944: 1200.

The Royal London Hospital League of Nurses Oral History Project, 'Back to the Future: Nurses' Knowledge for Change and Improvement' *RCN Centenary International Conference 2016 Poster*.

Thompson, Paul, *The Voice of the Past: Oral History* (Oxford: Oxford University Press, 1978).

Tosh, John, *The Pursuit of History. Aims, Methods and New Directions in the Study of History* (6th edn. Abingdon: Routledge, 2015).

Toynbee, Polly, *Hospital* (London: Arrow Books, 1977).

Trant, Kate and Susan Usher, (eds.), *Nurse: past, present and future* (London: Black Dog Publishing, 2010).

Ward, Alan, *A Manual of Sound Archive Administration* (Aldershot: Gower Pub. Co., 1990).

Worth, Jennifer, *Call the Midwife: A True Story of the East End in the 1950s* (London: Phoenix, 2002).

Young, Michael and Peter Willmott, *Family and kinship in East London* (London: Penguin, 1974).

Index